The Little Big Beat Book

Rory Hoy

NEW HAVEN PUBLISHING LTD

Published 2018
NEW HAVEN PUBLISHING LTD
www.newhavenpublishingltd.com
newhavenpublishing@gmail.com

Cover design © Pete Cunliffe
pcunliffe@blueyonder.co.uk

CONTENT

Introduction	4
Preface	5
A Beginner's Guide to Big Beat	7
The Weekend Starts Here	9
The Early Years & Birth of Big Beat (1973-1995)	
What's That Sound?	44
The Many Origins of the Name 'Big Beat'	
Start the Commotion	51
Big Beat Flourishes (1996-7)	
Life Is Sweet	89
The Golden Age (1997)	
Beats International	112
Big Beat Overseas	
You've Come A Long Way, Baby	147
Mainstream Success Peaks (1998)	
Stop the Rock	174
Big Beat's "Death" . . . or was it? (1999)	
A Little Less . . .	201
Big Beat's Curtain Call (2001-2)	
Sometimes I Feel So Deserted	214
The Wilderness Years (2003-10)	
Back Once Again . . .	229
The Possible Return of Big Beat (2010-Present)	
References	278
Acknowledgements	286
About the Author	290

Introduction

I have tried to make this 'History of Big Beat' as accurate as possible and, unless stated in a citation, all interviews, comments and quotes are new, as told to me during 2017/2018. If any aspects appear to run counter to previous accounts, I'm aware that people were often misquoted, so when archive material is used, I have tried to contact those responsible, or their management, to verify. I am very fortunate that so many people involved were willing and happy to share their stories; there were others who had been 'burned' along the way, who were less forthcoming, but nevertheless wished me every success. I hope this journey into the world of big beat brings back happy memories!

Rory Hoy

Preface

"The best thing about big beat was the idea that we broke all sorts of musical rules and yet made it sound accessible to people who found house music boring."

Norman Cook AKA Fatboy Slim to the author - October 31st 2017

It was 1999, my primary school summer dance, and I was 11. The DJ, looking like a circus clown who had got dressed without the aid of a mirror, was blasting out 5IVE, Steps, S Club 7 and Britney Spears, intermittently talking on the mic, muffled, like Bane from the *Batman* movies; you couldn't tell a word he was saying. I hated it, so I plucked up courage to ask if he could play Fatboy Slim 'Right Here Right Now'. He looked at me as if I were an alien (which, of course, I am) and said "Do you want me to clear the dance floor?" With trembling lip, I went back to stand with Mum and Dad, who were always there to see I was OK. They strode up to the DJ, and explained that I was autistic and if he didn't play 'Right Here Right Now' I may just scream the place down – and that *would* clear the dance floor for him! So he played the track, and I was in heaven, dancing/walking/mimicking the video on my own around the perimeters of the dance floor – which was empty.

Fast forward to the present, and I'm now a DJ/music producer myself (so I do have some sympathy for the poor fella) and have even shared the bill at festivals with people like 5IVE and S Club (!). I've had 6 albums released, countless singles, EPs, remixes, collaborations, been on British and American TV and radio many times and I am a multi-award-winning film maker. And I LOVE big beat.

So much so, I have embraced the music style throughout my career, and now I wanted to write a book about the genre, the music and the people involved, from DJs, singers, record labels, club nights, journalists from the time, punters… anyone and everyone. I started writing and contacting a few people, then put a posting up on social media inviting anyone with a story to get in touch… and they came from far and wide in their droves. Some are household names, some are well known in the big beat circle and some you may have never heard of... but they all have a fascinating tale to tell.

My own introduction to the movement was in 1999 which, funnily enough, was the beginning of the end of the movement's time in the sun. I was originally a Britpop kid, until one day I heard 'Right Here Right Now' by Fatboy Slim on an Adidas advert and it all changed. The first records I bought in the genre were 'Right Here Right Now', 'Hey Boy Hey Girl' by The Chemical Brothers and 'Ooh La La' by The Wiseguys in my local independent record shop (sadly, like many independents, no longer there) and, musically, it opened my ears. At the time, I didn't know the style was called big beat, and I just called all dance music "techno". I was drawn in by the catchy, repetitive hook lines, the loud syncopated drums and the raw energy - it really blew my very young 11-year-old mind.

In late 2005, when I got my first iPod, the 17-(soon to be 18)-year-old me rediscovered the music of my 11-year-old self; I finally did some detective work on the music of my childhood, and discovered a lot more of the sound I once loved. I even learned about the tag this elusive movement was given – 'big beat'. It was about this time that I wanted to become a music producer/DJ myself and, since then, I've been able to make my own big beat records.

Rory Hoy

A Beginner's Guide to Big Beat

Big beat was an oxymoron of a musical movement. It has produced some of the most famous and iconic acts that the electronic dance music scene has ever known, such as Fatboy Slim, The Prodigy and The Chemical Brothers – yet, in an ironic twist, the genre has almost completely faded to obscurity in the mainstream - outside of hearing the Fatboy on countless adverts and in football stadiums and seeing him, The Prodigy and the Chemicals headlining festivals and arena shows. Strange, as surely big beat was one of the most interesting movements in dance music's history, yet, at the start of the 2000s, the genre was eventually sidelined and ignored. Yes, the scene started to get a little formulaic and predictable, and yes, there were some tracks that weren't exactly "quality" (just like in all genres) but, unlike other types of music, big beat has never experienced a serious revival, outside of a few hardcore fans who grew up with it back in the day. Maybe one day things will change and more people will start to properly appreciate it once again... "with the ill behaviour".

The big beat scene is one bizarre enigma - yet I love it. Maybe that's the attraction to it? I also feel affection for the genre's irreverence, unpretentiousness and sense of humour. To quote Forrest Gump: "You never quite know what you're going to get." It's escapist music that makes you forget about the problems in the world. There isn't a message really with most big beat records, so it's not about "smashing the system"; it's just fun, happy party music. It was a patchwork mutation of 20th century music history mashed together, like Frankenstein's monster, that combined genres as disparate as rock & roll, hip-hop, acid house, techno, funk, disco, jazz, soul, easy listening, Latin and more, into one dancefloor-friendly package.

Interestingly, another fascinating nugget to the big beat oxymoron is that people actually still remember this short lived genre and its artists. Nowadays, sub-genres come and go really quickly and are very short lived – ironically, people still remember big beat with nostalgic fondness.

I feel the best way to get a genuine first-hand account of the era is to interview the people who were actually there, as I was only 10 when big beat was at its peak. What I've decided to do is to make the book something of an oral history, with mainly new and some archive interviews from the players involved. While the majority of the people I have contacted for this book have been more than happy to share their stories, there have been some who, as previously mentioned, felt they had been burned along the way, so some of the memories were not the happiest for them. I've also made a conscious effort to make the book positive in tone, but I'm not here to glamourise or romanticise the era.

There is really only one thing that unifies 98% of all records tagged under big beat, and that is that the records must have a big, syncopated drum beat, usually taken from a "breakbeat" (more on breakbeats in the next chapter!). Records considered to be "big beat" very rarely have a straight four on the floor beat. The movement is easily the loosest and most abstract of any genre of electronic dance music - there are very few rules. In November 2017, when I spoke to Robert Luis who runs Tru-Thoughts Records (Brighton UK), he told me that "Big beat was that freedom to play anything, and I think, as it got bigger, it got more difficult for people to figure out what it really was. It was not as clearly defined as a musical genre as, say, jungle, drum & bass or grime. 'Praise You' (by Fatboy Slim) was a big tune, but that was a slow electronic / hip-hop / soul tune."

Big beat doesn't have an instrument that's constant on all records, but if there had to be one, it would be the famous Roland TB-303 Bass Synthesiser, which was also the foundation for acid house's signature sound. Its squelchy sound was the template for many classic big beat records, notably 'Everybody Needs a 303' by Fatboy Slim. Outside of the occasional vocal snippet or loop (usually from an old school or golden age hip-hop record) it's a mostly instrumental genre of music, so it transcends language and cultural barriers.

The Weekend Starts Here – The Early Years & Birth of Big Beat (1973-1995)

Big Beat's Origins

How did big beat begin? The prototype of what would become the loud breakbeat orientated music, associated with the "big beat" tag (as well as all music genres that involve the looping of a "breakbeat"), had its origins in the genesis of the hip-hop genre/culture, back on August 11th 1973 at 1520 Sedgwick Avenue in South Bronx, New York, USA, when a DJ from Jamaica named DJ Kool Herc (real name Clive Campbell), who coincidentally coined the term breakbeat, held a block party for some local teenagers. In 1974, Kool Herc tried something new – in his sets, he was now elongating the percussion and bass led instrumental sections of classic funk (and sometimes rock) records called "the break", using two vinyl turntables (a technique that he would call 'The Merry-Go-Round'.) Kool Herc would loop this part, as this was the section of the record when the dance floor would go crazy, and also so that the MC (later to be known as a rapper) would spit some rhymes and breakdancers would dance (hence the term 'breakdancer'.) Other DJs who would adapt this method were Grand Wizzard Theodore (accidental inventor of DJ scratching, later to be known as turntablism), re-formed Black Spades gang leader Afrika Bambaataa (founder of the Universal Zulu Nation – a famous hip-hop awareness movement, who's best known for the groundbreaking Kraftwerk-sampling electro tune 'Planet Rock') and, most famously, Grandmaster Flash, who cleaned up Kool Herc's technique and perfected it. This would form the backbone of the hip-hop genre, as well as providing the genesis of all breakbeat-orientated music styles.

Music that would incorporate the use of a breakbeat as its basis wasn't released commercially until the early 1980s (practically all hip-hop releases prior to this used live instrumentation to recreate the samples and breaks.) This changed however in 1981, which saw the release of Grandmaster Flash's famous live DJ mix 'The Adventures Of

Grandmaster Flash On The Wheels Of Steel' on Sugarhill Records, which cut up 'Good Times' by Chic, 'Another One Bites The Dust' by Queen, and 'Rapture' by Blondie, among others. This was the first record release to incorporate the technique that would later be known as turntablism, as well as the very first non-experimental mainstream record to be made entirely from samples (a technique that a lot of big beat records would later adopt).

We should also not forget that, in the early 1980s, under the influence of disco, and pioneering songs like 'I Feel Love' by Donna Summer (produced by Giorgio Moroder), house music (arguably the most successful genre of contemporary electronic dance music) was emerging from Chicago, and was pioneered by the likes of Ron Hardy and the late, great, Frankie Knuckles. By 1987, a sub-genre would emerge from this movement called acid house. This was, according to legend, invented by accident by Marshall Jefferson and his protégé, Pierre, and featured deep basslines and the "squelching" sounds of the Roland TB-303 synthesiser (according to myth, the "acid" sound was "invented" when Pierre's 303's batteries went flat). It was very popular in the British Isles, and would form the basis of the rave movement (and was key to the big beat mutation.)

Moving back to early hip-hop, in 1983, under the influence of Flash's 'Wheels of Steel' cut-up, a hip-hop production duo named Double Dee and Steinski (Doug Di Franco and Steve Stein) entered a remix competition to rework the G.L.O.B.E. and Whiz Kid track, 'Play That Beat Mr. DJ', for the famous Tommy Boy Records, which was run by Tom Silverman. Their winning entry for the competition was rebranded as the first track in their 'Lessons' series ('Lesson 1 – The Payoff Mix'.) This pioneering tune incorporated samples from early hip-hop, as well as snippets from older artists, such as Little Richard and The Supremes. This was followed up with 'Lesson 2 – The James Brown Mix' in 1984, and 'Lesson 3 – The History Of Hip-Hop Mix' in 1985.

Following hot on the heels of Grandmaster Flash's 'Wheels of Steel', 1986 saw the release of the first record in the DJ Mega-Mix series for DJs. It was called 'The Finest Ingredients' and was mixed (uncredited) by none other than the artist who would, arguably, become the most important figure in the whole big beat scene – Norman Cook (later known as Fatboy Slim.) At this time, he was best known as a member of the popular indie pop band, The Housemartins, doing bass guitar duties, and it was considered a bit too much of a drastic change for the group's fanbase. This record was really ahead of its time, with young Norman cutting up and scratching the likes of Led Zeppelin, Indeep, The Mohawks, Run DMC, and even dialogue from TV shows such as *Batman* and *Doctor Who*. It didn't get a commercial release because of the heavy amount of samples (whosampled.com lists 27 uncleared samples.) There's even an alternate mix that featured Norman (along with future Beats International collaborator MC Wildski) doing some rapping.

Influenced by Double Dee and Steinski, January 1987 saw the release of the groundbreaking track 'Say Kids What Time Is It?' by Coldcut (Matt Black and Jonathan Moore.) It was their debut single, which sampled 'King Of The Swingers' from the Disney film *The Jungle Book*, James Brown's 'Funky Drummer', 'Shack Up' by Barbarra, and others. It is regarded as the first commercial UK breakbeat record, and was the first UK release to be made entirely from samples (Norman Cook's track preceded it by a year, but never officially came out.) Originally a white label, with a limited pressing of 500 copies, this (along with 'The Finest Ingredients') was, in many ways, an evolution of what US hip-hop cut-up artists, such as Double Dee and Steinski, were doing in their 'Lessons' series, and would evolve into what would be breakbeat (the genre, not the technique) and later big beat.

In fact, the first tune that may well be classed as a big beat track would, arguably, have to be Coldcut's follow-up tune, 'Beats + Pieces', which was released in May 1987. While not officially part of the big beat canon, it does contain many of the tropes that would be associated with the genre, such as its heavy drums (taken from 'When The Levee Breaks' by Led Zeppelin), liberal use of sampling, turntable scratching etc. The Chemical Brothers themselves consider it to be the first tune in the genre so, in essence, 'Beats + Pieces' was the first ever big beat track. Other notable proto big beat tracks included the early hip-hop influenced UK house hits such as 'Pump Up The Volume' by M|A|R|R|S, 'Beat 'Dis' by Bomb Da Bass, and 'Theme From S-Express' by S-Express, as well as tunes such as 'Hear The Drummer Get Wicked' by Chad Jackson and 'Radio Babylon' by Meat Beat Manifesto – all of these tracks were big club hits (as well as mainstream Top 40 hits) in their day. Other artists credited for creating the prototype for big beat were Renegade Soundwave and Bristol artist J Saul Kane AKA Depth Charge.

During this time, hip-hop was developing a more plunderphonic (sample-heavy) influence, and getting increasingly more based on the use of creative sampling – it should also be noted that early UK house music had a similar, sample-heavy ethos. This was during the period when sample clearance issues were a lot more lax than they are today, and this produced some of the best known and acclaimed works the genre has ever seen. Notable examples included De La Soul's debut album *3 Feet High and Rising*, Public Enemy's *It Takes A Nation Of Millions To Hold Us Back*, and The Beastie Boys' *Paul's Boutique* – this release is rather notable, as it is partially where the name 'Big Beat Boutique' comes from, and the album's producer, The Dust Brothers, was one of the early names for the Chemical Brothers. The album's ethos of mashing diverse record sources (along with the other acts stated above), such as Bob James, Led Zeppelin, Funkadelic, Johnny Cash, and The Beatles, was key in formulating the eclectic big beat sound.

By the end of the 1980s, during the "Second Summer Of Love" (1988-89), the rave movement was also starting to form. Initially, the music used was acid house from the US Chicago area, but the 4/4 house beat was slowly being replaced in the UK scene with sped-up hip-hop breakbeats, primarily from golden age hip-hop records (such as James Brown's 'Funky Drummer' and 'Amen Brother' by The Winstons, which would also become the basis for jungle/drum & bass). This genre was known as "hardcore" in later years, to distinguish it from later rave movements, and was a massive commercial success during the early 1990s. This scene has been very well documented many times, but it did, unfortunately, trough around 1993/4, as the genre got over-commercialised, and the hardcore movement would later evolve into jungle, which would eventually evolve into drum & bass.

Probably the most well known act of this movement was The Prodigy, whose line-up consisted, at the time, of producer Liam Howlett, dancer Keith Flint, MC Maxim (Keith Palmer), and Leeroy Thornhill (as well as a female dancer, Sharky, in their initial phase.) This band would later be included in the "big beat" tag and would form the "big 3" of the genre. February 1991 saw their first EP 'What Evil Lurks' released on XL Recordings (future home of Adele) and their first show was at the Four Aces club in Dalston, London. They didn't reach mainstream success until August of that year with the single 'Charly', which sampled the famous 'Charley Says' animated public information films and reached No.3 in the UK singles chart. The success of this spawned

12

many copycat singles such as 'A Trip to Trumpton' by Urban Hype and 'Sesame's Treet' by Smart E's with this short lived trend titled 'Toytown Techno' by the music press. 1992 saw the release of their first album *Experience*, which was a massive success with both the critics and the public, and it was certified Platinum by the British Phonographic Industry. Subsequent singles from the album included 'Out Of Space' and 'Everybody's In The Place' which were also very successful.

One other notable act that would form the basis of what was to be known as big beat would be US West Coast breakbeat act Bassbin Twins (who is, in fact, only one person, Pete Houser.) In 1992 he released the first Bassbin Twins EP, 'EP 1', which was a favourite among early UK pioneers of the genre. The music coming from the West Coast scene at the time was basically big beat, but it wasn't yet called big beat. In an interview for this book in April 2018, Pete Bassbin gave me a brief history of the West Coast breakbeat scene.

"To me the breakbeat scene in Los Angeles was primed by the sample-heavy hip-hop that was huge there from the mid-eighties on," Pete explains. "I was all-in with hip-hop and especially obsessed with sample production, so by the time SL2's 'Way In My Brain' was airing, the fuse had been lit: that was THE tune that set me off, as I'd been a fan of both Wayne Smith's original ('Under Me Sleng Teng') and the breaks that underpinned that track. What I loved most of that era was the juxtaposition in the music: the thrill of hearing things that shouldn't work together feeling amazing, which was also true of the earlier mentioned hip-hop, but the spirit was different: hip-hop had the toughness built in, while breakbeat felt more open-ended and celebratory.

"Raves, record stores and radio were all part of the wave swell rolling out a sort of loving punk rock movement. I was more focused on the music than anything and started making records as an outsider, feeling genuinely surprised that they resonated with anyone else. Mostly, I was making mini-homages to both the tracks I loved and filling the gaps of tracks I wish had existed.

"I'd go to underground raves (the stuff of secret location/map-point legend) then the record shops the following week to try and collect fractions of what I'd heard the weekend before. I moved up to San Francisco in the mid-90s and connected even more with the scene happening there, which might've been a timing thing: in LA I hadn't met many

13

other producers, while in SF there were several and multiple collectives releasing records and hosting parties. I loved both LA and SF but the latter felt more cohesive and mystically-tinged."

A style of music that experienced a spell of popularity and was not too dissimilar in sound to what would later be known as big beat was the UK hip-hop sub-genre Britcore (British hardcore hip-hop). This style of hip-hop was similar, sound-wise, to the early rave records, with uptempo, sped-up breakbeats, and funk samples with frantic, intense speed raps; it was a lot faster than most US hip-hop (around 110 to even 160 BPM). A noteworthy tune in this style was '20 Seconds to Comply' by Silver Bullet, which reached No.11 in the UK singles charts – a tune that would not feel out of place in a big beat set. DJ Spatts (Ian Allen) from the Britcore group The Criminal Minds would later produce big beat with Zak H Laycock and friends under the name of Environmental Science.

Another popular genre at the time was trip-hop, which started in the UK in Bristol at the beginning of the decade. It is a fusion of hip-hop beats with chilled and jazzy, trippy samples; notable acts include Massive Attack, Tricky, Portishead and DJ Shadow (in fact, one of Shadow's releases was the reason trip-hop became known as trip-hop, thanks to a 1994 review in *MixMag*). A lot of the early big beat releases were very similar to trip-hop in their sound and, in many ways, the early big beat records could be described as club-friendly trip-hop. Another honourable mention of a genre that was very similar in sound to big beat at the time was the early "hip-house" hits, with the likes of the Rob Base and DJ E-Z Rock song 'It Takes Two', 'Back By Dope Demand' by King Bee and 'Don't Scandalize Mine' by Sugar Bear.

In a 2017 interview for this book, Ben Willmott, a journalist for the *NME* and later *The Guardian*, who played a very important part in the story, explains the origins of where the big beat sound came from. "The scene had its roots in rave, like nearly all dance music genres and sub-genres. You could say that a record like SL2's 'DJs Take Control', 'We Are IE' by Lenny De Ice or 'Let's Go' by DJ Hype, records that are way before anyone started talking about big beat, fit into that mould musically. But to me, what became known as big beat was something that came out of the trip-hop movement. Rather like hardcore, which had split into the light and dark camps, trip-hop split in two somewhere around 93/94. Whereas it was anything with hip-hop beats driving it at the beginning, it became divided into clear camps, with the more

14

blunted, downbeat stuff like Portishead, Tricky etc. on one side, and then a new sound that was tougher and more for the dancefloor. You can hear it in something like David Holmes' mix of 'Live At The Opium Den' by Justin Warfield, which is still based on a kind of trip-hop template, but is much more intense, certainly not coffee table material. Also, look at the *Fried Funk Food Vol.2* album that Norman [Cook] and Ashley Slater did – it kind of fits into the trip-hop thing but you can hear it's on the way to something clubbier. When the Chemical Brothers' 'Chemical Beats' came out, that was considered trip-hop, but again it was clearly something distinct from Morcheeba etc. "

The Birth of the Chemical Brothers and the Heavenly Social

In 1992, an up-and-coming duo, Tom Rowlands and Ed Simons, called The Dust Brothers (as stated previously, named in tribute to the producers of the Beastie Boys) would release their debut single 'Song To The Siren' – one of the first "official" canonical records in the big beat genre. The record was pressed up as a white label with the help of a £300 loan from a friend. Barry Ashworth from the Dub Pistols describes the track's impact for an interview he conducted for *NPR* Magazine in 2011:

"At the time, dance music had run itself up an alley, with the 4/4 beat and the cheap, cheesy vocals. It had just run its course for me. And I heard this Chemical Brothers (then called Dust Brothers) track at the time, and it just blew my socks away. It was like hip-hop meets dance meets electronica and with the beats… it just totally and utterly changed what I wanted to do and the direction I was going in. Suddenly, that was what I wanted to do." [2]

The song's impact was far and wide…

"We used to run a night called Ask Yer Dad at Venus in Nottingham in the early 90s," remembers Daniel Curtis, who produced big beat under the name of Danielsan for Skint Under 5's. "I used to play upstairs, playing house, hip-hop, breaks, disco, anything. A key crossover track was 'Who's The Badman' by Dee Patten. I used to buy hardcore tunes and play them much slower, about 124 BPM, 'cos they had the biggest breaks and basslines. I used to play what was then called breakbeat house, but became rave.

"I can remember going into Selectadisc in Nottingham, and Fergus, who worked there, shouted to me as I came through the door 'Danny, they've started making records for you' whilst waving a copy of 'Song to the Siren' by The Dust (Chemical) Brothers. This was a pivotal record. For me, the start of big beat was The Prodigy and The Chemical Bros."

The underground success of 'Siren' led to The Dust Brothers getting an independent record deal with Junior Boy's Own. "I signed The Dust Brothers to my label Junior Boys Own in 1993," remembers Junior Boys Own's Boss and A&R man, Steven Hall, exclusively for this book. "Tom and Ed had self released 'Song to the Siren' on a limited edition 12", which Andrew Weatherall introduced me to, and he said he'd love to remix it. The track was pretty underground, but fitted where we were trying to go with the Boys Own/Junior labels, so the deal was done, which included the guys getting to meet Andrew in the studio... they were thrilled."

Tom and Ed from The Dust Brothers also had their own club night based in Manchester called Naked Under Leather, which was eclectic in its ideology, playing instrumental hip-hop records and doing unusual effects, or playing them at 45 RPM instead of 33 RPM. This "anything goes" style of DJing was described as being Balearic (named after the Balearic islands near Ibiza, where DJs shared an equally diverse music palette), and this was unusual in the UK at the time, as the DJ scenes were increasingly getting more homogenised with their musical approach. It was rare for clubbers circa 1992-94 to appreciate dance music, rock and hip-hop etc in the same night. "You could see the fun to be had out of music," says Ed Simons, "more than just sitting in a club, drunk, thinking 'This is OK.' We thought there was better stuff you could play. We'd really hunt hard for records – the second mix on the B-side of some house thing, then into this breakbeat sort of some instrumental hip-hop track. It was quite like the Heavenly Social [the successor club night] – a room full of 100 people out of their minds on beer." [3]

Another thing that set The Dust Brothers apart was their self-admitted lack of mixing skills on the decks. "We're not fantastic mixers," stated the band in an issue of the *DJ Times*. "We don't have the smooth, long continuous mix. But what we do get from DJing is a way of programming music, how you can shape a crowd, create ripples of energy and get people going crazy." [77]

Despite the supposed lack of mixing finesse, Tom and Ed managed to create an atmosphere on these nights that set them apart from other club DJs of the time.

"I remember they [The Dust Brothers] were supporting Primal Scream on their Give Out But Don't Give Up tour in '93 or '94 at the O2 Academy in Leeds which was then called Leeds Coliseum, I think," remembers Graham Chalmers, journalist for Johnston Press newspapers. "They were loud, the beats were big and I'd never heard anything like it before. Amazing – like The Beatles' 'Tomorrow Never Knows' had mutated into dance music."

"I was in Nottingham in '93 when I heard The Dust (before they became Chemical) Brothers' 'Chemical Beats', which sounded like the future of dance music – all the best bits of everything that had happened before," remembers Skint Records artist Kidda in an interview for this book. "1993 was peak golden era hip-hop, and that was all I was listening to. I'd been through the rave/acid house thing a few years before that, and it had worn itself out into a semi-commercial VIP hell of dress codes and bad drugs. To me, dance music was done, but 'Chemical Beats' sounded like a proper statement of intent. I was listening to and playing out a lot of Kenny Dope instrumental hip-hop joints at the time, just breakbeats with funk loops and a few vocal hooks. I liked it 'cos I got a bit tired with the ever-present ego of the MC that tended to loom over the production and with the 303 all over it. 'Chemical Beats' sounded a bit like a pill-charged British version of those early 90s NY Jeep beats."

On US Independence Day 1994, The Prodigy released their second album *Music For The Jilted Generation*. The album received rave reviews, and was a commercial smash, reaching No.1 in the UK charts, and going two times platinum, selling over 600,000 copies in the UK alone, as well as reaching the Top 10 in various European countries. While the album was an evolution of their classic rave sound (though a little grittier and edgier than before), a few of the tracks on the album would provide the prototype of what would be known as big beat – notably, the midtempo hip-hop meets acid house track 'Poison', which contained looping vocals and 'Their Law' which featured indie dance band Pop Will Eat Itself (whose lineup at the time included future big beat artists, Richard March from Bentley Rhythm Ace and Fuzz Townsend).

The Prodigy – One of big beat's most famous acts, who are Keith Flint (left), Liam Howlett (middle) and Maxim (right). With kind permission from JCF Management. Photo taken by Bartleberry Logan.

A similarly minded club night to The Dust Brothers' Naked Under Leather began on August 6th 1994. Indie label Heavenly Records from London, which consisted of Jeff Barratt, Martin Kelly and Robin Turner, who discovered the Manic Street Preachers, Beth Orton (who would later work with Tom and Ed) and others, started a Sunday club night in the Albany pub called The Heavenly Sunday Social – the aim was to make dance music fun again.

"The first Heavenly Sunday Social took place on the first Sunday of August 1994," states Robin Turner, co-founder and A&R/Press Officer of the Heavenly Social. "The original intention was for it to run for four weeks. The first week had about 40 people, all mates. The second about 100, the third was full; by the fourth week, we were turning a lot of people away. It eventually ran for 13 weeks. By the end, it was a real headache – we were turning away hundreds of people, people who were getting angry about not getting in. It took a lot of the fun out of what we were doing, so we stopped it.

18

"At the time I was a PR at Heavenly Recordings. Jeff and Martin, who ran the label, were my partners in the club – Jeff came up with the name, Martin found the venue, I sorted the DJs, it was a team effort the whole time. I didn't like the name initially – I thought it needed to be a bit more exciting. Now I think it was our strongest asset – it's never dated and it did what it said on the tin – it was a social, nothing else.

"The original '94 version of the Sunday Social was dreamt up as a reaction to what was going on in mainstream clubbing. I'd first been attracted to going out clubbing by listening to the music that the Boy's Own crew were making in the late '80s/early '90s. By '94 it had completely polarised. You had very dark techno music on one hand; on the other, you had big room house music played to crowds of very dressed up clubbers. I didn't feel part of either scene, neither felt or looked like much fun. The Sunday Social was always supposed to be about the music – the music the residents played and the music the guests played in support. The guest was booked with the intention of playing their 'other box' – the kind of records you'd play back at someone's house rather than on a Saturday night at Cream or wherever. Most of the time this worked out amazingly well – I still listen to a recording of Andrew Weatherall's warm up set even now, it's a masterclass in how to make a room start swaying."

To create a party that was free from the snobbery that was going on at the time, the Heavenly Sunday Social's music policy was like Naked Under Leather's – anything goes – so you could hear everything from funk, soul, disco, hip-hop, acid house, Madchester, rock, punk, reggae, ska – just anything that would make the party fun and not take itself too seriously. The most distinctive style of music that was played in these nights was a style of breakbeat influenced electronic dance music that had loud, syncopated drums, often with acid house influenced Roland TB-303 Synthesisers, rock guitars, as well as funk and hip-hop samples, which, at the time, didn't really have a proper name. The Social became (along with the Big Beat Boutique later on) the equivalent of the Cavern Club in Liverpool for this new genre of music.

As stated previously, you have to remember that in that time period, club nights were starting to get increasingly more homogenised in their musical palette, so pretty much all club nights were restricted to a narrow sub-genre. The eclecticism of Naked Under Leather and the Heavenly Sunday Social were a reaction to these trends. "It just felt like if you were playing a certain kind of house or techno, you couldn't do anything else," remembers Alex Gifford from the Propellerheads in an interview for *DJ Mag* in 2014. "People would start by coming up and complaining, and it felt really ludicrous. We just couldn't find enough good stuff in one style to play a whole night. My roots were in jazz and funk, and we started hearing what the then Dust Brothers were doing, Depth Charge and some of the other labels, and thought 'This is definitely the way forward'. So we tried to put tunes together that we could play out. We forget nowadays how easy it is to get exposed to all different styles of music — without spending any time or money finding it. You can educate yourself really easily now, and it's much easier to have eclectic tastes. Back then, you had to go to the right kind of record shop, and if your town didn't have that kind of record shop you would never hear that kind of music. It was much harder for people to develop eclectic tastes." [90]

The nickname of the regulars of the Sunday Social were given the rather apt title of Socialists, seeing as they had a liberal and open-minded approach to music tastes. However, the concept of the Social wasn't original. Preceding the Social, other diverse club nights that were based around pubs existed, such as Full Circle, which was based in Slough, founded by Phil Perry, the rather humorously named Disco Pogo based in Manchester (where The Dust Brothers were regulars), and there was even a free entry Saturday night event at a pub called The Swan, based in Windsor, which shared a similar musical ethos. Another similar minded night was Athletico in the Midlands, which was set up in 1994 by Alex Sparro, Kirsty McAra and Simon Fathead, which had residencies at London's famous Blue Note venue, and Sanctuary in Birmingham. Social resident Justin Robertson also had his own club night called Most Excellent, which also followed the eclectic DJing ethos.

Naked Under Leather founders, and future megastars, The Dust Brothers, would become the Heavenly Social's most prolific residents. During this time, their status in the dance music field would only go up and their success was unbelievable. "The success of The Dust Brothers wasn't immediate," A&R Man for Junior Boys Own, Steven Hall, told me back in December 2017. "The sound was challenging for the times, but the label had a lot of strong supporters who were beginning to become influential. Tom and Ed themselves had some good connections in the so-called 'Balearic network', so things grew steadily and quite naturally. The 'Fourteen Century Sky' EP really took things up a notch and got massive club play from Darren Emerson, Justin Robertson and

20

the DJs at the 'harder' end of the Balearic/progressive house scene. Sales were really good especially on export to the USA, but it was all just relative to underground success at this point. The singles 'Leave Home', 'Life is Sweet' and the album *Exit Planet Dust* were when we all thought we'd really done something, the album went into the charts at number 9 which was amazing for all of us."

Because The Dust Brothers were threatened with a potential lawsuit from their US namesakes, by early 1995 the duo became known as The Chemical Brothers (after their track 'Chemical Beats' from the 'Fourteenth Century Sky' EP), but they did occasionally slip into the habit of referring to themselves as their original name. The duo also produced music with this new style that was starting to emerge, and they would often bring in DATs and acetates of tunes that would later end up on their full length debut album *Exit Planet Dust...* but the punters at the Social were so high on amyl nitrates that any critique was impossible. The clientele that were attracted to these nights were mainly kids from the Britpop/indie scene looking for a dance movement where they didn't feel embarrassed, and also veteran clubbers from the original 1980s Balearic era. Often there would be queues of over 200 people waiting to go in to the Albany for a night out at the Social, and it wasn't just Londoners wanting to come – it was a nationwide craze.

The Chemical Brothers performing at the Big Beat Boutique circa 1996-98 with permission from Damian Harris

21

"The Dust [Chemical] Brothers were the reason we actually started the club," remembers Robin Turner. "There would never have been a Sunday Social without Tom and Ed. I'd started doing their PR in early '94 and was spending a lot of time with them and their mates. Every weekend I'd go to some mad club they were DJing at, and I'd witness proper wild abandon – people jumping off speaker stacks to 'Tomorrow Never Knows' and mad Brooklyn hip-hop 12s. They were the best DJs in the country, but they were always booked for the back room. You'd have Paul Oakenfold or someone playing some mad cobblers in the main room, and Tom and Ed playing this kind of punk rock mutant disco in the back to their crazed mates. I had the idea to start the club as a shop window for them – from a PR perspective, it was massively helpful to have that visibility. They played the last set every week (Tom missed one due to a accident that sent him to A&E); by the end of the 13 week run, I think they were ready to stop – it was pretty chaotic down there. For my money, they're still the best DJs around – I'm going to see them play in a couple of weeks, 25 years or so after first hearing them. Can't wait."

One of the most famous regulars of the Social was Essex DJ Jon Carter, who also DJed and produced under the name of Monkey Mafia. He was previously in several reggae bands and his own DJing and productions heavily leaned towards it. "At the end of the first one, I knew most of the people there," Jon remembers in a May 2000 issue of 7 magazine. "The main enticement at the Albany was just the sheer mayhem. We all used to go back to Beth Orton's flat in Ladbroke Groove to carry on the party. I lived a few doors down, so I used to go home, get my records and kick Tom and Ed Chemical off the decks and put on my beats and Cutty Ranks and that sort of stuff. When it moved, that's when it started getting silly." [106]

Jon would later end up being one of the most prolific and biggest figures in this brand new movement which was emerging. "I can't hack going to house clubs," Jon recalled. "Total respect to The Chemical Brothers, they changed people's minds and opened people's minds up to it." [3]. He was also signed to Heavenly Records – the label that spawned the Social Nights. Jon was known as the "wild boy" of this new movement, famous for his hedonistic and sometimes humorous antics, on and off stage.

Another notable figure in the Social's early days was Irish DJ David Holmes, who dumped his initial techno style for a night of classic northern soul 7 inch singles, as well as Andrew Weatherall, who mashed up classic hip-hop with dub reggae. One other well-known resident at the Social, outside of the Chemicals, was Justin Robertson, who was also in the band Lionrock. Like Jon Carter/Monkey Mafia, his interpretation of this new style of music was heavily influenced by reggae and Jamaican dancehall.

The Social also gave way to an up-and-coming band called Dead Elvis, which was led by Richard Fearless (real name Richard Maguire) – they had many line-up changes over the years. Their name had to be changed to Death In Vegas, as explained by Richard himself in an interview for the Ransom Note: "We were called Dead Elvis and then we had to change the name because there was a record label called Dead Elvis. And my friend had made a film about the last 15 minutes of Elvis' life, with Lee Bowrey playing Elvis, who was my flatmate at the time, and that was the name of the film, and I had a day to change the name, I think." [91]

Death In Vegas would later become one of the most influential acts in this new musical movement (though Fearless told me that he denied being a part of it).

The nights at the Heavenly Sunday Social were also known for being very rowdy. There were instances of punters setting fire to bottles of highly flammable stuff, then dancing in the resulting ring of flames. One time, Ed from The Chemical Brothers had to dodge a flaming shoe hurled towards the decks by some nut job. A person's leg even went up in flames after a potentially lethal spillage caught fire. Talk about a bunch of fire starters!

"I don't really remember that much," recalls Alex Hardee, who represented the Skint and Wall of Sound roster and would later become Special Agent for the world-famous CODA Agency and one of the biggest music agents in the UK. "I remember someone putting amyl nitrate on the floor and setting fire to it at the Heavenly Social."

"The first night I went to the Heavenly Social, Norman Cook was warming up, imagine that now!" remembers DJ Aldo Vanucci. "Leftfield were on next and Chemical Brothers were headlining. I'd been at a wedding or something, as I was wearing a suit, which I rarely did in those days. Musically, you heard everything from Latin and dancehall to house, and what would later be called big beat, but then wasn't. It

23

was literally a life changing experience; it was such a laugh and such a difference from a lot of moody clubbing in those days. You need to understand that big beat came along when you'd had a few years of house nights being all about dressing a certain way, and notorious for people being turned away for not looking right. With big beat anything went, musically, dress wise, it was just a breath of fresh air."

The events at the Albany had become so popular that after its initial 13 weeks, in November 1994 it moved to a temporary stopgap location at Smithfields in the Farringdon area and then finally to its main destination, Turnmills on a Saturday, under the shortened name of The Heavenly Social (obviously, as it didn't take place on a Sunday anymore) as well as a second destination at the Deluxe Club in Nottingham and curating stages at several music festivals. Robin Turner remembers the venue upgrade in an interview for this book in November 2017: "There was a stop-off point prior to Turnmills – eight weeks at a venue called Smithfields which backed onto Smithfields Meat Market in Farringdon. It was an amazing venue – has been empty since about 1998, and was the only thing in the area. After it shut, Fabric opened.

"Turnmills felt like a massive jump. It wasn't one we managed to make work every week – it was a big venue, you needed a lot of DJs to cover the whole place all night. We all loved it, but it was hard work doing it week after week whilst trying to hold down a proper job in the week.

"Festival–wise, we've always loved doing stages. Jeff and myself still do festival things under the Caught By The River banner – it's a slightly less frantic version of what we used to do. That said, Andrew Weatherall has closed Saturday night for us for the last five years, so maybe it's not that different."

Because of the night's massive success, similarly minded club nights started to emerge – one of these was called the Big Kahuna Burger Club based in London and named after the fast food joint in the film *Pulp Fiction*. This was set up in May 1995 by Jon Nowell and Dan Oromdroyd, and followed an identical ethos to the Social; the guys also DJed under the name of FC Kahuna. This originally took place in Finsbury Park, but moved to Smithfields (one of the original haunting grounds of the Social), and gained a huge following. Like The Chemical Brothers, they were known for their chaotic and (possibly deliberately) dubious mixing skills, and they had a notorious reputation for being as drunk and out-there as the punters! They would also have a monthly residency in a venue called Mars, which was based in the centre of London. They also ran the successful label Kuhuna Kuts, which lasted until the early 2000s.

A collection of Heavenly Social and Heavenly Jukebox flyers circa 1994-1998 with permission from Paul Kelly.

Unlike most nights that were associated with the drug culture, drugs were not a big deal at the Social and similar nights. (Though amyl, AKA Poppers, were popular, thus the name amyl house given to the music at the time). Robin Turner remembers in the book *The Nineties: What the F**k Was That About*: "It was not a big drug club, it was a boozer club.

Being on a Sunday meant that people couldn't get so caned. They've got to go to work, and they are skint after the excess of the night before, so it was booze instead" [4]. In an interview for *Spin* magazine in 1998, Damian Harris, founder of Skint Records, states that "I do think England's love affair with Ecstasy is on the wane. A lot of people have gotten bored with E, and they can't handle the comedowns. Big beat's drugs of choice are lager and amyl nitrate." [6]

Drugs however weren't everybody's cup of tea in the new movement – "Both of us don't really do drugs," stated Ed Simons in a 1996 interview for *Melody Maker*. "It's melted our brains over the years. Drugs are nothing to us." [7]

Whilst illegal substances were not as big a deal in the DJ and live circuit, on the production side for some DJ/producers it was a different story, as told by DJ Jadell (James Hatt), who remembers an insightful incident in an interview for this book in December 2017, when he recorded the scratch lines for the Appleseed track 'Mile High Express'.

"We went to Kingsize studio in East Molesey; Nick Faber had laid most of the backing track, and I spent an hour or so doing several types of scratches and cuts for the tune. The phrase I was scratching was a rapper saying 'Let me scratch it in your brain!'

"After finishing the cuts, Nick pulled out a blunt he had rolled, which was full of 'scuff' – I think it's some type of cannabis pollen?

"We passed it back and forth until we had smoked the whole thing between us. When it was done, we sort of looked at each other and began to crack up laughing. Then Nick looked at me and said 'WHOOOAAH!', as he felt a wave of buzz come over him. I had felt another wave surge through me just then also, so I pissed myself laughing a bit more.

"Then, the NEXT wave hit me – and I looked at Nick, whose face had changed from smiling to sort of 'holy fuck!' I was feeling really high. All the shadows in the studio were starting to take on red and green outlines. Then another wave hit me, then another and another all in fast succession. Nick turned around and said something like 'Well, I'd better get back to this tune...' And he got back onto his computer, trying to edit my scratches to fit in the right places he wanted them over the song.

"I stood up, and the room started to sort of melt upwards. The wallpaper seemed to be breathing, and the 3D of the room seemed to be all over the place. I remember thinking 'I'm really not up for this, right now'. I turned to the studio engineer and said 'I'm just going to the bathroom…' but I really just wanted to get the fuck out of there. Nick, who was obviously completely done in also, kept repeatedly trying to get the scratches to land on time, so over and over, all that was playing, loudly, was 'let me scratch it in your brain, brain, br-br-br-br brain'.

"I went out to the bathroom and sat down on the toilet, because sometimes just getting anything out of your body has a helpful purging effect. As I sat there, I was hit with ANOTHER wave, and my visuals intensified further. In the cubicle, a friend of the Kingsize studio had painted a nice kind of magical painting, with hills, mountains, fairies and wizards all holding up magic wands and jumping and skipping about, with speech bubbles saying 'we love Kingsize' and 'love and nice vibes', etc. I just thought, 'fuck… I really don't want to look at anything to make me feel even more trippy than I already am'. As it was, I believe the drawings were done in biro, and my mind was already adding colours, animating the characters, and adding depth of field to the background of the picture. All of this while 'let me scratch it in your brain, brain, br-br-br-br brain' was going on in the next room.

"I couldn't get away from the music, no matter how hard I tried. I put my hands over my ears, walked to the furthest, quietest place in the room. Nick had to have the music up loud, as he was having trouble focusing on it. I looked out of the window. Outside it was raining and dark. The raindrops landed on the pavement with electric crackles. It looked like the pavement was actually pulling the rain down onto itself. The pavement was thirsty.

"I decided that I really had to properly get the fuck out of the building completely, so I walked back into the studio and announced to Nick and the engineer, 'I'm stepping outside to get some fresh air'. Then I opened the door to the back garden and stood in the rain. It was freezing cold, and I could still hear 'let me scratch it in your brain, brain br-br-br-br brain' coming from inside. So, I went back in. I really didn't know what to do. I was miles away from my house, so I couldn't walk it. Nick's label were paying for this studio session, so he couldn't leave. I had no money, so I couldn't get a taxi. I wouldn't have been able to look at money anyway, because my vision was so fucked up. All these thoughts were going round my head really fast, repeating.

"In the end, I took Nick's car keys, borrowed a blanket, and sat in the back seat of his car, trying to get to sleep. I could still hear the music a bit, but it was much, much better. I closed my eyes, and I entered a vortex of 1960s spiky *Tom and Jerry* characters whirling around endlessly sort of punching and kicking each other in fast succession. Really black outlines, lots of blue, red, green colours. I took some deep breaths and tried to get my heartbeat down, and tried to imagine being on a nice sunny beach, and slowly walking up to the blue sea's edge. Eventually it worked, and I dropped off to sleep.

"I woke up when Nick opened his car door to leave. I was feeling alright, and felt utterly relieved. I asked Nick how it all went, and he looked at me and just shook his head, smiling. I put Harvey Mandel's version of 'Wade in the Water' on the cassette player for the ride home. It sounded INCREDIBLE.

"It took quite a few days for me to feel completely normal, however. I thought maybe that was the last time I should do psychedelics. That thought didn't last for very long."

It probably also didn't help that the main music loop of that particular track was based on the soundtrack to the very druggy French 1970s children's film *The Magic Roundabout – Dougal and the Blue Cat* – a movie very fondly remembered by British baby boomers.

Early Success and the Birth of Skint, Wall of Sound and Fatboy Slim

Moving on to The Chemical Brothers – in 1995, because of their astronomical success, Tom and Ed had now outgrown being on an indie label, and opted to sign to major label Virgin (set up by famous businessman Richard Branson) under their own sub-label, Freestyle Dust. "When Tom and Ed left the label to sign with Virgin, it was bittersweet to say the least," remembers Steven Hall, A&R Man for Junior Boy's Own. "It didn't happen overnight and it all happened in a very friendly and 'above board' manner, but I would have loved to have continued working with them. They were very ambitious, and I had only signed them for one album originally, so when the success they were having built and built during the single releases, we all knew that their 'worth' in the business was going up and up. Obviously it was going to be hard for me to offer them an onward deal to compete with the majors, so in the end they signed with Virgin for future albums and I did a deal with Virgin to release *Exit...* jointly on Junior Boys Own/Virgin."

On the 26th June 1995, The Chemical Brothers released their million-selling debut album *Exit Planet Dust*, which was a critical and commercial success.

The *NME* magazine described it as "brash, raw, rule-bending gear made by open-minded music fans for open-minded music fans" [8] and it was even included in the book *1001 Albums You Must Hear Before You Die*, which also contained many future big beat releases such as *The Fat Of The Land* by The Prodigy and *You've Come A Long Way, Baby* by Fatboy Slim. *Exit Planet Dust* was, in many ways, the first "proper" big beat full-length release, and the start of this new genre's rise to commercial glory. In an interview for *Muzik* magazine in June 1995, Ed Simons stated that "Nobody from the dance world has come up with an album to reflect these times. Why is that? Why is it left to a group like Oasis to express the way that young people want to go out and get battered every weekend?" [9]

What made the album special was the structuring of the tracks, like regular rock tunes, rather than the standard textural shapes of contemporary dance music of the time, employing vocalists from the rock and indie fields, such as Tim Burgess from The Charlatans and folk singer Beth Orton, rather than the standard dance divas. They were also not afraid of showing their rock influence by using guitars, cementing the rock/indie/dance crossover further.

Returning to the Social – the club nights were starting to attract some very famous clientele from the Britpop and indie rock scene, such as the Gallagher brothers from Oasis, Primal Scream and The Charlatans (Tim Burgess from the band would sometimes be a guest DJ at the Social). They had grown tired of the soulless corporate afterparties – their infatuation with the Heavenly Social scene led to these artists asking The Chemical Brothers to do remixes for them. "We often used to get asked to remix the Endsleigh league of indie bands" [7] stated Tom Rowlands in a January 1996 issue of *Melody Maker*. Because of the amount of offers they received, they did, however, have to turn a lot down, including big names such as Massive Attack, Echobelly, Consolidated, Fatima Mansions and Deee-Lite. Despite agreeing to remix the likes of Primal Scream, Method Man, Bomb The Bass and the Manic Street Preachers, sometimes they only received paltry sums for their services. They also remixed the classic track 'Packet Of Peace' by Lionrock (fellow Heavenly Socialist, Justin Robertson), which would become one of the de-facto tunes in this new movement. "They are old friends of mine so I was obviously delighted," Justin told me in January 2018. "This was quite early on in their career, but even then you could tell they had a unique and beautiful sound. Psychedelic and irresistibly rhythmic."

Speaking of this new movement's association with Britpop, former *NME* journalist Ben Willmott told me in 2017 that this new genre's crossover with rock was vital to its success and became the gateway for rock and indie kids into the world of dance music.

"As a music journalist, I think the rock element is something that people at *NME* and *Melody Maker*, who weren't necessarily dance heads, could latch on to. Stuart Bailie, who was a big cheese at the *NME* at the time, was always telling me to get down to the Heavenly Social nights because people like Weller and Oasis were hanging out with The Chemical Brothers. That sounded like my idea of hell! Very much against the anti-celebrity ethos that I'd grown up with, going to illegal raves and free parties. And it also indicated the return of alcohol to the equation. I didn't drink at the time, again coming from that rave generation who'd seen the big brewers funding the Tory party and trying to crush the drug culture with quite heavy handed legislation like the Criminal Justice Bill. But he was right, there was something going on there, a kind of freedom away from the snobbier elements of techno culture and a continuation of the kind of cross-pollination that had started with the Stone Roses, Mondays and Weatherall creating 'Loaded' with Primal Scream."

To top things off, in 1995 a then semi-unknown yet very special duo from France, consisting of Thomas Bangalter and Guy-Manuel De Homen-Christo, would sometimes come and play at the Social. They would arguably become one of the most famous and influential acts ever in the electronic dance music scene: Daft Punk. "Well, I wasn't there so everything I say is picked up from people who lived to tell their tales," remembers Robin Turner regarding a set they played at the Social in Turnmills. "We'd had Daft Punk playing before (at Smithfields, our second venue). They were phenomenally brilliant, I loved their early records so much, but I was quite surprised by how they came across. One of them pretended not to speak English, just so he didn't have to bother talking to us. I'm sure he thought we were pricks – maybe we were – but it seemed like a pretty hardcore start point. Anyway, we were all quite surprised when they agreed to do Nottingham a few months later. From all accounts, the party started on the bus trip up – we'd hired a coach to get regulars up there for a smash up. Not sure what they made of their support act, Earl Brutus (one of whom was naked from the waist down during the gig). The bus back sounded utterly riotous – Daft Punk later complained that they weren't part of the Heavenly Social scene and that they'd been kept awake by the smell of amyl all the way back to London. I'd imagine if you'd been kept awake by amyl all night, you'd end up having a good time, but there you go. Pretty sure we put on two of their only British DJ sets – every time they came over afterwards they played live and, presumably, they never needed to pretend they couldn't speak English ever again. "

Daft Punk, while not canonically a big beat act, were very influential in the scene, and their early single 'Da Funk' (which reached No.7 in the UK singles charts) was a staple at the Heavenly Social. Their befriending of Tom and Ed Chemical led to them remixing the Chemicals' single 'Life Is Sweet' in their trademark funked-up house sound (it was also their first remix). Daft Punk would later end up being one of the most successful and acclaimed acts in dance music history.

The Chemical Brothers were now one of the most influential artists in the country at the time. One of the most notable acts to come from this new wave of music was the Dub Pistols. Barry Ashworth from the band remembers how they came to be – all thanks to hearing the sounds of Tom and Ed, and also how they came up with the name Dub Pistols. "It was kinda us trying to think of a name for somebody else's band, my ex-girlfriend and me came up with the name Dub Pistols and she said 'That's great, can I have that?' and I said 'No – I think I'll keep that one!' And it just went on from there – I was just finishing my time with a band I was with previously – I was bored of the 4/4 house sound, and I was just listening to a Chemical Brothers track, who were known as the Dust Brothers then, and decided that was the way I was going to go and that was the sort of music I was going to start making."

Barry was known for his wild on-stage antics – one time, when he was playing at the night RAW he was kicked off the decks after he headbutted one of the turntables – ouch!

A series of compilations on React Records that were very influential in the genesis of the soon-to-be named big beat movement was the *Dope on Plastic!* series compiled by John Stapleton, which had 8 volumes from 1994-2001. Listening to the series from start to finish in itself is pretty much the audial history of the genre, from its evolution from trip-hop to Brit-hop/amyl house to big beat to eventually nu-skool breaks/breaks. Stapleton would also be the man responsible for setting up the popular Bristol big beat night, BlowPop, which lasted from 1998-2013, and the short lived BlowPop record label.

The two biggest labels that would define this brand new genre of music were Skint Records, based in Brighton, and Wall of Sound, based in London.

Skint Records (which was set up by Damian Harris AKA Midfield General) is a sister label to the house label Loaded. The label's initial concept was music with the raw energy of hip-hop and its breakbeats, but at house music tempo. In an interview for this book in January 2018, Damian Harris recalls how the iconic label came to be. "In 1993 I was offered a job by Tim Jeffrey & JC Reid; they ran Loaded Records – an independent house label in Brighton that had released 12"s by Wildchild, Luke Slater and Pizzaman. At the time I was two years out of Brighton Art College and DJing, working in record shops, writing for *DJ Magazine* and *i-D* and doing bits of artwork, flyers and the odd record sleeve. I was in charge of the day to day running of the label, getting records cut and pressed, labels designed and printed, mailing out to DJs and sold to distributors. It was a very good grounding.

"The money was pretty terrible, but it did give me access to a recording studio. Once I'd learnt how to use it, I was obsessed, and was in there at every opportunity. I was naturally drawn to my favourite breaks and samples, as well as squelchy analogue synths, and found myself making a hybrid of all my favourite styles. I liked the stuff, but couldn't think of anyone that might release it.

"Unfortunately my actual job suffered, 'amiable but useless' they said. They were about to sack me, but somehow I managed to convince them to allow me to start my own label instead. The infrastructure was there, so they told me to get my first three releases together. I wasn't allowed to release any house music – as Loaded did that – and I wasn't allowed to lose any money.

"I immediately rang Norman (Cook) and asked if he would make me a record. About a week later he gave me 'Santa Cruz'."

Damian Harris (Midfield General - founder of Skint Records) performing at the Big Beat Boutique with kind permission from Damian himself.

The label began with the debut single from easily one of the biggest artists in the whole genre – former member of 1980s indie pop band the Housemartins, Norman Cook, under his new pseudonym Fatboy Slim. As previously stated by Damian, his debut single was the Lulu sampling 'Santa Cruz'. When I spoke with him in October 2017, Norman explained the origins of the name of his most well known alter ego:

"We just needed another name, at the time I was in Freak Power and I was also Pizzaman and the Mighty Dub Katz, so the last thing I really needed was another alter ego, but Damian Harris bullied me into making records for him. It just came to me when I was trashed one night. I love dirty old blues records and if you are a fat blues singer you get called 'Slim' – there was Pinetop Slim, Memphis Slim, Bumble Bee Slim etc. so I thought, why not the ultimate oxymoron bluesman. It sounded kinda cool, yet wrong at the same time..."

It should also be noted at the time that, due to contractual reasons, he had to keep the fact that Fatboy Slim was Norman Cook a secret.

"Because I was signed to Island Records as Freak Power, it was in my contract that I couldn't make records under false names for independent labels. So for ages I had to pretend it wasn't me. It was a pretty badly kept secret but, legally, we had to keep up the façade. If you saw me DJ it was pretty obvious! At the first ever Big Beat Boutique I was billed as Norman Cook and Fatboy Slim like they were two different people!"

"We couldn't tell anyone who Fatboy Slim was," recalls Damian Harris in an *XFM* interview in 2007, "because he was still under contract for Freak Power. He really wasn't meant to be having any more alter egos. We remember we had to find this picture of someone who we thought could be a Fatboy Slim for the first couple of records and then, people twigged – and then people started to get it and realise it was him." [11]

Fatboy Slim DJ-ing in an Oxfam Shop(!) in Dalston, London for a Charity gig circa October 2007. Picture by Tom Hoy

'Santa Cruz' was a modest seller and sold around 800 copies, but it was a favourite of the Heavenly Social residents, the Chemical Brothers among others. "I was a huge fan of Norman," recalls DJ Aldo Vanucci, "so followed everything he did avidly. I remember the first time I heard 'Santa Cruz' was Norman doing a mix on Kiss FM, I think as part of Freak Power and he played a bunch of his, as yet, unreleased Skint tracks, I used to record all his radio appearances so played the mixes in the car for weeks after." Despite the less than impressive sales, every time Damian Harris played it in his DJ dates, without exception, he would get at least two or three people asking about it, so via word of mouth the career of Fatboy Slim would begin – little knowing that three years later, Norman would become the biggest and most famous DJ on the planet.

One man who witnessed the transition from Norman Cook to big beat icon Fatboy Slim was Robert Luis, who runs the record label Tru-Thoughts. In 1999, he set up Tru-Thoughts, which was funded because of the wild success of Fatboy Slim's remix of his tune with Deeds Plus Thoughts 'The World Is Made Up Of This And That'. In an interview for this book in November 2017, Robert talks about this transitional period, and a little bit about the nights Shake Your Wig and Vibez Express in Brighton.

"I had been running club nights in Brighton from around 1992. That is how I first met Norman. I ran a night called Shake Yer Wig every Wednesday at the Jazz Place and played hip-hop (alongside the original tracks being sampled) plus soul, jazz, hip-hop, reggae/dancehall and beats. The night started doing very well and Norman was booked by a promoter to play at a rival night trying to do a similar style as my night, but it was quiet, so Norman ended up coming down to Shake Yer Wig and asked if he could play a set. He was very humble about it and acknowledged it was a bit cheeky, as I did not know him. Normally I would say no to someone asking to DJ, but I knew Norman had good tunes and was into his music and remixes he had done. This was around the Freak Power era for Norman, but before the big Levi's advert tune. Norman played a great set with Ashley Slater on Trombone. It went down really well and I started booking Norman regularly from then to play at my nights. I did a monthly Saturday night at the Concorde called Vibez Express soon after and booked Norman and Ashley to play there too.

"So I was booking Norman regularly for a few years and booked him to play in November 1995 at the Concorde, and his set was now a bit different, playing the breakbeat/acid/house tracks alongside the hip-hop, funk and soul he used to play. I remember we had a few regulars complain to me about Norman's set, but I knew that this scene was going on (not yet called big beat) so I did not mind the music, and was always quite open if DJs I booked tried different styles out. There was also another part of the crowd well into the music too.

"In December 1995 I booked a Wall Of Sound night with Jon Carter and Derek Dahlarge. It was a busy night and, again, they played some more harder breakbeat/house tunes which some people in the crowd were not into but, again, others were really into it. From my side as a promoter/DJ, part of Norman, Jon and Derek's sets were not where I was going, but they were also playing tunes I was spinning too. But there was definitely a buzz in Brighton about their DJ sets in those two months and I could tell a change was happening musically. Early in January/February 1996 Norman called me and said that he was planning to start a night at the Concorde and was going to book Jon Carter to play alongside himself and asked if I was OK with that, which of course I was. This showed me how nice Norman was, as often in Brighton, promoters and DJs would just go behind my back and try and book people I had been booking. I knew there was a scene developing for them and I always enjoyed booking Norman, but also knew that they were pushing their sound and obviously wanted to have their place to do that in Brighton.

"The last night at the original Concorde ending up being on my Saturday night and the big beat had moved to another venue by then. We wanted to have a big celebration on that last night, and Chris, the owner, asked if I could get everyone together for it, so I ended up booking all the Brighton DJs from the other Saturday night events at the Concorde, and asked Norman if he would play with us and he agreed. All the DJs got the same fee (which was not much as I recall). I told Norman everyone is getting the same fee and he was totally fine about that, he really was a serious headliner at that point."

The other label that would be another de-facto record label in this new movement was Wall Of Sound Records (which has nothing to do with the famous and controversial producer Phil Spector). It was set up by a rather eccentric former singer of boy band Perfect Day, Mark Jones, and his colleague Mark Lessner, in 1994.

"I was originally in a band called Perfect Day, and we got dropped," remembers Mark Jones when we spoke in December 2017. "I wanted to know more about the other side of the industry and how it worked. I was originally doing visual work, and my label partner, Mark Lessner, used to sell records, and I contacted him and worked there for three days a week, and we started Wall Of Sound. We were the first people to sign Basement Jaxx - we were discovering all these new artists, and we thought, let's do a compilation of all these great new artists! We changed people's thoughts on music."

Their debut release was the aforementioned compilation, which was called *Give 'Em Enough Dope* – it contained artists from the trip-hop movement, such as Kruder & Dorfmeister and future signees, such as The Wiseguys (DJ Touché and DJ Regal). Wall Of Sound also saw some big tunes coming out in its first two years. This included 'Trick-shot' by Ceasefire (Jason O'Bryan, Derek Dahlarge and Mark Pember, who was also Meat Katie), the laid back 'Nil By Mouth' by The Wise-guys and EPs from Dirty Beatniks, Zoot Woman, Rootless, and Artery. Mark Jones himself even recorded under the name E-Klectik (with Lessner), and recorded the Brazilian themed 'Maracana Madness', which was done to capitalise on the 1994 World Cup in Brazil. How-ever, they didn't have any signings yet, so their first official signing was none other than Mekon (John Gosing). "I started doing Mekon around 1990," John told me in February 2018. "Later on, I put out a self-re-leased track called 'Phatty's Lunchbox', and Mark Lessner's distribu-tion label Soul Trader were interested in it, and I became the first act to be signed to Wall of Sound."

"The term big beat had yet to land like a clod of mud lobbed on to what was, to my mind, a pretty eclectic music scene," remembers Jemma Kennedy, who used to be label manager for Wall of Sound. "The label had plenty of beatmakers, but also artists like Akasha who were brilliant jazz musicians. I remember everything changing when the Propellerheads arrived with their demo for 'Take California'. It was one of those moments when one record became an aural zeitgeist mo-ment. The phones started ringing and didn't really stop from that point on. By the time I'd become label manager a year later, the whole scene had exploded."

Mark Jones with the Wall of Sound roster circa 1990s with kind permission from Mark Jones himself.

As mentioned previously, one of the acts to emerge from Wall of Sound was The Wiseguys, who would end up being one of the most influential groups in this new genre. DJ Regal from the band, in an interview I conducted in October 2017, recalls the genesis of one of the greatest duos to embrace the scene. "I was first introduced to Theo [DJ Touché] in early '89, by the two rappers from Stockwell I was making demos with, CJ Ace and MC Dynamo. I'd met them the previous year, after a very drunken night out in Covent Garden, where, bizarrely, Hijack were handing out promo 12"s of their new single – was quite an evening! Anyway they introduced me to another DJ they had met in Hammersmith, and so Theo and I hit it off pretty sharpish, both admiring each other's breakbeat finds and turntable skills.

"By the summer of '89 we'd all four become Direct Current MCs (2 MCs, 2 DJs) and we co-won a competition on City FM to get a demo produced by Simon Harris (Music Of Life). That didn't pan out, but the impetus to make our first 12" together resulted in a self-made and self-pressed 12" EP, 'Keep In Step', where we sampled together Talking

Heads, Wilson Pickett and James Brown, for a pretty hype groove. It achieved its highest position of #2 on the Echoes Hip-Hop Chart in April of 1990.

"After another year of unsuccessful demos, Ace and Dynamo went back to college and Theo and I began our next step: forming Fifth Column and working with Solo E. Our Fifth Column demos (x4), feat Sense Live from NYC, got us played on Westwood's Capital Rap Show and DJ 279's Choice FM Hip-Hop show in late '92. It was while working with Sense Live and getting knocked back for deals for our straight up hip-hop demos that we decided to make an instrumental EP, after encouragement from Black Market Records boss, Rene Gelston.

"So, in the winter of '93, after a few months of writing, we went into a studio near Soho, and spent one VERY long weekend, and produced three tracks: 'Ladies Say Ow!' / 'If The Style Fits' and 'The Real Vibes'. We needed a name at this point, and so we thought The Wiseguys would be cool, more so for our sense of humour than anything else. Theo has said that he was inspired by hearing DJ Shadow's debut for Mo' Wax at this time, but me personally, I never heard his stuff until I started working in Notting Hill over a year later...

"Still grieving about our demos being declined, I found the seedling trip-hop scene pretty tame and couldn't stand to be associated with it. However, Pete Rock was making amazing remixes at this time, and his instros were getting banged out everywhere by non-hip-hop DJs too, so we thought fuck it, let's make some instrumental hip-hop. So really, 93/94 was a very fluid time for us – firmly camped in hip-hop culture, but having to stretch our vision out left, in order to make our music... satisfying and unsatisfying at the same time to be honest."

Regal also added how he was discovered by Mark Jones from Wall of Sound, as well as the early success on that label. "In the summer of '94, Mark Jones put together his first Wall Of Sound compilation album – of other labels' work. He had no artists at this point, but the comp *Give 'Em Enough Dope Vol. 1* was a statement of intent, rounding up some of the more leftfield funk, jazz and breakbeat independent 12"s that were swirling around the Sole Trader Warehouse, where he worked. This happened to include our recently released B-side 'The Real Vibes' and soon after he called us in to ask us if we wanted to record a proper 12" for his new label. And so from there, he put us in touch with Jon Carter, in whose Ladbroke Grove flat we spent the week recording our two new tracks, 'Nil By Mouth' and 'Too Easy'.

"Lucky for us, the reception for 'Too Easy' on the promo circuit was massive, so that was finally our door into the business proper. We were released as WALLT008 in June '95 and alongside being placed on the *Back To Mono* comp, it gave us all the boost we needed to finish writing our debut album."

Publicity photograph of The Wiseguys (Regal on the left, Touché on the right) from 1996 taken by Chris Clunn with kind permission from Fake Blood (formally DJ Touché), Regal and Mark Jones from Wall of Sound

The early Wiseguys releases such as 'Ladies Say Ow!' and 'Nil By Mouth' were very influential records in their time. When I spoke to producer Nick Faber in November 2017, he remembers how he got to know about this new movement, thanks to The Wiseguys.

"I discovered the music that would eventually come to be called big beat in 1994, probably when I first heard The Wiseguys' 'Ladies Say Ow' EP that had just been released on Black Market. It was the first time I'd heard a record made by somebody I knew – or knew of, as I hadn't actually met Theo at that point, despite hearing all about him from Jadell.

"The track that really struck me was 'The Real Vibes'; it had a massive effect on me and remains not just one of my favourite tracks from the genre, but simply one of my favourite tracks ever! It inspired me, along with the music that Jadell was making at the time, to start creating sample-based, breakbeat music – we just considered it 'instrumental hip-hop' – and started my journey towards being a producer and beat maker."

Another graduate from the school of Touché and Regal was Jadell. "I was from Hampton, and had quite a few 'best' mates who I would see pretty darn often back then," he recalls. "Theo, who I had been pretty firm with since we met in 1989, had put his first record out as The Wiseguys along with another old graffiti/DJ/record collecting mate from Teddington called Regal. Their first single came out on Black Market records, but then they got talking to Mark Jones and started working 24/7 on their music for his label Wall of Sound.

"In my 2nd year at Uni, which would have been 1995, one of my other best mates from Hampton called Nick Faber got signed too, with Greg Belson, another DJ buddy from Kingston going under the name The Hightower Set. I thought to myself 'Fuck this! What am I doing?' so I started trying to get 3-4 decent tracks together in my bedroom as a demo.

"I had been 'digging in the crates' since about the age of 15; pretty much every weekend all my money went on old and new records. I'd bought a plug-in sampler program for my Amiga A600 computer, and I also had a 4-track tape recorder. So, I'd loop up drum beats and sample things off old tunes nobody had used yet, record them into my 4-track, and then record another layer of me scratching/cutting and adding sound effects.

"I didn't know anyone who was an MC, so I just had to make it sound interesting as strong instrumental hip-hop tracks. I took my demo to Mark Jones at Wall of Sound, but he thought I was a bit too close to The Wiseguys in sound; so my 2nd port of call was to Max Lousada at Ultimate Dilemma records. I got in touch with him as another good graffiti mate, SheOne, was designing their cover art at the time. He loved all of it, wanted to hear more, so boooom that was it, I was getting stuff out at last."

A notable Wall of Sound release in its formative years was 'Trickshot' by the act Ceasefire, who, as previously stated, were Derek

Dahlarge, Jason O'Bryan and Mark Pember (who is also breaks producer Meat Katie). This tune was an underground smash, which sampled the Al Pacino movie *Carlito's Way*, and had a Blaxploitation or *Sweeney*-esque vibe. In an interview for this book in October 2017, Derek Dahlarge remembers vividly when the track went big. "It was amazing – it was the time of my life. It was one of the best summers I've ever had! People like Afrika Bambaataa were playing it, The Chemical Brothers championed it, it was amazing, it blew me away. I'll never forget receiving the test pressing, because it was the first record I'd ever made. I was shaking with anticipation – I took it out of the sleeve, put it on the record player, put the needle on the groove – to hear your own record, it was beautiful. I was blown away by the way it was received – it was mind-blowing – it was a spiritual experience!"

Another act to be signed to Wall of Sound was a duo known as the Dirty Beatniks. "The Beatniks grew out of [the band] Rootless - it was the same people originally - Rory Carlile, Neil Higgins & Justin Underhill, " remembers Rory Carlile when we spoke in December 2017. "We were one of the first acts on WoS: us, The Wiseguys, Jacques Lu Cont, Artery, Mekon, Ceasefire and Akasha all came along at the same time I think - 1994? 1993? We got *Give 'Em Enough Dope Vol 1* when it came out, and realized there were other people out there making music like us. Dirty Beatniks were an uptempo version of the same thing - we were mixing house and breaks, at a higher tempo than what was then being called trip-hop, and not as fast as jungle."

Moving away from Skint and Wall of Sound, one track that was highly influential in this unnamed new style of music was 'Higher State Of Consciousness' by Josh Wink. The 'Original Tweekin' Acid Funk Mix' reached No.7 in the UK singles charts, and its mixture of rave breakbeats and squelchy Roland TB-303 hook was imitated endlessly by the founders of the genre currently without a name, notably Fatboy Slim on his track 'Everybody Needs a 303'. Interestingly, the tune started off life as a Kruder & Dorfmeister-esque trip-hop track, which was featured on the Strictly Rhythm compilation *The Deep & Slow* in 1994 – other than having a big breakbeat and a 303, the original version and the famous 'Tweekin' Acid Funk Mix' are worlds apart in style.

Not everybody discovered this new kind of music in the clubs (some were too young, like myself - I was only 7 in 1995) but instead some found it through a very popular video game for the Sony Playstation (the original) that was released in September 1995 called 'Wipeout'.

This futuristic racing game was set in the year 2052, and featured an electronic inspired soundtrack containing many big tunes from the day, including The Chemical Brothers. One DJ who discovered this new genre via 'Wipeout' was none other than Richard Marshall, who would later make music in this style under the name of Scanty Sandwich.

"I remember the very first Playstation came out in 1995 and there was a driving game called 'Wipeout' which had this fantastic soundtrack – artists like Leftfield and Orbital – but there was this one blistering track – 'Chemical Beats' by the Dust Brothers (later known as The Chemical Brothers) – that just blew me away."

There was now only one piece missing in the puzzle – a name for this new genre of music, so the next chapter will look at the many origins of why big beat came to be known as big beat.

What's That Sound? - The Many Origins of the Name 'Big Beat'

This is where things get hazy, as people I've spoken to for the book seem to have different takes on where the name 'big beat' originates. It was probably a simple case of similar minded people thinking along the same lines at different times. There was even a band from the late 1980s who were doing a concept that they called "big beat", which was almost identical in style to the "big beat" we know today – more on this later.

As previously stated, at around 1994-5, this new style of music didn't really have an established name, so journalists at the time often referred to it as either Chemical Beats (after The Chemical Brothers track of the same name), Brit-hop (as a play on Britpop, during the press' infatuation with the genre at the time), hardhop (coined by famous hardcore techno producer, Omar Santana), tripno (a hybrid of trip-hop and techno) which was also spelt as trypno, Brighton breaks (probably because of Norman Cook), hard hypo, and rip-hop (coined by Keith Cameron of the *NME* to describe Fatboy Slim's first album). The most popular of these names at the time was amyl house (based on the fact that a lot of the clubbers were fond of amyl nitrates). Another of the terms that journalists were using, which seemed to stick, comes from a friend of the journalist Ben Willmott, who used to work for the *NME* (*New Musical Express*) magazine (he's now working for the broadsheet newspaper *The Guardian*). Ben coined the phrase 'big beat' in a 1995 issue of the *NME*. In an interview for this book in September 2017, Willmott explains his genesis of how big beat became known as big beat.

"The first time I ever heard the name was when a mate of mine called Flee was staying on my floor and DJing at nights around the UK with the Cyclorama sound system. He came up with this phrase 'Big Beat' to describe the mixes on various 12"s that concentrated mainly on the beats, which were quite stripped down. So stuff like the DJ Food albums on Ninja Tune would fit into that, stuff by the Ballistic Brothers too - just the odd mix though - we'd be playing those mixes alongside tracks like 'Theme' by Sabres Of Paradise and 'Coup' by 23 Skidoo, which was a lot older, but strangely bore a close resemblance to 'Block Rocking Beats' by The Chemical Brothers, which was a long way in the future. So I just started using the 'Big Beat' tag in my reviews, and when things like 'Take California' or the first Mekon tune arrived, and the same with the early Skint tunes, it was a name that seemed to fit."

On April 23rd 1996, promoter and part-time DJ and producer, Gareth Hansome (AKA G Money and one half of Norman Cook's project, the Mighty Dub Katz), Norman Cook (Fatboy Slim) and DJ/Producer Damian Harris (Midfield General) set up a club night in Brighton with a very similar ethos to the Heavenly Social called the Big Beat Boutique (originally to be called The Social on Sea or more humorously, Kung Fu Jim Jams) - a night with the appropriate subheading of 'Party Rocking, Genre Trashing Bollocks', which took place in a tiny wobbly wooden hut known as The Concorde (which was named after the famous plane and was amusingly, during the daytime, a bingo hall for the elderly!). It was chosen because of its grotty, sweaty, rock & roll atmosphere - the antithesis of the sexy, glamorous clubs of the more mainstream scenes.

When I spoke to Gareth Hansome in November 2017, he told me that the Big Beat part of Big Beat Boutique was suggested to him by Mark Jones from Wall of Sound, who had heard the term being used by Ben Willmott to describe the acts on Wall of Sound and Skint, and the Boutique part of the name was a nod to the Beastie Boys' seminal album *Paul's Boutique*.

Big Beat Boutique flyer from 1998, courtesy of Freddy Fresh

"I think I first heard the term 'big beat' at a night in Brighton - or it could have been something at the Blue Note in Hoxton Square, London," remembers producer Jadell. "By 1998 I realised we were sort of involved in a 'scene', as you would often see the same people each week. If you were DJing three nights a week or more, you'd get to become pretty good friends with these guys, and that's how a lot of collaborations came about. I would regularly see people like Deadly Avenger, Barry Ashworth, Jon Carter, Stuart Price, Richard Norris, Aim and the Grand Central crew, the Pussyfoot crew who used to work out of Milo / Miloco studios in Hoxton Square, the Skint records crew, and of course all of the Wall of Sound crew, as my best mate Theo [DJ Touché from the Wiseguys] was constantly doing things with all of them. So yes. I'd say virtually every night, I was out having a massive laugh with all that lot. Then it would be on to somewhere else... then back to someone's flat... then on to the next day. Every day seemed like a Saturday to me."

When I spoke to Norman Cook (Fatboy Slim) in October 2017, he told me what he considered to be the thing he was most proud of. He said: "Having the genre [big beat] named after our club. There were all kinds of names as the scene was growing, trypno, Brit hop, amyl house, but if you think house music was named after the Warehouse Club in Chicago and garage after the Paradise Garage, it is a tremendous honour to have a genre named after your club!"

When speaking to Ben Willmott in September 2017, I asked him how he felt when he saw a club named Big Beat Boutique.

"Very flattered, obviously, although the name is so simple it could have easily been put together by someone who hadn't seen my reviews."

Funnily enough, this new genre wasn't the first to be called 'big beat' - it's a name that has been used to describe various styles of music since at least (to the author's knowledge) the dawn of the 20th century. An example is its use as an alternate name for rock & roll in its early years, probably coming from the ABC TV show from the 1950s *The Big Beat* hosted by Alan Freed, who also organised package tours with the likes of Chuck Berry, The Everly Brothers and Buddy Holly & The Crickets.

There was also a popular rock & roll magazine from the 1960s called *Big Beat*, and The Beatles in their pre-Ringo Starr years played at several events called Operation Big Beat (coined by Liverpool promoter Sam Leach, who I met in Liverpool at the famous Grapes pub). On their US second album (*The Beatles' Second Album*) the front cover states

'Electrifying Big Beat Performances,' not to mention a 1963 newspaper article for The Beatles by Donald Zec of the *Daily Mirror* containing the headline 'The Big Beat Craze'.

Coincidentally, their 1966 psychedelic masterpiece from the *Revolver* album 'Tomorrow Never Knows' feels like the prototype for every Chemical Brothers track ever, and was a staple in Tom and Ed's early DJ sets (I personally think that tune was the "first" ever modern big beat track). This trippy song had tape loop samples (often in reverse), an unusual drum beat that sounded like it was looped, and John Lennon reciting the Tibetan Book Of The Dead, with his voice filtered through a Leslie speaker. The Chemical Brothers track 'Setting Sun' (which features later in the book) is a direct tribute to it, and Paul McCartney's lawyers thought they were directly copying 'Tomorrow Never Knows'.

Also in the 1960s 'big beat' (alternately 'big bit') was a term for homegrown rock & roll in Eastern Bloc countries such as Poland and the Czech Republic. This was because the name 'rock & roll' was considered an element of American imperialism by the authorities of the time, and musicians who wanted to play rock & roll had to think of an alternative name for this genre. 'Big beat' was a natural fit. It was coined by Polish journalist, Franciszek Walicki, who was a member of the first Polish 'big beat' band called Rhythm & Blues. Arguably the most popular of these 'big beat' acts was Czerwono-Czarni, who had many big hits in their home country and even opened for the Rolling Stones in 1967, but the term fell out of favour by the 1970s. "Because of the ambiguity caused by the names," recalls Michal Borczon aka BMD, a Polish big beat DJ and founder of XLNT Records and Tru-Funk Records, "some people in Poland were quite confused when I was telling them that I play big beat and it actually sounded like breakbeat, and not at all like rock & roll."

A 1960s/70s bandleader from Portsmouth, Jack Hawkins (d.2015 - not to be confused with the famous actor of the same name), even had his sound described as 'big beat' and was known for Go-Go-Pop covers of tracks as diverse as the theme from *Shaft, Match Of The Day, Hawaii Five-0* and even *The Wombles* theme. In the classic 1971 Michael Caine movie *Get Carter* Caine's character (Jack Carter) visits a nightclub, where Jack Hawkins and his band make a cameo, playing a cover of the Willie Mitchell tune '30-60-90' and the poster outside the club states 'BIG BEAT NIGHT with Jack Hawkins' - though obviously, this has nothing do with the modern term for 'big beat' music... Not a lot of people know that.

Unbeknownst to many, there was an act who described their music as 'big beat' and had an identical concept to modern big beat by mashing disparate styles of music together - the 1980s electronica band, Big Bang (Laurence Malice, who's best known as promoter for the LGBT Club night, Trade, and Iain Williams, with vocalists Teresa Revill and Jasmine Ventura), who were formed in 1988.

"Laurence Malice and I of Big Bang had previously been in a band together called You You You, along with singer Karen O'Connor and backing vocalist Alice Shaw," Iain told me in January 2018. "The band had built a sizeable following on the club circuit, and throughout 1987 performed a series of sell-out shows in London, the south of England, and in Paris, France. By the summer of 1988, the band was in the process of signing a record deal with Tom Astor who owned Orinoco Studios in London, where we had been recording tracks. When Karen announced in July that she was leaving to pursue an acting career, You You You disbanded. Soon after, Laurence and I decided to continue working together musically and formed Big Bang, originally as a studio-based band employing guest vocalists. No sooner did this happen than Big Bang secured a record deal with Swanyard Records. Margarita Hamilton, who owned the Swanyard Recording Studio complex in Islington, London, created the record company in order to sign Big Bang to it."

Iain Williams from the band described their music as "big beat" and he explained the concept in an issue of the *London Metropolitan Magazine*, which was also featured on the press release of their debut single, a Middle-Eastern flavoured cover of the ABBA classic 'Voulez-Vous?'

When I spoke to Iain, he told me how he came up with their big beat sound (as well as getting clearance from Benny and Bjorn from ABBA).

"Prior to Big Bang signing to Swanyard Records in January 1989, Laurence and I had, for several months, been experimenting and recording in a demo studio that belonged to the hugely talented musician and producer Simon Thomas. Thomas co-produced all the tracks with Big Bang that were demoed at the studio. As with You You You, Big Bang were primarily interested in producing dance tracks, with catchy, memorable tunes, with the aim of achieving chart success.

"In doing so, we took on board various elements and music genres already established, and some newer electronic ideas, and mixed it all up. New Beat from Belgium greatly interested us, as did the whole European dance sound. At Swanyard Studios, we worked with engineer/producer Steve Toth, who was managing and co-producing the band Nitzer Ebb, another band we admired. Laurence's musical background hailed from London's club land, in as much that he ran club nights and knew all the right DJs in the city that mattered. I coined the term big beat to describe our sound and our musical ethos, taking 'big' from our band's name, and 'beat' from the music that was coming from Belgium, new beat. The name big beat instantly stuck. Our agent, 10 X Better, even produced a press release in 1989 to accompany our first record release, in which it states our musical direction was termed big beat.

"Big Bang's sound consisted of various experimental musical elements, including heavy hard rock drum beats, and synthesizer-generated loops, as well as an added suggestion of European and Arabic influences that, at times, had a trance-like quality. In the demo studio, we would first produce an instrumental dance track and then later add vocals to it, at which time, most of the track would already be laid down. We brought the vocalists Teresa Revill and Jasmine Ventura on board, to sing on most of the tracks. When our first white label, an Arabic-inspired version of Abba's 'Voulez Vous?', was distributed to UK clubs and hit #1 in the club dance charts, that inspired us and Swanyard to release it to the public commercially.

"However, we were walking on dangerous terrain here, because we hadn't just recorded an Abba song, and re-arranged it with Arabic melodies, we had also rewritten the instrumental part of the song. The recording was sent over to Abba's management company, Polar Music in Sweden, for clearance before we were able to release it commercially. No one at Swanyard expected to get clearance from Benny and Björn, the songwriters in Abba. Amazingly, our version was given clearance by Abba's management and Benny and Björn. In fact, later that same year, our vocalist Teresa Revill was introduced to Benny and Bjorn backstage at the London musical, 'Metropolis'. Teresa was a featured singer in the production and Benny and Bjorn had come along to see the show. When Teresa met them she mentioned she was the singer on Big Bang's recording of 'Voulez Vous?' to which the Abba songwriters said they thought the recording was one of the best covers of an Abba song they had ever heard. I believe Big Bang are, to this day, the only

49

musicians ever to have been given clearance by Benny and Björn to alter one of their songs. For reference purposes, Madonna only sampled the instrumental introduction to Abba's song 'Gimme! Gimme! Gimme!' for her song 'Hung Up,' she never rewrote any part of Abba's music."

Big Bang's version of big beat is probably best shown in their track 'Cold Nights in Cairo' ('Voulez-Vous?'' B-Side). One major difference with Big Bang's version of big beat was that the music was done with live instrumentation, while the more well-known version of big beat is, in general, plunderphonic, using chopped up breakbeat loops and samples.

I also asked Iain how he thought when other people started to make big beat music.

"It's always interesting to hear, and to see how music in any genre develops and expands over time, and that's exactly what has happened to big beat."

Big Bang disbanded in 1991 (but briefly reformed in 2013 after renewed interest in the band) – Laurence Malice would later set up the famous LGBT Club night, Trade, specialising in the hard house genre, which took place at Turnmills in London where, coincidently, the Heavenly Social (later Heavenly Jukebox) took place. "My favourite moment with Big Bang has to be working with Laurence," remembers Iain. "He truly is a genius and deserves all the accolades that are given him. His rich career lays testament to that fact. Laurence encourages an artist to grow, and experiment, and develop. That's exactly what he has always allowed me to do. I hope I did, and still do, the same for him."

Also in a very strange coincidence, the original US Dust Brothers, who The Chemical Brothers named themselves after, had a weekly hip-hop radio show on Pomana College Radio Station KSPC, which started in 1983, called 'The Big Beat Showcase'. There was also a BBC Radio 1 show in 1987 that was the first weekly dance show on that station hosted by Jeff Young. Its name – 'Big Beat'. Also in 1987, a record label called Big Beat was set up in New York by DJ Craig Kallman, and is part of the major label Atlantic Records. While the label does specialise in dance music and hip-hop, it isn't really a label that specialises in the big beat music style that we know.

In a nutshell - why big beat ended up being called big beat is a very confusing story.

Start the Commotion - Big Beat Flourishes (1996-7)

Big Beat Rises and Mix CDs Emerge

By 1996, the big beat movement had finally been set in stone. Big beat-themed mix CDs were starting to appear on the market. The first of these was released in January '96 and mixed by an uncredited Tom Rowlands from The Chemical Brothers called *Brit Hop and Amyl House* on Concrete Records. It's a fantastic time capsule of the genre in its initial phase, though Ed Simons wasn't keen on the amyl reference in the compilation's title and described it as "the worst title for a record I've ever heard in my life" [3]. The liner notes of the CD were provided by none other than the co-founder of the Heavenly Social himself, Robin Turner. Here is a small extract -

"It's not about electronic Easy Listening music or ambient Trip-Hop by numbers, it's not about chin stroking stoner music. This is Dance music, music that makes you jump around until you can't jump no more... maybe it's a generation thing, but, to me, this is about feeling good, getting high. It's a rush." [98]

Other mix CD releases in 1996 saw the *Heavenly Presents - Live at The Social Vol. 1* CD mixed by the Chemical Brothers in May of that year. It was a very eclectic showcase of the Social nights, featuring classic cuts from Eric B & Rakim, Davy DMX, Meat Beat Manifesto, Lionrock, The Charlatans, Eddie Bo and, of course, Tom and Ed themselves. The success of this CD also saw a subsequent compilation mixed by Jon Carter (also in 1996) and another one by Andrew Weatherall and Richard Fearless in 1999, during big beat's twilight year in the mainstream (though the latter compilation is about as un-big beat as possible.) More and more people were discovering this brand new musical movement, which had now been given a proper name - big beat (though it was still being referred to as other things, and it didn't really become standardised as the name for this new form of music until late '96/early '97).

Leeds DJ, Andy Halstead, aka Ictus, remembers when he discovered this new form of music via The Chemical Brothers in an interview for this book in October 2017:

"I am not actually 100% sure when I 'discovered' big beat as a 'genre', but I know I have always loved drum breaks in songs - anything that I heard with a break in it - even as a kid - was a sure thing for me. I suppose if we're talking about big beat as a style of music, then The Chemical Brothers spring to mind first, to have made me think 'ooh, that's different' – very, very raw and trippy tracks, with heavily processed breakbeats that still make me nod my head today – 'Chico's Groove' being my fave from the Chems."

"For me, big beat always offered something a bit different and refreshing from a lot of the house music that was around at the time," remembers James Glenton, journalist for *Mixmag* who reviews breakbeat releases, and produces under the name of Lebrosk. "Those infectious broken beats and massive breakdowns made such an impact on the dance floors. I remember seeing Oasis play their huge Knebworth gig in 1996, but it was the lesser known warm-up act, The Chemical Brothers, who made the most impact for me that day. It was the first time I really heard this kind of music and it completely blew me away! After that, I heard Fatboy's *Better Living Through Chemistry* album and I was truly onboard. The internet was in its infancy in the mid-90s and there was something exciting about scouring the record shops for the latest Skint or Wall Of Sound releases and getting them home and playing them out loud."

"I guess, as with most genres of music, I didn't find it – it found me," remembers Harrogate artist, DJ Trev Broadbank. "That is to say, I already had a lot of tunes like that, before I heard the term big beat. Certainly I'd been playing artists like The Wiseguys and Fatboy Slim before really realising it was a break-away genre of its own."

"I'd grown up listening to (and learning to drum to) a lot of '70s funk and soul, so it was logical that those influences, mixed with electronic bleeps, beats and basslines, was where my music was going," big beat DJ/Producer Max Sedgley told me in February 2018. "Hip-hop was a huge force to be reckoned with when I was a teen in the late '80s, and I loved it, but always wanted something a bit faster to dance to, but with that kind of fat production. When I heard the Propellerheads or The Chemical Brothers, I knew that mixture was where a lot of artists saw things heading, too. "

"I've always been a pretty committed record collector, and would continually be trawling for new records to play while DJing," remembers Andrew Divine, who was the co-founder of the Scottish big beat night, Hi-Karate. "Although my roots were definitely indie, I loved seeking out influences - so quickly became obsessive about obscure old '60s and '70s stuff like the Velvet Underground, The Stooges and Funkadelic. I loved hip-hop, like the Beastie Boys, De La Soul, and A Tribe Called Quest, but probably more for the old samples than the raps - so hearing things like Fatboy Slim and Bentley Rhythm Ace in the mid-'90s really just clicked with me. Suddenly there were records which sampled things like 'Love Loves To Love' by Lulu (yes, LULU!) which I'd played out for years, which I could now mix with - I could totally relate to a style of music which was focused on obscure samples, crate-digging and the dancefloor. David Holmes tracks sampling old jazz instrumentals, the Bassbin Twins taking Skatalites tunes and knocking them out the park, The Chemical Brothers sampling Schoolly D and the Cocteau Twins, the Propellerheads sampling old spy soundtracks - for a brief period of time, it was like a bunch of old mods, punks and indie-kids were creating a style of music just for me.

"I remember in an interview, The Chemical Brothers talking about how The Jesus & Mary Chain tried to get Marley Marl to produce them, round about the time of 'Sidewalking' - and how if this had happened, they wouldn't have had to make their own music! That, to me, pretty much summed up what big beat was all about. I also remember talking to The Chemical Brothers in the toilets at an MTV Awards party in New York about how Belle & Sebastian wanted to do a cover of 'Block Rockin' Beats' but I don't think they really believed me... "

One of the most well known faces on the underground tip for big beat was Damon Baxter, who DJed under the name of Deadly Avenger. "When I first signed to DC Recordings (Depth Charge's label) in London, I hung about Portobello Rd, met a few people, did a few local gigs and started hearing it (might have been Chems' [Chemical Brothers] track)," remembers Damon. "Coming from hip-hop and breaks etc seemed like a natural step for me."

"If you think about it, big beat had the all the existing elements of dance music rolled into one phat sound: breakbeats, 303 acidy effects, flowing with hip-hop samples and a funky house foundation," states Bristol DJ and Producer, Lee Mathias (aka Stepping Tones) in a 2018 essay. "It could, as well, be fast like techno, and with the build-ups and release of drum & bass, so it moulded into many different shapes of 'electronica'. In terms of club nights, it reflected an eclectic vibe and gave DJs more freedom to impress their influences and different styles into one set. In a sense, it was a goofy rebellion against the generic club nights for those who preferred more mash-up type DJ sets, with plenty of old funk records thrown in for good measure."

The Start of Big Beat Boutique

As stated in the last chapter, 1996 saw the start of probably the most well-known night in the big beat canon - Big Beat Boutique.

"It's all my fault," says promoter Gareth Hansome in an interview for *The List* magazine in December 1998 on the success of the Boutique. "It's like you go to the pub and listen to Oasis in the jukebox, go round the corner and go to a small student night and hear some really good scratch DJs playing hip-hop, then a raging house night, then an illegal techno party and end up at some dodgy place hearing a bloke playing an acoustic guitar singing folk songs. I just wanted to put all that into one." [74]

The concept for Big Beat Boutique started in 1995, but couldn't be staged until a year later, because Gareth couldn't find an appropriate venue (as previously mentioned, he settled for the unglamorous venue known as The Concorde). Like Naked Under Leather, The Heavenly Social and the Big Kahuna Burger, this was done as a reaction to industry trends of the time... and because he heard a certain 'Santa Cruz' record by a certain Fatboy Slim! In an interview for this book in January 2018, Damian Harris (Midfield General) remembers how the famous club night came to be:

"I had been putting on club nights ever since I was 16, so I was always going to have a Skint label night. I did try one with some friends from college but it didn't really take off.

"The problem was, the flyers would always look great, but we were terrible promoters, so when Gareth and I first talked about doing something, it worked because he was really good at actually getting people to come along.

"The Boutique was an extension of the house parties were having at Norman's - doing them at The Concorde meant we didn't have to clear up afterwards. We were also heavily inspired by The Heavenly Social, which was happening in London at the time. It was the first time you could feel something resembling a scene was happening.

"The first one only had 70 people there, but we had a blast. Every night after that was packed. We had a really good crowd who went with us, allowed us to play what we liked, take risks. Nothing was defined back then, and it's so liberating. As DJs, we both felt incredibly lucky to experience it.

"This might sound a bit weird, but I would often be at clubs and have this feeling 'I bet there's a better party going on somewhere else'. The Boutique was the first time I ever felt at one of my nights that there was no better place to be."

"The first time I was aware of the big beat movement and big beat becoming a 'thing' was when the Big Beat Boutique started in Brighton down at the old Concorde venue opposite the Brighton Pier," remembers DJ Cut La Roc in an interview for this book in October 2017. "We'd (me and a few friends) all been making semi eclectic weird tracks for a while, that encompassed hip-hop, funk, indie, acid etc etc… all forms of music really, just a bit mashed up and crazy, I'd heard about (and then later played at) The Heavenly Social, and was also aware that Norman FBS [Fatboy Slim] had also been making similar music in his spare time, in between being Pizzaman and all of his other musical pseudonyms - all of this was literally when Skint launched, an idea that came from Damian 'Midfield General' Harris, who was also making this 'new sound' music as well, and we all needed an output for it. I'd been recording music for Loaded Records and several offshoot labels that they were doing, but the music didn't really sit with those labels, so Skint was a real blessing to have been involved with and, quite frankly, totally changed my life forever, so I owe Damian, JC and Tim (and the Skint staff!) a lifetime of gratitude. It was a great feeling being signed to Skint, it all just weirdly came together, and with the success that the Fatboy Slim material had from the off, it propelled us all to dizzying heights of demand really quickly and, before we knew it, the Big Beat Boutique was hugely popular, and we were all off on our travels around the world DJing in crazy places all over the shop, something I'm still doing now."

The most well-known resident from the night was Norman Cook, who also DJed under his new alter ego Fatboy Slim. As previously stated by Damian Harris, an inspiration for the Big Beat Boutique nights were the infamous after parties Norman Cook held at his house at the time called the 'House Of Love' - these were known for being very wild get togethers, that sucked people in and didn't let them go for days on end. Like Naked Under Leather, the Social and the succeeding Big Beat Boutique nights - the diverse "anything goes" musical ethos was identical.

Fatboy Slim discovered the big beat scene via his good friend and former Beats International vocalist, Lindy Layton, who took him to a Heavenly Social night, and he befriended The Chemical Brothers, who he considers "kindred spirits" - who coincidentally, were playing the first Fatboy Slim single 'Santa Cruz' when he walked in (Tom and Ed were shocked that Fatboy Slim was Norman Cook). He was amazed that there was a night that shared a similar ethos to his 'House Of Love' parties, that championed eclecticism over purism. In an interview for XFM Radio in 2007, Norman remembers this pivotal moment: "Lindy Layton from Beats International phoned me up one day and said 'You know that music you like that no-one else likes, I've just found a club with other people who like it' and she took me to the Social, and to the Big Kahuna Burger… and it was like meeting the rest of my long lost family." [11]

The Big Beat Boutique's debut night's lineup included Norman Cook (and Fatboy Slim too!), Midfield General, Jon Carter, Sean Rowley (Britpop band Oasis' warm-up DJ) and Gareth Hansome himself under the DJ name of G-Money. As previously stated by Damian, the very first night only attracted a very paltry 70 punters, though the night was considered successful enough to carry on with subsequent nights.

Former *NME* journalist Ben Willmott remembers going to the Boutique fondly. In an interview with me in September 2017, he told me about his favourite moment. "On a personal level it was the night I went to Brighton to cover the Big Beat Boutique and ended up being put up in Norman Cook's house, the famous House of Love. The room I slept in had all his master tapes, and I remember thinking I'd never been close to that much musical history, because he was someone who had, even then, had hits in a number of different incarnations and across several generations. I also quite fondly remember Fabio slagging me off on the Radio 1 Jungle show for wearing a Big Beat Boutique t-shirt down to the Metalheadz night, which was almost why I did it. Not to wind him, I mean, but to oppose puritan thinking whenever I had an opportunity to do so."

"The first time we played the Big Beat Boutique, we arrived really early," remembers DJ Spatts from Environmental Science, who were signed to Skint Records, and were a proper live act. "The place was locked up. So, bored of sitting on our flight cases, we broke in through a toilet window (or something). We got caught and ended up having a huge row with what we assumed was the cleaner/caretaker. It turned out to be Tim Jeffery, who had just signed us. This was all before Facebook, so we didn't know what the guy looked like. How we laughed!

"When we performed live, myself and Seamus would be on all the samplers, synths and drum machines, Stranik would be on guitar, with Zak and a lady singer called FZA out front. It was unlike anything anyone was doing in the big beat scene at the time. It owed a lot to the OTT showmanship of Parliament/Funkadelic. Everything blended into a continuous 'funked up' journey. The live show was high on drama, to say the least."

In an interview for this book in November 2017, I asked the co-founder of the Heavenly Social, Robin Turner, if there was any rivalry between the Social and the Boutique.

"I never thought of the BBB as a copycat club, it was a brother/sister club that we bounced ideas and DJs off. I'm a firm believer that ideas sit there in the ether and wait for people to pluck them out. The way I see it, the Sunday Social was an inevitable reaction to what was going on elsewhere in club world. Made sense that around the country, people were thinking the same thing. There were amazing records being made – slower, heavier, funkier, punkier, odder – but they would never have been spun in your average city centre discotheque. Record shops were selling them though – you only need to look at the amount of records The Chemical Brothers were selling at that point."

"I think what people liked about nights like the Social and the Boutique were the prevailing 'anything-goes' attitude," states Carl Loben, editor for *DJ Mag* who at the time worked for *Melody Maker*, in an exclusive interview for this book in 2017. "This extended to — or partly emanated from — the tracks that were getting made under the big beat umbrella. A DJ or producer could throw in a guitar riff, a huge stonkin hip-hop beat, an air-raid siren or a sample from a TV western - it didn't matter, there were no rules. It didn't matter what you wore either - just as long as you were there.

"Big beat's early 'do it yourself', 'anything-goes', 'bung it all in' (chiefly in terms of samples) attitude was a counterpoint to the homogenisation of mainstream house music and the purism of techno. It also served as a bridge between the rock and the dance worlds — something which was very important. Writing for weekly inkie *Melody Maker* at the time, big beat was a godsend. There was little understanding of dance music by most of the editors and writers on the paper - with some notable exceptions - but take them to a club night where they played a bit of Public Enemy or the Beach Boys and The Clash alongside some mainframe-wrekkin' breakbeat or whatever, and they were reeled in.

"Big beat helped convert a whole swathe of 90s youth to the wonders of dance music. People who were sold on Britpop would also like to go on to a club night after the Elastica gig or whatever - and, already a few pints to the good, maybe drop a cheeky pill to extend their night out by a few hours? Big beat was all about a sense of abandon; hedonism with a rock & roll attitude; a love of an eclectic range of music; having a fun-packed party. Big beat never forgot that it was a party - not much po-faced, booth-hanging trainspotting went on at big beat nights."

While the DJ and producer side of big beat was very male-centric, in an ironic twist, the Boutique's clientele was very female heavy. "About 70% of the people who come down to the club are women, which proves to me that the club had very little to do with the whole dull thing about playing big beat stuff all night - that's for the lads," stated Gareth Hansome in an 1997 issue for *Jockey Slut*. "Last Friday, for example, Norman Cook was playing The Kinks next to Transglobal Underground, that sort of thing. It's about playing a party set." [97]

One of the great things about big beat was that it was for everybody - the genre didn't have a dress code or the like. It brought people together. Lee Mathias aka Stepping Tones states in this essay how the power of big beat brought different cultures together:

"Another unique element was it helped a mixed generation of youths dance side by side. When goths, punks, hippies and 'townies' are all grooving to the same beat, you know you have a winning formula. And at a time when Britpop was top of the charts, the two simply went hand in hand. Big beat didn't just cover the big party tunes, it also gave birth to the experimental and darker sounds of Skint Records, Wall of Sound, Athletico, Fused & Bruised and whatever Freddy Fresh was up to in his basement-dwelling drum machine days. It could be argued that big beat and trip-hop were different sides of the same coin."

The world of big beat also had a strong presence on radio, most notably BBC Radio 1. "A huge thanks must go to Mary Anne Hobbs, as growing up in the rural Welsh countryside, both her and John Peel were my main source of music from the outside world that I truly connected to," remembers Lee Mathias. "I actually found that their selection of reggae, hip-hop, breakbeat, drum & bass and anything independent sounding were better than the DJs who specialized in those areas. And the fact that it was all jumbled up and diverse made it even more special. From memory there were two hours of John Peel starting at 9pm, followed by four hours of Mary Anne Hobbs, which included a guest Breezeblock DJ mix, this was on Monday and Tuesday evenings.

"This began my quest for this new funky breakbeat sound and everything that came with it. I couldn't find or buy blank tapes quickly enough to record all the shows and mixes; I'd swap recorded mix-tapes with mates who stayed up late to 'turn the tape over' as some of us had stereos that would do this automatically. Some of us didn't.

"Again the 'Breezeblock DJ mixes' were always far more interesting, compared to what Radio 1 was providing on the weekend, which often seemed dull to whatever was happening on Mary Anne's show. Her guests had the chance to dig really deep into their record collections and create some memorable mixes; it always seemed to be about how far they could mash styles together rather than seamless mixing. I think this had a profound effect on my DJ and production style, both good and bad! Any fans of the 'Breezeblock' will recall fond memories of these far-out guest mixes."

Big Beat Begins to Get Big

1996 saw the release of many massive tunes from the Big Three (Fatboy, The Prodigy and The Chemical Brothers) including The Chemical Brothers' crossover anthem 'Setting Sun' with Oasis co-frontman Noel Gallagher, Fatboy Slim's debut LP *Better Living Through Chemistry* and the singles by the Prodigy 'Firestarter' and 'Breathe' which were number ones worldwide.

Starting with 'Setting Sun', this tribute to The Beatles psychedelic classic 'Tomorrow Never Knows' was a hit in September of that year and was No.1 in the UK charts. The vocalist on the track was Noel Gallagher from the Britpop band Oasis, who, at the time, were at the height

59

of their fame and tabloid infamy, and this collaboration came about when Tom and Ed met Noel backstage when he was drunk and offered his vocals. In an interview for *Addicted to Noise* in 1997, Ed Simons describes working with Noel as being "Very entertaining. He was very funny. He's very charming. He just makes everyone laugh." [61]

"I think it's one of the best things I've ever done," recalls Noel Gallagher. "Very disappointed they didn't ask me to be in the video. Never forgiven them for that." [86]

Due to contractual reasons between Virgin and Creation Records (Oasis' label at the time) Noel was not allowed to promote the single or appear in the video, but he was allowed to be credited in the sleeve notes (though in small letters).

Previously, The Chemicals opened for Oasis to a surprisingly positive reception, considering the 'Hang The DJ' stereotype of indie rock fans of the time - Ed Simons recollects in a 1996 *Melody Maker* interview: "We played support with Oasis in Manchester, this huge gig, that was wicked. You can't turn that down, playing to a 14,000-seat ice hockey arena. Even though we thought we were going to get bottled off, which we didn't at all." [7] The Chemical Brothers (as well as The Prodigy) also supported Oasis at their legendary open-air show at Knebworth Park on the 10th and 11th August 1996 to an audience of 125,000 people over the two nights, which was one of the most famous music gigs of the 1990s (think the decade's equivalent to The Beatles at Shea Stadium). "I remember the day well," remembers Prodigy frontman Liam Howlett in an interview for this book in May 2018. "I think it was Noel who asked Keith if we could do the gig; he had seen him out one night. It wasn't like a rock festival, it was more like an old school massive rave. I remember walking on stage, and Noel grabbed my arm and said 'Play 'Poison'!' - We smashed it up! We enjoyed playing the gig, then after, went in the crowd and got fucked up, can't remember fuck all about Oasis coming on though! Good times - one of the best."

"I went to Knebworth the day Chems and Prodigy played," remembers DJ and Producer Graham Scullin. "Only passed my driving test two days before. Got there with my friends and the sun was shining, so had my prescription sunglasses on. Left my regular glasses in the car. Security wouldn't let me out into car park to retrieve them. Had to watch all the night-time stuff with my prescription shades on. Must've looked like a right 'try-hard rockstar wannabe!' Amazing concert. I also remember thinking that the whole place was full of Londoners pretending to be Mancunians for the day. Very amusing.

Set times for Oasis' legendary 1996 Knebworth Park show featuring both The Chemical Brothers and The Prodigy courtesy of www.knebworthhouse.com

In the process, it was the gateway drug for Oasis/Britpop fans into the sounds of big beat, thanks to The Prodigy and The Chemical Brothers opening for them, and, in many ways, (as well as Oasis and Britpop music being at their zenith) it was the start of big beat's very quick rise to the top.

In September of that year, Norman Cook would release his debut album as Fatboy Slim, *Better Living Through Chemistry* - a title which he borrowed from a flyer for a rave in San Francisco, which was, in turn, a shout out to the old advertising slogan of the American conglomerate, DuPont. In an interview for XFM radio in 2007, Norman remembers how he came up with the album's unique sound: "We used to play trip-hop records at 45[RPM], dropping the Kinks or The Beatles... and the first album, *Better Living Through Chemistry* was basically me making records I wanted to play, but there weren't enough people making them." [11]

This was, in fact, not a traditional debut album of sorts, but a compilation of previous singles (such as 'Santa Cruz' and 'Everybody Needs a 303') and some "new" material such as 'Song For Lindy' - a tribute to Beats International vocalist (and one half of Hardknox) Lindy Layton - material that Norman had been working on for a few years, with some even pre-dating the Fatboy Slim alias. The album wasn't a big commercial hit at first, but it did receive rave critical reviews, with Simon Reynolds from the *Village Voice* magazine saying "I can't think of a more entertaining dance album released this year" [82] and, over time, the album did very well with over 1 million copies sold worldwide. "There was a feeling that the first album had established a new genre," explains Fatboy Slim in a BBC 2015 interview, "and if we refined it, it could go bigger. But we never dreamed how big it could go." [10]

As previously mentioned, the album contained the funky Josh Wink-inspired single 'Everybody Needs a 303'. "I remember getting 'Everybody Needs a 303' on a promo 12" and loving it, but not having a clue what was going on," remembers DJ Trev Broadbank. "It had fairly obvious parallels with the 'Higher State of Consciousness' by Josh Wink, but whilst that tune had an out and out techno feel to it, this felt a lot more soulful. So, before I had any idea that big beat was a movement, I had the tunes from the likes of The Propellerheads and just thought of it as funky breakbeat. Sadly, I can remember my first (and worse, not my last) experience of being a know-it-all music snob, when a fellow DJ mentioned that the remix of 'Brimful of Asha' sounded just like "that tripping record" and I – not for the last time I'm afraid – said "Well that's because it's Fatboy Slim. It's the same producer. I've been into him for ages. He was in The Housemartins you know". I've since discovered that being smug over widely available information is not only unimpressive, it makes poor anecdotes."

Easily the biggest big beat hit of 1996 (and easily one of the biggest tracks of the genre as a whole) was the now legendary 'Firestarter' by The Prodigy, with dancer Keith Flint doing a very John Lydon-esque (of Sex Pistols) vocal delivery, which came out earlier in March of that year. "I don't think either of us could quite believe it was me," stated Keith Flint for *Rolling Stone* magazine in 1997. "I'm not a singer. I love the fact that there's people out there that have been trying since the age of 9 to sing and get the voice right - do, re, mi and all that - and I can roar in, not ever written anything or performed lyrically anything, and write a tune that's so successful. I think that's a brilliant piss take on a lot of people, and that gives me a buzz." [13] This tune was a gigantic hit in its day and was number one (their first) in the UK and also in Finland and Norway. The song did attract some controversy, and the music video, featuring the band in an abandoned London Underground tunnel, didn't go down well with the moral guardians, because of Keith Flint's punk rock appearance, which unfortunately upset some young kids. In an interview for this book in May 2018, Keith explained: "If anybody is offended, than fuck off and listen and look at something you feel more at ease with. We are not here to try to appeal to people, if you wanna jump on our mad ride, than you are welcome to get on and be a part of it, we aren't interested in the part timers, the casual tourists."

"If anything annoys people," says Maxim for *Rolling Stone* in 1997, "then it is good. You're not killing anybody on TV or shooting somebody or harming anybody in any way. He's just being himself, and if that can frighten people, well, the world needs to sit down." [13] Because of the controversy, Keith became the most recognised member of the group, and, unofficially, was the face of the band – in fact he became a symbol of 1990s pop culture, and was even parodied in a Lucozade advert from the time, featuring an old man, donning a Keith Flint-esque wig dancing about to 'Leave You Far Behind' by fellow big beat artists, Lunatic Calm.

This was followed up with 'Breathe' in November - another massive hit which topped the UK charts and was a Top 10 all over Europe, though it didn't attract the amount of controversy that the previous single and the following would get, despite the music video featuring creepy insects in a rotten looking room.

1996 saw Wall Of Sound sign one of the most well known acts of the entire scene - a duo, known as The Propellerheads (Alex Gifford and Will White), who debuted onto wax with the EP 'Dive', which had an initial run of 5000 copies. The year also saw them release the track 'Take California' which was a massive tune in the big beat underground at the time, and would be one of the signature tunes of the genre. "We formed in 1994, in Bath. I'd been messing around in the studio (aka my spare bedroom) with some beats and an old Hammond organ, which I'd bought from Dave Greenfield back when I was playing with the Stranglers," Alex Gifford from the band told me in March 2018. "At the same time I'd been learning some DJ skills and getting involved with nights being put on by my mates in the Hub club in Bath. It was an amazing time — although the Hub was a pretty small venue, it had gained a reputation which was drawing top names from all over the world. It was all about trying to achieve a positive, social vibe, and doing things in whatever way felt right. The main force and inspiration behind it was a young Paddy Malone (more recently the founder of Spiritland) and as I recall he basically dared me one night to put a live act together to perform the tunes I'd been producing, which sounded like a fine idea to me.

"At that time, you would very occasionally see live PAs at house and techno spots in the UK, but rarely anything more than a live vocal. I wanted to do something that was genuinely live, where what you saw was what you were hearing — no CDs, DATs or lip syncing. Being a fairly old school muso, the idea of doing live shows with a bunch of samplers and laptops has always sounded like a nightmare to me, so I started trying to think of possible alternative approaches. Hip-hop culture had long established vinyl as being a legitimate live instrument, and around that time, Masters at Work had played an inspiring four-deck set at the Hub, which started me thinking about what might be possible with two guys at four decks, beat-mixing backing tracks and scratching in top lines, and also jumping over to live drums and Hammond organ whenever they could spare a few minutes from the decks. You'd get the kind of fat, compressed, analogue sound which people expect to hear in clubs from the decks, the energy and vibe of live drums and Hammond, and a kind of ghoulish buzz from knowing that at any time it could all go horribly wrong — needles might jump, cues might be missed, critical mixes might be train-wrecked and so on.

"I knew Will from seeing him playing in various local bands and I knew he could drive a pair of decks. He also had a sick pair of green Airwalk Ones, which sealed the deal from my point of view. I played him the material I'd been working on - he said he was up for trying to do it live. We had a few initial jams in a mate's basement, cutting up DJ breakbeat records and playing drums and Hammond over them. The racket sounded promising enough to justify paying to have a few acetates cut of simplified mixes of the new material, and a few weeks later we played our first gig at the Hub, with the four decks supported on a framework built out of rusty scaffold poles set up in front of Will's kit and a real live Hammond B3 and Leslie speaker. We shared the bill with Jon Carter and Krash Slaughta, and an exceptionally fine night was had by all. Everyone who was there has stories they could tell from that night, I think. As far as the Propellerheads part of the night went, we got the general impression that although a lot of people hadn't known exactly what had hit them, they were all bang up for having it hit them again.

"It was either Carter or John Gosling (Mekon) who passed on some of those early tunes to Mark Jones. He cold-called me one afternoon and said, 'Hi, I'm Mark Jones from Wall of Sound — do you fancy making a record?' A few days later we all met up at a WoS night at the Thekla, a club built in an old ship moored in Bristol docks, where The Wiseguys and The Dirty Beatniks were playing. I don't remember everything that happened that night, I just recall vivid fragments of it — Jonesy galloping around the sweltering ship inexplicably swathed in an enormous, brown, fake fur coat, lurching out of hatchways like a hyperactive grizzly — Will nodding contentedly while rolling a smoke, standing with his head actually inside a bass bin — he and I being firmly escorted off the premises by the management along with what felt like a very narrow and perilous gangplank, I don't remember why exactly... 'we were veh, veh drunk' (see *The Fast Show*). Anyway, it was clear by the end of the night that we were all on roughly the same page, so that was that, really. I think it was 1995. Probably."

Another notable release on the Wall Of Sound label was the debut album by The Wiseguys, *Executive Suite* - an album on the more mellow end of big beat, which wouldn't feel out of place with the trip-hop/ninja tune crowd. The album also featured guest vocals on several of the tracks from a Bronx hip-hop posse called DJMC, which consisted of Sense Live (who would later work with the Black Eyed Peas and the Jungle Brothers), Joey Bunsen, Season and Tito-T. The same hip-hop crew would also appear on the second Wiseguys album *The Antidote*. Coincidentally, Norman Cook was in a group called DJMC in the early 1980s (pre-Housemartins) but other than the namesake, it has no relation to the US DJMC. [79] DJ Regal from the band remembers making the album in an interview for this book in October 2017: "Getting a final pressed ready-for-the-shops copy of your first album, on vinyl, is a wonderful thing. It was also sweet relief after the 7 years or so we had spent working together, sometimes wondering if we'd ever break through. But ultimately, it was testament to our love of hip-hop and digging for breakbeats, which had reached a point of frenzy by '94/'95. It also, in hindsight, probably reflects the input of two minds rather than one, as Theo's follow up shows. Where *Executive Suite* is rough, hazy, dream-like and the sound of mucking about in Theo's top-floor bedroom studio, showing our progression from its earliest demos in '92, to the final produced track in the winter of '95, Theo's *The Antidote*, is a tighter, more focused and better produced album, ultimately successful, with proper hit videos too!

Wall of Sound Crew publicity photograph from 1996, Courtesy of DJ Regal. From left to right are DJ Regal, DJ Touché, Mark Jones (back), Jon Carter (middle), Derek Dahlarge (front) and Agent Dan (Right).

"I could bore you for years with behind the scenes notes, except to say that copious amounts of Topps Pizza washed down with Pepsi Max, alongside Theo's dad's all-time spaghetti bolognese, kept us going long into most nights!"

Other big Wall of Sound releases that year included Les Rythmes Digitales' debut long player *Liberation* and The Dirty Beatniks' *One One Seven In The Shade*, as well as albums by former acid jazz act, Hustlers of Culture, and a crossover compilation with Pussyfoot records called *Wall of Pussy*. These albums would receive positive reviews from the critics. "It was nice to have the opportunity to put records out, we enjoyed ourselves," remembers Rory Carlile, who was signed to Wall of Sound as part of the band Dirty Beatniks.

Justin Robertson's Lionrock band also saw their debut album *An Instinct For Detection* being released that year on Deconstruction Records in the UK and Time Bomb Records in the US. The album was critically acclaimed, and contained the singles 'Packet Of Peace', 'Straight At Yer Head', and 'Fire Up The Shoeshaw'.

Another notable act that was gaining traction in the big beat front was Liverpool band Apollo 440, who, at the time, consisted of Noko (Norman Fisher-Jones), Howard and Trevor Grey and James Gardner, and were formed in 1990. They had already released tunes before then, which included the rave track 'Lolita', 'Liquid Cool' and the 1994 album *Millennium Fever*, as well as remixing all the singles from U2's *Achtung Baby* LP. "It's all relative," Noko from the band told me back in November 2017 regarding their increasing success. "I can remember being absolutely blown away the weekend we dropped 'Lolita', bumping into a couple of the 808 State guys who were all raving about it and Roy The Roach telling me that he'd heard Judge Jules playing it on the radio the night before.

"That sense of having engaged with the community was ace. The thrill of hearing Mark Goodier on Radio 1 announcing our 'Astral America' in at number 36 in the singles charts too.

"Things really started to take off in '96 when 'Krupa', the first single from the second LP, went huge all over Europe, followed by 'Ain't Talkin' 'Bout Dub', which was a game-changer, establishing us first and fanatically in Germany and going top 10 pretty much everywhere in Europe, especially the old Eastern Bloc. 'Stop The Rock' and our third LP took us even further, harder, faster, louder and even bigger into Japan and the US. Things kinda get out of your control and everyone wants a piece: the domino effect of success is exhilarating to be in the middle of."

The band's singles 'Krupa' and 'Ain't Talkin' 'Bout Dub' were released in 1996, and 1997 respectively, and were very big tunes of their day reaching No.23 and No.7 in the UK singles charts.

The Skint side (other than the Fatboy) saw the release of a compilation called *Brassic Beats Volume One* featuring a collection of the best songs from the Skint catalogue to date, including a duo that would start to gain a lot of buzz consisting of Mike Strokes and Richard March (formally of Pop Will Eat Itself) - Bentley Rhythm Ace (or BRA). In an interview for this book in December 2017, Richard March remembers how they came to be: "I met Mike at a party where he was DJing, he played some of my all time favourite records and we got talking about music. I was involved in a band called Pop Will Eat Itself and we weren't doing much at the time. We'd just come off a long tour, and we were having some downtime. I had access to the Pop Will Eat Itself studio so I invited Mike down to work on some ideas. We had three or four tracks on the go, and a friend of ours heard them, liked them, and suggested some labels who might be interested. So, we finished four tracks and sent a tape off to the first label on the list which was Skint in Brighton. They loved it and put out the four tracks as a 12" EP. In the meantime Pop Will Eat Itself had split, so it all worked out really well for me…"

Their early input was so successful that they attracted a major label deal with Parlophone records in 1997. The track on the compilation 'Bentley's Gonna Sort You Out' featured a very memorable music video directed by the legendary Hammer & Tongs. Their sound was unique, as their sample sources were taken from really cheap and naff bargain bin records rather than the usual funky James Brown and George Clinton records that their contemporaries would use. "We used to go to car boot sales to pick up cheap records," remembers Richard March. "This was before the resurgence of vinyl as a collectible high value thing; you could pick up 20/30 albums for £10. We'd pick up stuff with interesting covers and trawl them for usable samples. Just crazy loops from obscure German covers albums etc. Old sound effects records and just weird stuff we'd never heard of. Then sit in the studio adding drum beats and synth lines, that's how the first album got made. It was great fun, we weren't trying to fit into a particular genre, but certainly the first album has its own idiosyncratic groove that people really seemed to enjoy."

The unofficial third member of Bentley Rhythm Ace was a drummer (and another former Pop Will Eat Itself member), who would end up being a producer (and later TV Presenter) in his own right – Fuzz Townsend. "I was kind of in from the start, as 'Bentley's Gonna Sort You Out' was recorded in my living room, at my flat, although Rich and Mike's good mate, Dy' was originally going to go out live on hand percussion," he told me back in December 2017. "I did one show, at The Rocket, London, with a set of congas mounted in a shopping trolley, before I suggested that the live work could be done with a drum kit instead. The next gig was at the original Concorde, in Brighton, and when James Atkin (EMF and live BRA) turned out with a new bottle green suit for each of us, each one costing £5.00 in total, one size fits all and knocked out in 10 minutes flat, the real-life cartoon that was BRA really got going."

As well as Skint and Wall Of Sound, another notable big beat label was formed - Freskanova, which was the home of one of big beat's biggest acts, The Freestylers (Matt Cantor and Aston Harvey). "Matt and myself were signed to the same record label called Fresh Records," recalls Aston for this book in November 2017. "We used to hang out at their studios whilst recording as separate acts, talking about music and food mainly. Matt came to me with an idea to sample something and it kind of snowballed from there."

Other acts coming from this label included Cut & Paste, Hal 9000 (probably named after the character from the Stanley Kubrick film, *2001 - A Space Odyssey*), 2 Fat Buddhas, Mad Doctor X, Bowser (possibly named after the Super Mario villain of the same name), Agent Sumo and Soul Hooligan (who would later be signed to Madonna's label, Maverick). Another noteworthy label was Concrete Records, run by Tom Chemical's girlfriend at the time, Vanessa Rand, who hosted releases by some of the biggest names in the genre such as The Dub Pistols, Death In Vegas and Lionrock. We should also not forget other legendary indie labels such as Kingsize Records and Fused and Bruised, who were also influential in the big beat circles.

Another record company that would become influential was London label Bolshi Records - a sub label of Big Life Records, which was formed by Jazz Summers and Tim Parry. A notable signee was Jason Cohen, who, at the time, DJed and produced under the name of

Laidback. "I signed to Bolshi Records under the pseudonym Laidback and wrote 'The Laidback EP' in 1996 which was the label's first release," he remembers. "I knew all those vinyl buying trips to Groove Records in Soho as a kid would come in handy one day! The EP was inspired by my hip-hop addiction to breakbeats, and by the energy of the first Chemical Brothers album, *Exit Planet Dust*. I was already signed to Big Life by Jazz Summers and his forward thinking gave Sarah Bolshi the chance to set up a new big beat label, as she, too, was influenced by the Chems eclectic DJing at the now legendary Heavenly Sunday Social sessions. We all knew something special was happening that was fresh and exciting!"

The label would also see releases from Rasmus, Hijinx and US act LHB. The company disbanded in 2003.

One notable label to emerge in the early years, which was vital to this new musical wave, was trip-hop label Pussyfoot Records, which was set up by Glasgow DJ, Howie B. "I started Pussyfoot with Nick Young and Harriet Dell, around 1992/93," Howie told me in February 2018. "The reason was I had knocked on many record label doors asking them to release my music. I got the same answer 'we really like it but…' So I decided to do it myself." As a producer, Howie recorded numerous singles (such as 'Angels Go Bald', which was No.36 in the UK singles charts) and albums, as well as some big name remixes including U2, Garbage, UNKLE, Simply Red, Annie Lennox, New Order, Leftfield, Jeff Beck and Serge Gainsbourg and also the theme tune to *Mission Impossible* with members of U2 (it reached No.7 in the UK charts). He was very proud of Pussyfoot Records, and was kind enough to share some memories of this iconic label. "Every day is my favourite moment to be honest. I love the chance I have to make music and produce several bands and artists. I think one of my favourite moments is when Ry Cooder shouts at the tape op on our session when I'm producing a record for him. He is complaining about the wiring in the studio as he was listening to that fucken noise. I said, 'Hold on a minute I've spent all morning making that.' Another favourite moment was when Dobie lifted me off the decks in a Paris Pussyfoot party because I was lining up the slip mat - that was a great moment. Then when we got our first licence deal from Wall of Sound that was a great moment for us on the label."

One of the more popular acts in big beat was Lunatic Calm (Simon Shackleton, Howie Saunders and Jez Noble), who formed that year. Simon from the band explains how they were formed: "We'd been playing as Flicker Noise prior to that and released a couple of singles on Concrete records before folding. I formed Lunatic Calm with Howie Saunders in 1996 I think, and we released our debut album the following year. They were really interesting times to be making electronic music, as there was a real open-mindedness from a whole raft of producers, all looking to merge the energy of indie/rock music with that of electronica. It was a time of possibility where genres seemed happily ill-defined."

While not a big beat release per se, 1996 was the year when Californian turntablist wizard DJ Shadow released his legendary debut album *Entroducing*, which received universal acclaim and is considered a landmark album in the electronic music field. This release has been covered in several other books, blogs and websites already, but many of the album's tracks, notably 'Organ Donor' and 'The Number Song', became staples in the sets of many big beat DJs from this period, as they fitted in so well because of the tracks' loud, syncopated beats - maybe Shadow was partially influenced by prototypical big beat when making the album (coincidentally, it came out on the same day as Fatboy Slim's equally influential debut long player!).

One of the de-facto grapevines for big beat back in the day was the magazine *Jockey Slut*, which ran from 1993-2004 (remember - this was when the World Wide Web was in its formative years, so most people still bought physical magazines). While it did focus on other dance music styles, it did have a very large focus on the big beat genre (similar to that *Select* magazine had to Britpop), with many of big beat's biggest artists appearing on the front cover. In 1993, they were the first magazine to interview The Chemical Brothers (when they were still known as The Dust Brothers).

The magazine also had a short-lived label called Slut Trax, which was established in 1997, with one of the releases ('I'm A Disco Dancer' by Christopher Just) being licensed by Deejay Gigolos, and getting a well-known remix by Fatboy Slim. They also gave away free 7 inch vinyls and CDs with certain issues, (which were referred to as Slut Smalls), which included tunes from Freddy Fresh, Lionrock and Midfield General. It was a great source for trivia and facts for the big beat enthusiast - there is probably no other magazine that reveals that Liam

Howlett from the Prodigy's favourite piece of classical music is the theme tune to the 1980s UK dart-themed game show, *Bullseye* (Super Smashing Great piece of Trivia, eh?).

Other magazines that covered big beat included the obvious ones (*Mixmag, DJ Mag* and *DMC*) as well as indie rags such as *Select* and the *NME*.

The genre also started to become synonymous with its boozy and hedonistic (but mostly good natured) undertone (Jon Carter and Derek Dahlarge were masters of this sort of behaviour back in the day!). Big beat nights were known for their alcohol-fuelled rowdiness, and to quote the slang of the day, the punters were "Having it Large" or "Largin' It". Despite being mostly harmless fun, Jemma Kennedy, who was label manager for Wall of Sound, remembers in an exclusive interview for this book in January 2018 one of the more unpleasant nights of boozy tomfoolery: "The memory etched in – and on – my head was when, at a Wall of Sound party in the infamous Hobgoblin pub in Portobello, I was on the decks (playing 'Don't Scandalize Mine' by Sugar Bear: I still have the bloodstained copy) and somebody decided to throw a pint glass at me from across the room. It smashed on my head, just missing my eye. I was carted off in an ambulance to have my head stitched up. A wasted but gallant WOS recording artist, who shall remain nameless, escorted me to the hospital. He held my hand, dried my tears, wiped away the blood and then proceeded to chop out large lines of gear on the toilet in the hospital cubicle while I was having shards of glass picked out of my cleavage. If there's a better moment to encapsulate the entire big beat movement, I can't think of one. It has to be said that the scene was relentlessly laddish and fuelled by lager and other substances, which was all a bit wearing, but for sheer jumping-up-and-down-on-the-dancefloor hysteria and good times, it was pretty great. Everyone wanted to come to our parties. We really knew how to throw one."

Big Beat Becomes Nationwide

Big beat wasn't just now being restricted to The Social, The Kahuna and The Boutique in London and Brighton - big beat nights were appearing all around the country. These included Molotov Pop in Manchester, Tweakyhousediscobreaks in Cardiff, Planet of The Breaks in Shrewsbury, Hi-Karate in Glasgow, and D:Funked and It's Obvious in

Leeds. Other big beat nights also popped up in London such as Airswaraj at Mass, Passenger at The Islington and Happiness Stans at Smithfields (originally a stopgap location for the Heavenly Social in 1994, and also home of the Big Kahuna Burger), as well as It's On! run by Gareth Currie and It's A Finger Lickin' Thang. Big beat would also have followings in Liverpool (home of the "original" big beat group - The Beatles), Newcastle, Fungle Junk in Birmingham, as well as nights in Nottingham and Leicester.

Wall of Sound had their own club night too called Back 2 Mono, which took place at the Blue Note Jazz Club in London. As Mark Jones (the Wall of Sound founder) told me "Fun days - memory is wiped, but hey." Rory Carlile from The Dirty Beatniks remembers what Back 2 Mono was like: "Yep, we played there as the Beatniks live band quite a few times, and myself and Neil DJed a lot in the upstairs bar," he told me in December 2017. "It was a brilliant club - absolutely rammed, really exciting. It was the first time I realised people were into it. Not long after it started, there were queues all the way round the block to get in. Metalheadz was on the Sunday I think, and Ninja Tune on the Friday, with Back To Mono on the Saturday - you knew there was something exciting happening musically. The details could be wrong, it's hard to remember exactly - it got a bit hazy."

Andy Harlstead, who DJs under the name of Ictus, remembers what the big beat scene was like in the Yorkshire town of Leeds in an October 2017 interview for this book: "From what I remember, in the late 90s, crowds at clubs like The Elbow Room in Leeds, which is where I used to sometimes warm up for Utah Saints, loved the big beat sound… dope breakbeat based tracks mixed then with funk, hip-hop, then back to big beat… yeah… the crowds all loved it… and especially when you got DJ Tim mixing it all up, it was always a great party!!! I don't really know what it was like in other cities, as I never travelled around, but I can only assume it will have been the same sort of vibe in the 'Funk Hip-Hop Soul Disco' clubs at that time."

Despite "Up North" generally preferring more straight up four on the floor beats, big beat did develop something of a cult following up there, because of the genre's crossover nature. "As a DJ in the north, there are always musical movements that don't seem to happen up here," recalls DJ Trev Broadbank from the northern town of Harrogate. "This is certainly true in smaller towns. For example, the 2-step garage sound never really penetrated into North Yorkshire – but that sound was still quite a force in more urban areas... At the same time, on the underground, a lot of styles involving breakbeats don't have quite the same traction as a straight 4/4 kick does in the north – hardcore techno then happy hardcore had more pull up here, compared to jungle and 'dark' down south... but these comparisons don't quite work for big beat; I think that's because the overall sound was a bit more 'party orientated'. The biggest tunes could almost be classified as straightforward pop, so the tunes always worked in the north, in both mainstream and less commercial places. I guess some people would say that means the music isn't as cool – but who cares about cool, so long as it's good! I also think that there are a few roots of the sound in northern soul, which also helped... Certainly when I first became aware of big beat, there was almost a 'cultural memory' there for me... These were new tunes in a fresh style, but there was something lovely and familiar about the sound. I still play northern soul and big beat alongside each other."

A friend, who wishes to remain anonymous for this book, remembers the euphoric moment of discovering big beat for the first time.

"Acid jazz and trip-hop came along – I recognised something new, something different for people who liked lots of genres, something for trainspotters – and I got into it in a deep way. I really developed my scratching, sampling and mixing techniques and I geeked it up – BIG TIME. I was a nerd discussing every nuance of the scratch techniques, roots of a sample blah blah blah. Going out was a totally different club experience, much more cerebral fun, if you think getting a smug sense of being respected by sycophants is fun. I was walking past a club and out of the blue a voice said 'You're late!' It was one of my old crew who I hadn't seen in years – he was now promoting a club night in a well known venue. He grabbed me and laughingly said 'Do me a favour, sit here and take the money, it's a fiver each, here's the guest-list.' I had nothing better to do.

"I sat at his till for about an hour - listening to the usual motley crew of blaggers, clubbers, geeks and happy-heads trying to get in for free. I'd done this job back in the early days, so when it came to the guest list, I knew to let in anyone who I thought would bring a vibe to the party. And I charged all the 'don't you know who I ams' full price.

"Meanwhile, in the background was this interesting mix of sample and bass heavy beats, a lot like trip-hop to my ears, but faster, and harder, but not hardcore or rave. There were no cheesy synths or chipmunked vocals. It wasn't house, as the beats weren't four on the floor, they were all like drum fills, or hip-hop breaks, but deeper than hip-hop, more produced. It wasn't jungle as it wasn't that fast, or that processed. It was new. It had a variety of tempos. It had a much wider variety of rhythms, timbres and dynamics than any other of the separate genres I had got bored of already. To my ears it sounded like someone was mixing all the best bits of jungle, hip-hop, trip-hop, acid jazz and house at just the right tempo to suit them. I liked it. The main thing was though, it didn't make me want to find out who made it, or how it was made, or who released it, or any detail – it just made me want to dance.

"After a while the queue died down. I looked in the till and thought I'd done a reasonable job. I knew better than to ask the security lads to watch it, and asked a few people to find my mate. He came back, took the till and said 'nice one.' That was my cue to wander into the club proper – I see the DJ booth, I see the dancefloor. I'd been in this club before and I knew my bearings – so I head for where I know there are speaker stacks, with subs.

"Euphoria.

"I wasn't cool, attractive, hip, on-trend or any of those things. I found myself doing the 'running man' dance, skipping on my feet. There were flashing lights in my eyes, dry ice helping me feel hidden, I was happily losing my ego, occasionally making old-skool cheesy-raver hand motions. I may have let out comments about how nice I was feeling; 'oh aye' and the like. Then the lights came on. It had been three hours. I hadn't moved. I hadn't spoken to anyone. I hadn't drunk. I hadn't taken anything. But I was high. Suddenly I was making wild-eyed contact with complete strangers and excitedly saying 'nice one' 'top one' 'sorted'. It was my first experience of being high on life, and it was directly caused by big beat."

Probably the most infamous of the Leeds-based big beat nights was one called It's Obvious! It began before big beat's rise at the start of the 1990s and was considered the 'Anti-Club' club night. Its residents were DJ Crash and DJ Burn (Simon Landin and Rich Williams), and they had very surreal methods of promoting the nights, such as removing baked bean tin can labels and replacing them with the club's logo, without any indication of what the night was about – the whole point being it wasn't obvious! It mashed DJ acts with circus performers, and took place in a venue called the Warehouse which is still an incredibly popular venue to this day.

Another well-known northern big beat night was one called D:Funked, which began in 1997. "We ran D.Funked every fortnight on Thursdays circa 1997 and packed it out at the Faversham (700 capacity) in Leeds, eventually going weekly," remembers the night's promoter, Tony Green. "It was pre-internet boom - no mobiles/social media, so I didn't know what was going off at the Big Beat Boutique (or anywhere else for that matter). I was given a job of bookings, and because I had bought the Skint compilation and started buying their music, I booked the first Skint artist I could find and it was Hardknox (with Lindy Layton)... it was a road block, so I knew we were onto something, so I just kept on booking more and more big beat artists."

Big beat had an obviously natural following in Manchester, which is the home of The Chemical Brothers (as well as the entire Madchester scene, The Smiths, New Order and of course, Oasis, and many others). In an interview for this book in October 2017, Jane Winterbottom (aka Funk Boutique), who was the resident of a big beat club night called Molotov Pop, which ran for three years at the Music Box venue, remembers what the scene was like in Manchester: "Back in the day, I promoted two of my own breakbeat/big beat nights: one called Humbug with a friend of mine, Melanie Crawley. We had some amazing guest DJs including The Runaways, JC 001 and Freddy Fresh. The other night was called Bassbum, which I ran and DJed with fellow DJs Tin Tin and Terry Andow.

"There were a couple of other big beat nights in Manchester, including Tangled and Molotov Pop, where I also DJed.

"There was a fantastic big beat scene in Manchester from the mid 90s onwards. All these nights were part of the underground scene of Manchester, which was Manchester's strength and where it was at. I DJed with acid house pioneers, 808 State, who also played breaks, who were quite often on the same breaks/big beat club circuit as me around Britain.

"Many breakbeat/big beat DJs came from the original acid house scene. I also came from an electro and hip-hop background from the early 80s in Manchester, hanging out with Street Machine, who were the UK breakdancing champions. For me, my love of breaks and big beat came from my background in these musical genres: a mixture of acid house, electro and hip-hop."

Mancunian DJ legend Mr Scruff (Andy Carthy) also shared some memories of what the breaks and big beat scenes were like in Manchester. Here he states, in an exclusive interview, that specialist big beat nights were in short supply.

"As far as specialist breaks nights, I remember Tangled (Steve Thorpe from Tangled is an old school friend of mine) and Breakdown & Recovery, although there may well have been more that were not on my radar. There were strong house/D&B/soul/reggae/hip-hop scenes, but not really one that focussed on breaks. I was personally involved in several scenes, either playing at specialist house/soul/reggae/hip-hop nights, or playing at more open/freestyle events that covered many genres, such as the Electric Chair, Headfunk and One Tree Island. Manchester is a very hedonistic city with a love of all types of underground music, which means that you can play very deep and the crowd will still go crazy. With this in mind, it wasn't a naturally fertile place for a scene such as big beat. "

Flyer for Mr. Scruff show in North Wales for the big beat night, Ba'da Boom from 2001, where he performed one of his legendary extended marathon sets. By kind permission of DJ Hadj.

There was also a big beat scene in Wales. US big beat DJ Freddy Fresh told me in October 2017 he has some memories of playing in the region.

"I played big beat parties in Wales, but the only thing I recall were the impossible to read street names where all words appeared to end in Gwyned."

The popular venue for big beat nights in Cardiff was one called Club Ifor Bach, which was established in 1983, and is still going today (though they don't play big beat anymore). Another Welsh big beat night was one in the North called Ba'da Boom run by DJ Hadj, which was in Bangor, and lasted until 2005. In an interview for this book in December 2017, Hadj remembers the big beat scene in North Wales:

"I started a night in St Albans called Fungle Junk with a guy called Hansi Kopke. Our first night was massive and I remember Fatboy's 'Everybody Needs a 303' absolutely tearing the roof off the place. We'd never seen anything like it, and neither had the crowd. I went off to Uni in North Wales literally a week later, and Hansi carried on the night I think.

"Up in Bangor, North Wales, there was a really special free party scene happening. Every weekend there were multiple sound systems in the most amazing locations, like slate quarries, beaches, forests, amazing! But the overwhelming soundtrack up there at the time was techno, trance and more hard techno, with some gabba thrown in for good measure. It was a tough scene.

"So, I started asking about some chillout rooms; the guy who was doing PAs was a deep house head, and I talked him into setting up some speakers round the corner from a couple of the raves, and I'd play chillout and big beat (slower stuff initially). I got a residency in the back room of the main trance night (Transience) in the main student venue (1000+ capacity and full every month). It was with a lovely couple of guys playing a really eclectic music selection (they were called the Heavenly Music Corporation I think, but not related to the group of the same name).

"I ended up playing more big beat there, and after a few months, I got the chance to run my own little night in a smaller venue in the Student Union (300 capacity) and I called that Ba'da Boom. The title came from the line in the movie *The Fifth Element* released that year - 1997. We went from playing that venue for a while into the bigger 1000 capacity venue, and that's where it went crazy. We went all out on decor, visuals with VJ's (using two VHS decks and crossfading), and after a couple of successful nights we started booking in people from all over the scene. After a few more years we found another venue called Hendre Hall, the kind of wild place out in the countryside where everyone could truly go nuts. It was an amazing time.

"A huge part of the success was the rest of the crew. Adam Isbell was my main partner, and he'd grown up in London and knew a lot of the guys who were in the scene down there, particularly the guys at Vinyl Addiction in Camden, who went on to start the Finger Lickin' Records crew. That was a big way in for us to start booking folks up to us. Another big part of the team was Piwi, he was a funk 45 collector and he ended up playing the back room, starting a new night in the process called Racubah! We're still running that night today, with a new residency in Brighton, lots of guest gigs in London, festivals like Glastonbury, Shambala, Green Gathering etc, and occasional big events in Bangor. It's more tropical music now, but it's still going.

"Anyway, we got a really strong following for Ba'da Boom in Bangor, we were able to get folks like Krafty Kuts to become a resident, and had most of the main players come up to us at some point. The night ran until around 2005. It was good times for sure."

The scene also had something of a following in Scotland, though it was more of a "Room 2" thing rather than something that would be in the main room of a club. In October 2017, I spoke to Dan Lurinsky, from the famous record shop, Rubadub Records in Glasgow. When I was chatting to him, he mentioned some interesting titbits of what the big beat scene was like in Scotland back in the day…

"I was probably about 15 or 16 when I first heard it. We used to go up to my friend's flat and listen to all sorts of music, techno, acid, and then big beat. It didn't really have that name at the time - we heard the first Fatboy Slim album with 'Everybody Needs a 303' and the Big Beat Boutique compilations - it was quite a fresh sounding thing at the time - there was some quite organic sounding big beat, with proper live drummers, and there was stuff with amen breaks with acid lines over the top of it - it was kind of different for the time.

"When I was old enough to start going to clubs, that's what was getting played - the first room played techno and in the second room would be a big beat room. When I was at art school in Dumfries, there was a club called The Loft, which was owned by the same people who owned the venue in Edinburgh. The venue would have people like Twitch or

Optimal playing in one room, and in the second room it would be guys playing big beat. It was really energetic and we would go to the techno room, and then go to the big beat room for a bounce about."

Dan was also happy to share some memories of seeing American big beat DJ, Freddy Fresh.

"When I first moved to Glasgow when I was 18, at Thursday nights at the Art School there was a club night called Hi-Karate, that was pretty much exclusively big beat, and the second room would be more funk & soul from Divine - I remember seeing Freddy Fresh there, and that was a pretty memorable night from my late teens, and he was banging out the acid and the big beat at the time. He was one of the first guys that I knew from the techno scene to adopt big beat, as I always thought of him as a techno or house DJ, though he had a hip-hop background as well, obviously. It was a pleasure to see him and it was the only time I've ever seen him live, actually."

Crawford Tait, who was the resident of the Scottish big beat night Hi-Karate, remembers when he discovered the genre when I interviewed him in October 2017: "The order of events here is a bit hazy for me, but... I'd DJed at a weekly Friday funk night in the Sub Club, then started playing Mo Wax and trip-hop. I'd always been trying to track down stuff I couldn't quite put my finger on, which usually led me to instrumental hip-hop and breakbeat tracks, and I was also into old school hip-hop, electro, rave and random old club tracks like 'Alarm Clock' by Westbam. Round about then, Andrew told me about Neil, who he'd met through Divine, and the night he'd just started Hi-Karate, which he thought I'd be into. Also at that time, I'd go to London regularly and, though I don't think I went to Heavenly Social in the early days, I did go to the Big Kahuna Burger. What I heard there and what Neil was playing just clicked, it was what I'd been looking for."

Crawford also remembers how things were in Scotland back in the day. "When Hi-Karate started, there wasn't a lot of diversity in Glasgow clubs - house and techno dominated, and there wasn't even much hip-hop going on. Clubs also tended to be limited to a genre, with only 'student nights' playing a more eclectic mix, and even then they had their own formula. Bar DJs were much more prevalent than they were in places like London at that time, and you'd hear a lot more variety there.

"That's why Neil hooked up with Andrew originally - back then Divine was more mixed and you'd hear funk, soul, indie, 60s and new music too; it was the closest thing to a big beat night there was at the time. I can't recall another big beat night to be honest, and I can only really talk about Glasgow."

"There really wasn't much," remembers Neil McMillan from Hi-Karate. "There were the Jengaheads, who I think were into the more uptempo breaks stuff. Prior to Hi-Karate, I used to go to a night upstairs from Divine at the Art School whose name escapes me now, but it was eclectic and funky."

"I was DJing pretty much every Friday and Saturday night, so didn't really go to many other club nights," recalls Andrew Divine, Hi-Karate's co-founder. "But I don't think there really was much of a scene - Glasgow seemed to be dominated by house and techno, and anything else was pretty underground. Paul Cawley and Alex Horton ran a night called Phar Out at the Art School (and got Mo Wax and drum 'n' bass DJs up to Scotland) and the Jengaheads DJed in bars and clothes shops on a Saturday afternoon. I started DJing at the Glasgow School of Art doing a night called Divine in 1990, where I played a pretty random mix of all the music I loved. I still run the night, and nowadays it's focussed on obscure 60s and 70s soul, funk, psych and ska.

"But back then in the early 90s, it was far more eclectic and I was playing indie, disco, hip-hop, drum & bass, funk, techno, soul, psych, soundtracks and weird moog tracks. Eclectic is often a by-word for 'crap DJing' but I genuinely tried to fit all the pieces of the jigsaw together in a coherent fashion, getting things to blend and flow and obviously sample based big beat tracks fitted in nicely. Neil introduced himself outside the club one night, and invited me down to the night he and his brother were starting in Blackfriars basement - needless to say, the music was fantastic, most of it I didn't know, but I could tell that what the night really needed was a proper crowd, not just a handful of mates, to get the party started.

"After a few venue changes, it turned out that Thursdays at the Art School were looking to expand and, rather than shift the busy club from the bar into the cavernous hall upstairs, they decided to give some newbies the task of getting 500 people a week in. Fortunately, they decided to make it free entry and pints of lager cost a whole pound so, as you can imagine, it very quickly became very busy.

"And that's when Hi-Karate clicked. We had lots of guests at Hi-Karate over the years, and pretty much every DJ we invited to the club eventually travelled up, usually because we didn't have to deal with agents and huge egos - they tended to be like-minded fans of music and

I still keep in touch with a few. Andy Smith & Scott Hendy (Dynamo Productions / Boca 45), Matt Cantor (Freestylers), another guy called Matt (who gave us a *Star Wars* single he produced called 'Slave One' which my small children now love!), Deadly Avenger, DJ Format, Rahzel, Jeru The Damaja, Tim Love Lee (Tummy Touch), The Runaways, Mr Scruff, Freddy Fresh, Mushroom (Massive Attack), Jadell (Illicit) and Cash Money all played. But, cheesy as it may sound, it was the packed out residents nights at the Art School and the cheers of 'one more tune' at the end of the night which really made it for me. Oh, and the time we got asked to play at the opening of the Levi's Store in Glasgow and we got free shirts and a pair of denims... ;-}"

Hi-Karate's Co-Founder, Neil McMillan, recalls: "I was going to house and techno clubs in the early 90s, but I was getting bored with the monotony. I was quite into hip-hop and reggae and had been an indie kid in guitar bands, so when friends of mine in London took me to Heavenly Social and Big Kahuna parties I was blown away. There was so much variety - electro, old school hip-hop, funk, dancehall, rock records, techno... it's difficult to say what united it all (apart from breakbeats) but I'd venture that a reckless and fun-filled lack of subtlety was probably it! I'd been pissing around on decks and rinsing the record shops (mainly in London at that time) that dealt with this kind of thing. My brother Colin and I came up with the idea of doing Hi-Karate, then we doorstepped Andrew Divine because he was the only Glasgow DJ I'd heard that was mixing things up in a similar way.

"Andrew quickly got Crawford on board and that was it. It started in a small basement (Blackfriars) in 1996. We dotted around a few venues including Tin Pan Alley and The Volcano before settling into a Thursday night residency at Glasgow School of Art. Those were the peak years, probably 97 to around 2000. It was free or very cheap entry, very boozy, a lot of students - and art students at that, who were quite open-minded. We were getting the venue full, some great guests, and good press. We had a nice line in self-deprecating humour going with a weekly newsletter that some people have held onto over the years!

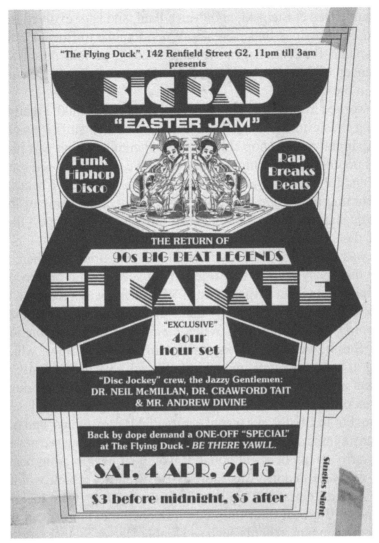

Poster for Hi-Karate reunion night from 2015 with kind permission from Andrew Divine

"Anyway, after that ran its course, we did smaller residences at The Liquid Lounge and The Reading Rooms in Dundee before, I guess, the vogue for what we did had gone, enthusiasm was waning, life was taking over, etc. I think we did our last nights around 2003 or 2004."

Outside of London and Brighton, the region in the UK where big beat would see its largest following would be the city of Bristol. Their take on big beat was more influenced by early hip-hop producers such as Double Dee & Steinski, and Prince Paul, and later evolved into what would be known as funky breaks. When I spoke to Boca 45 (formally of Dynamo Productions) in November 2017, he told me how he got influenced by big beat, and a titbit of what the scene was like in Bristol back in the day:

"I worked in a record shop in Bristol from 1996-2000. I really started making music in the late 1990s, and a lot of this stuff I was actually selling in the record shop called Purple Penguin, which was in Bristol. It was predominantly a hip-hop store, but we would also sell breaks and beats and funk records, jazz records and obviously the big beat stuff that was coming through at the time. We were stocking some of the Skint Records and the Wall of Sound stuff and also Ninja Tune - they were staple diets of what we were selling in the store.

"I was DJing a lot, mostly in Bristol at that time, and there weren't really that many records that fitted in between the hip-hop records and the funk records that I was playing - when there was a Krafty Kuts kind of thing, I got really excited by that - there weren't many of those type of records, believe it or not! When I was in Dynamo Productions with Andy Smith, we were making tracks for the dance floor, which were fitting in between a funk and a hip-hop track - we didn't really see it as big beat at the time. In Bristol, there's much more of a hip-hop thing. In London and Brighton, they were embracing more styles such as techno, but in Bristol, we were keeping the B-Boy ethics, and not using so many synths and things. That was our take on it, but we never saw it necessarily as big beat - although it would sit next to a big beat track - what we were making was more B-Boy centric, which would be, in some regards, classed as big beat, because the beats were fucking loud, I suppose. Big beat didn't directly influence me, but instead the more cut-and-paste type records such as Double Dee & Steinski, Prince Paul and the [US] Dust Brothers."

Ireland also had a small big beat scene back in the day. DJ Johnny Pluse remembers in an interview for this book in September 2017: "I left Ireland at that stage, but local DJs like Johnny Moy were putting on shows with the Chemical Brothers and Fatboy Sim."

In January 2018, I spoke to Irish DJ Decky Hedrock, who has given a very comprehensive look at what the big beat scene was like in Ireland back in the day (with a little bit about his involvement in the big beat act Hedrock Valley Beats):

"Back in the late nineties, dance music in Ireland was made up of two genres, either happy hardcore or 'funky house', as the natives liked to call it. The commercial club sound of Ireland hadn't really evolved much over the years and it wouldn't really 'till around 2006.

"When I started to get into big beat, I used to pick up what I could from BBC Radio 1, and what I read about on forums online or magazines. The internet, in its fledgling years, was a great resource to reach out to other music lovers who had similar tastes. So I trawled through websites to hear of new acts, DJs and producers which might inspire me or introduce me to a new sound.

"Since seeing The Prodigy play live at a music festival in Ireland in 1994, I was instantly attracted to something more hip-hop orientated but with rock tinges, so when big beat came along, I had found my favourite new genre! But it was in short supply in N.Ireland.

"The clubs here focused on the likes of Tall Paul, Anne Savage and Judge Jules; possibly a great night out, but not exactly what I wanted to hear.

"I was lucky enough to find some like-minded friends who became band mates, Frankie Kane (scratch DJ) and Kevin 'Foxy' Fox (bass guitar) who made up the Hedrock Valley Beats live show at the time. Also Vinnie Neff (Django Django) was part of our friends circle and sharing the whole experience with us, as well as popping into the studio to record his own ideas.

"We just needed somewhere to play now!

"Smaller clubs started popping up to play less mainstream dance music, and these were more eclectic, allowing the minority, who didn't like the typical dance music sound, to have a great Saturday night listening to a wide selection of everything the DJ could find that was outside the box. But we still never really saw any proper big beat DJs play yet.

"We actually hosted our own night, which we called Club 303, through a young DJ called Gary Curran (who later I would form The Japanese Popstars with) to allow us to play our first gig. Gary was playing a local club at the time and he was dropping HVB demos there that I gave him during his sets. We took this as a sign that we might attract a crowd for a big beat themed event that we could headline. It went very well!

"Around '98, as the genre became more commercialised by radio, these smaller clubs started to go out on a limb and bring the likes of the Freestylers, Deadly Avenger, Midfield General over. The scene had started to grow but you had to travel maybe 100+ miles to see these guys.

"Whilst I enviously read about clubs like the Big Beat Boutique in Brighton and the Social in London, in *DJ Mag* and *Mixmag*, over in Belfast there were club nights like Breakdown and Hydroponic that pushed a weekly diet of big beat successfully; but outside of the major cities, the other clubs struggled to attract an audience, they persevered only with a small group of loyal regulars who appreciated something different.

"My own first real taste of this bigger picture was when a local Irish promoter named Rich McGinnis (who later would start up Chibuku Shake Shake and Warehouse Project) had gone up against possibly the biggest club in Ireland at the time called Lush!, providing his own alternative eclectic sound at The Retro Bar in the very same town of Portrush.

"When I heard of his club, I rang him and had arranged to travel 40 miles to personally hand him a demo cassette of my Hedrock Valley Beats music, in the hopes of gaining a gig at the club! A week later he called me to say he had 'rolled his car off the road' whilst listening to my demo and thought it was THAT good that he had a slot supporting Bentley Rhythm Ace in his club! Result! (He was unhurt, by the way, in case you where wondering).

"This lucky accident helped launch awareness of HVB and allowed us to start playing the local Irish/UK scene, as well as international festivals and all the clubs that had only been a dream. Over the next few years the likes of Celtronic Festival became a popular dance music occurrence in Derry, which has grown each year and is still running even now, bringing all sorts of acts and DJs from around the world to play alongside local homegrown Irish artists. With that development, Ireland started to have a lot of local heroes in its own electronic dance scene like Phil Kieran, HVB and also David Holmes, who began his career as a techno DJ, but became more of an eclectic producer after his second album, which went down the big beat avenue, sampling old obscure rare groove records. This actually led him into soundtracking major Hollywood movies like *Oceans Eleven* and much more.

"Music festivals started adding big beat artists to their billing, and even though it was still a small underground club scene, its commercial acceptance had finally reached these shores.

"One of my best memories was playing Homelands Festival in Ireland back in 2000. It was the off-shoot event of superclub Home which, at the time, was a franchise, much like Cream, but unfortunately didn't have a similar lifespan. This year the popularity had grown for the scene that the likes of Hedrock Valley Beats and David Holmes are playing alongside Paul Oakenfold, Judge Jules and Leftfield. We had just signed to Infectious Records and their A&R man had flown over to watch us play. It was all pretty exciting.

"The festival site was being held on the old Butlins holidays site and we had secured two apartments behind the main stage for an overnight stay, so we landed down with our large entourage the night before to make the most of the festival. Being Irish, we raided an off-licence on the way down and bought as much alcohol as our cars could fit, just to help us sleep.

"So, as festivities kicked off in our apartment, I got a call from the A&R guy to tell us he had arrived and asked me to come and meet up. When I left the room, I noticed that there were 50 or more firemen and at least 4 fire engines right outside setting up health and safety points and running drills etc on site. It was like *Close Encounters of the Third Kind* outside.

"Up until this point, I was oblivious to all the commotion going on outside our door, as we were basically swimming in vodka indoors. So I called over to one of the firemen and asked him to do us a favour. I explained there was a bunch of alcoholics inside that didn't know this was going on outside and could he knock on the door and tell them they'd have to leave because the place was on fire! He had a mischievous grin and called over two more firemen and off they went to knock on the door. I stood far enough back to watch and the door opened...

"Our tour manager's mouth dropped when he saw the blue lights and firemen, he immediately turned around and shouted at the top of his voice 'GRAB THE FUCKING DRINK!!!' Within about 5 seconds the apartment emptied, and everyone came running out carrying as many bottles of vodka and beers as they could hold! Course they weren't that impressed when they came running towards me, 47 other firemen and our A&R guy all doubled over in fits of laughter at them. The gig the next day was epic."

Moving back to 1996, to top off the year, Ministry of Sound in London held one of the most epic big beat nights that the genre had ever seen called Night Of The Big Drums. In conjunction with the big two -

Skint and Wall of Sound (and of course, Big Beat Boutique and Back 2 Mono), on the bill were Fatboy Slim, Jon Carter, Midfield General, Derek Dahlarge, The Wiseguys, Dirty Beatniks, Cut La Roc, Basement Jaxx, Nuphonic/Dave Hill, The Propellerheads, Bentley Rhythm Ace, Les Rythmes Digitales and special guest, hip-hop pioneer Afrika Bambaataa. If anybody knows Doctor Who, who could help with the time travel - I need tickets to go to this event now!

Outside of the world of big beat, 1996 may not have been the greatest year in history, but the beats kept us happy - and the best was yet to come!

Life Is Sweet - The Golden Age (1997)

DJs and Producers Deny the Tag "Big Beat"

One year over - another one begins, and the big beat scene was rising. It was also the year when the term 'big beat' would almost be universally accepted as the name of this style of music, though not everybody was happy about that.

"I, myself or anyone else at the label never referred to the music as 'big beat'," recalls Steven Hall, A&R Man for Junior Boys Own, who originally signed The Chemical Brothers, when they were still known as The Dust Brothers. "That was a term I only heard later when the press started calling The Chemical Brothers part of, or leaders of, the Heavenly Social scene. Personally I wasn't happy or unhappy with the label, I didn't give it a second thought, as Tom and Ed were making great dance music that was played by loads of different DJs. At Junior Boys Own, we released all kinds of dance tracks - house, techno, breakbeat, trip-hop... you name it, we released it. We came from what you could call the Balearic scene of '87/'88, Alfredo at Amnesia, Shoom, Future, Spectrum, which meant all music was music and there were no barriers or restrictive genres as far as we were concerned."

During the heyday of big beat, it seemed like every electronic act with uptempo breakbeats seemed to be labelled under the big beat tag. The Skint and Wall of Sound head honchos, Damian Harris and Mark Jones, declared this to be "lazy journalism" at the 'In The City' Industry Conference [27]. The thing with "big beat" was that it was a very loose genre, so The Chemical Brothers' psychedelic multi-layered take on acid house was lumped in the same bag as Bentley Rhythm Ace's bargain bin charity cut-ups (or how they described it, carboottechnodisco) and The Propellerheads' bombastic 'Spy Beats' sound was very different to Les Rythmes Digitales' hark back to 1980s electro pop or The Wiseguys' jazzy hip-hop vibes and The Bronx Dogs' funky B-Boy block parties. Even trip-hop artists such as DJ Shadow were sometimes lumped into the big beat camp. History would repeat itself in the early

2010s during the "EDM" craze when, after the massive success of Skrillex, it seemed that all dance music was called "dubstep". Maybe the beauty of big beat was the fact that it was such a loose, open-minded and eclectic genre of music. Not every artist who had the "big beat" tag was happy about it, as Liam Howlett from the Prodigy explained to me in May 2018:

"It's easy now to look back at all these stupid names that get pinned on electronic music, usually by American journalists, so they can put it neatly in their genre box. We always tried to piss on that box as much as possible. Nonsense such as 'electronica' - we were never that, were were never big beat, we were never techno, we certainly didn't want anything to do with EDM. Fair play and respect to the Brighton Underground scene, where it first emerged from though, a lot of good tunes came out at the beginning."

Ed Simons from The Chemical Brothers was also critical of records under the big beat tag, as stated in an issue of *Spin* magazine in 1998

"My problem with big beat records is that everything's done for the DJ. It's all huge drops and builds, whereas a good record should groove a bit more." [6]

"Although we shamelessly adopted it at the time, I'm not too happy with the term 'big beat' as it homogenises what are, for me, very diverse kinds of party music," recalls Neil McMillan, who was the co-founder and resident at the Scottish Club night, Hi-Karate.

"I don't think anyone was really trying to make 'big beat' tunes, as it were," recalls Jadell. "I think most were trying to do a sort of UK take on hip-hop that was instrumental, and would work in clubs. There really weren't that many MCs about back then! I certainly never met that many. As time went on I worked with singers and ONE rapper from the Bronx... who I'd not work with again until many years later."

In a December 1997 issue for *Jockey Slut*, the very diverse DJ Mr. Scruff was not happy when what he does (playing across the board) was starting to get pigeon-holed as big beat by the press. He told them that "Personally, I'm not arsed by such categories, because they mean nothing about the music I play. A label such as big beat has no effect on the DJ who plays a lot of different types of music." [97]

Scruff at the time referred to big beat as 'handbag hip-hop'.

The irony was that a lot of the artists who were lumped in the big beat tag didn't set out to create a new genre of music, but rather just share a diverse musical palette; in many ways, a BIG range of BEATs rather than just making and playing records with big heavily compressed breakbeats, dusty funk loops, guitars, hip-hop hooks, and acid house squelches. "One of the healthiest things about big beat was the eclecticism about it," Wall of Sound artist Mekon told me in February 2018.

It wasn't all negativity regarding the "big beat" tag - Pete Houser, the West Coast breakbeat DJ who goes under the name of the Bassbin Twins, was delighted to see that a style of music that he helped pioneer was flourishing in such a big way. In April 2018, Pete told me how he felt when DJs and producers were making a sound not too dissimilar to his, but given the elusive tag "big beat".

"Elated. Norman [Cook] was a hero of mine since Beats International, and he seemed to articulate the whole swirling stew that had been bubbling up into concise artefacts that set the bar."

Despite the backlash, the two main players in the big beat scene, Skint Records and Wall of Sound Records, would join the roster of MPI Agency - one of the most acclaimed and successful music agencies in the UK at the time. "I was at school, and I was a music agent and I asked my best friend if he wanted to be an agent too. He said yes and he was very good at it, " remembers Alex Hardee from MPI, when I spoke to him in November 2017 as he was getting ready to mentor one of his acts, Liam Gallagher, before he embarked on his world tour. Alex is now a partner at CODA Agency, one of the biggest music agents worldwide. "I was more interested in going out and having a good time, and my friend secured some big artists like Fatboy Slim and The Propellerheads... and then he lost those acts. He happened to also be a drummer, and he became the drummer for The Wiseguys live shows. I said 'are you mad?' – I couldn't get it, that he wanted to be a drummer rather than an agent. I went to see Mark Jones and Midfield General [Damian Harris], and the like, and they had acts like The Wiseguys and Jon Carter, Dirty Beatniks, Big Beat Boutique Brand... and I said 'We can represent all of these and all the other acts,' and Mark Jones said 'Yes'... and we just built up the MPI brand from there."

CODA Agency represent The Prodigy to this day, and now also represent some of the biggest acts in the world.

The Prodigy Become Superstars and Face Super Controversy

1997 was the year that the Prodigy released one of the genre's finest hours - their incredible third long player *The Fat Of The Land* which came out in June of that year. It was a tremendous success, both critically and commercially, and was a hit both in the UK and Stateside (and in fact the world, as it was No. 1 in at least 12 countries) selling over 200,000 copies in America in its first week alone (eventually selling over 2,600,000 just in the US). Overall, by 2012, the album had sold over 10 million copies worldwide making it, by far, the best-selling album in the big beat genre. Because of this, they gained an army of famous fans including Sir Paul McCartney, Madonna (who asked them to produce for her, but they declined), U2, Dave Grohl of the Foo Fighters and David Bowie. In 1999, it entered the Guinness World Records for being the fastest selling album in UK history.

In a Q&A session for *Spin* magazine in 2015, Liam Howlett was asked if he had any idea that *Fat Of The Land* was going to take off like it did.

"In a way, yeah, because what happened was, 'Firestarter' came out a year before *Fat of the Land*. Of course, we had no idea how big it was going to be in America, that was a big surprise. There were very few breakthrough bands, English bands, so we were really the ones. Electronic music does get forgotten about, sometimes, it's good to remind people how important it was in the '90s." [19]

In an interview for this book in May 2018, Liam Howlett also said:

"I will add again though, we were Number 1 in the album charts, and that was great, because there were loads of Middle Americans scratching their heads going 'What is this kind of music?' We always liked that, and always will have a laugh trying not to be pinned down to a certain set of musical rules and genres - Fuck that! Just remember, when The Prodigy rock, it pisses on rock itself!"

Containing the already massive 1996 singles 'Firestarter' and 'Breathe', its most famous (and easily most controversial) track was the opener 'Smack My Bitch Up', which was based on a sample from the classic Ultramagnetic MCs track 'Give The Drummer Some' rapped by Kool Keith, who, coincidentally, does a guest spot on the track 'Diesel Power'. Its famous hookline goes "Change my pitch up, smack my bitch up" . Women's rights groups were up in arms, especially feminist groups including the Feminist National Organisation of Women of The

United States, a situation not helped by an even more controversial music video that contained graphic depictions of sex, drinking, vandalism, violence... and partying (which is revealed at the end of the video to be the deeds of a woman). When it was released as a single in November of that year, it wasn't quite as successful commercially as 'Firestarter' or 'Breathe', but was still a big hit reaching No.8 in the UK singles charts, probably helped by the controversy.

The tune's hook was taken out of context. "People take things too literally," recalls Leeroy Thornhill, former member of The Prodigy. "If you said to a girl 'change my pitch up, smack my bitch up' - she probably wouldn't understand what 'change my pitch up' means. It just works. It's just a hook. That's the only thing behind it. The bitch is the music, not a girl thing. A lot of the girls I know say that's their favourite track. There is no message in Prodigy music really, it's just an expression of hardness. We're not trying to put messages in about 'It's cool to beat up women,' because that's just pathetic." [83]

"I played this at The End about a month ago and someone threw a bottle at me," remembers Fatboy Slim in a 1997 issue of *Jockey Slut*. "Just as I put it on, someone bounced a bottle off my head onto the record. It's another record where I knew where I was first time I heard it. The track was rockin' and I thought 'what a tune' then the sample came in, and I was on the floor in hysterics. I totally got the joke. I can't explain it, it's just old school rap records with stupid lines like 'you can't beat that with a baseball bat' which mean absolutely nothing." [97]

In 2017, Fatboy Slim would later release a track called 'Where U Iz', which featured the hook "You can't beat that with a baseball bat, you can't beat that with a bat" - quite funny in hindsight.

To add even more to the 'Smack My Bitch Up' controversy, the cover for the single release was originally going to be a picture of a VW Beetle wrapped around a lamp-post but it had to be changed after the tragic death of Princess Diana earlier that year, so it was altered to a picture of a breakdancer.

In a 2010 poll conducted by *PRS* (Performing Rights Society) Magazine, 'Smack My Bitch Up' was recognised as the most scandalous song in music history.

Big Beat's Success Continues

The other big release of 1997 was The Chemical Brothers' second album *Dig Your Own Hole*, out a couple of months earlier than The Prodigy's album, and like *Fat of the Land*, *Dig Your Own Hole* was successful both critically and commercially. The opening track 'Block Rockin' Beats' was a Number One hit single - the *NME* named it 'Single Of The Week' and said "It throbs like your head might if you had just done a length underwater in a swimming pool full of amyl." [63] It even won a Grammy award for Best Rock Instrumental - quite a monumental feat for a big beat record. The album also contained the previous mega-hit 'Setting Sun', and other highlights included 'Elektrobank' featuring guest vocals from the founder of hip-hop culture himself, DJ Kool Herc, 'It Doesn't Matter', 'Where Do I Begin' (featuring folk rock star Beth Orton, who was previously on their first album *Exit Planet Dust*) and the nine minute epic 'The Private Psychedelic Reel'. In a review for *Mixmag* they describe it as "Take anything you've ever heard about dance or rock, and drop it in the garbage, because this is the best this fusion has ever got: imagine The Chemicals doing an acid drenched cover of The Stone Roses' 'I Am The Resurrection'. Grateful Dead fans are going to be frying their brains out on LSD to this track for the next 20 years." [64].

Jon Carter, in an interview for *NPR* magazine in 2011, also summed up the track's immense power:

"I think big beat peaked with the song 'Private Psychedelic Reel' by The Chemical Brothers, when there was still amazing creativity going on. Real efforts to make something different, not just use obvious samples. The Beatles' record company went for them, thinking they'd sampled the Beatles. They'd just layered so much to get the sound like that. The Beatles had their musicologist all over it. That's how intensely worked upon it was. It's got the magic of being really uplifting, yet taking such old influences, being progressive and pushing it forward. And also putting real soul flavour and a good quality of darkness into an instrumental track." [2]

"I did put on the 'Private Psychedelic Reel' one night at my house," remembers Noel Gallagher from Oasis, "and a couple of people were left frightened, which I really liked, especially as the couple of people that left were a pair of twats anyway. I like the fact it can be quite scary, and it can be quite soulful as well." [86]

As well as the Chemicals and The Prodigy, Bentley Rhythm Ace released their self-titled debut album that year, initially on Skint, but it was moved to a major label release on Parlophone in the same year, and spawned the hit single 'Bentley's Gonna Sort You Out' (No.17 in the UK charts), which was originally on the *Brassic Beats* compilation. "Our proudest moment was when the re-released version of 'Sort You Out' made the top twenty," remembers Richard from BRA. "We had a massive celebration and drank loads of champagne until the early hours. It was the same day Princess Diana died. Goodness knows what my neighbours thought..."

He also remembers what it was like being a big beat artist signed to a major label. "Because I'd been in Pop Will Eat Itself for maybe 10 years before Bentley Rhythm Ace started, I had a good idea of how major labels operated. So I approached the whole thing with a degree of cynicism and healthy disregard." Being signed to Parlophone also led them to remix some major artists including hip-hop legends the Beastie Boys and Britpop trio Supergrass. The BRA album was a smash hit with its unique brand of 'carboottechnodisco' (Car Boot Techno Disco), which was based on sampling sources as diverse as Brian Auger, Juicy Luck, the BBC Radiophonic Workshop, the Weber Muller Orchestra... not to mention the album beginning with a sample from the classic 1980s children's TV show, *Fireman Sam* (the episode in question being 'Bentley the Robot'). In many ways it was a forerunner to the plunderphonics stylings of The Avalanches, whose music is mostly created from charity shop vinyl.

Heavenly Social residents Death in Vegas also released their debut album called *Dead Elvis* (which was also their formative mantra). The album received healthy reviews and would later go on to sell 60,000 units in the UK. A noteworthy tune from the album 'GBH' would later be used in the 1998 stoner flick, *Homegrown*. The album contained the previous singles, 'Rocco', 'Dirt', and 'Rekkit'.

1997 saw Ministry Of Sound set up a big beat sub-label called FSUK (Future Sound Of The United Kingdom). Early releases on the label saw singles and EPs from Krafty Kuts, Skeewiff and Furry Phreaks, but the sub-label was best known for its acclaimed compilation series. *FSUK Vol.1* was mixed by Derek Dahlarge, and its cover featured the *Transformers* character Red Alert (The Freestylers would emulate this on their 'Electro Science' mix by featuring the *Transformers* character Astrotrain.) Unlike most mainstream Ministry mixes, the FSUK mixes were more interesting, had more character, and were mixed by actual DJs rather than software. Derek Dahlarge remembers making the first FSUK mix CD in an interview I conducted in October 2017: "They were exciting times. The Ministry of Sound had never done anything like that before - it was a bit of an honour. It's always nice to be honoured for your work in any field - I was really down with it - it was great."

The commercial success of *FSUK Volume 1* (100,000 copies sold) prompted Ministry to release three further volumes from The Freestylers and Bentley Rhythm Ace in 1998, and Cut La Roc in 1999. The FSUK label, however, folded by 2000 once the big beat backlash hit.

It wasn't just Ministry who were cashing in on big beat - Acid Jazz Records set up their own big beat label, Athletico, that year, which saw releases from Psychedeliasmith, Sir Drew, Selectah, Dubz Deluxe, Subsonic Legacy, Mao, and the Athletico Borough Upsetters.

Some trailblazing releases were coming out in 1997. The Lacerba label released a compilation called *Big Beat Elite* on June 9th and it is one of the best time capsules from this period. The first track was one of the genre's highlights, 'That Elvis Track' by Sol Brothers, which was originally released on Fresh Music, and is a mashup of Ultramagnetic MC's vocals, the bassline being taken from the Rose Royce track 'Put Your Money Where Your Mouth Is' - making it a really funky track and also the forerunner to the funky breaks/nu-funk movement of the 2000s.

Other highlights included the Cut La Roc single 'Hip-Hop Bibbedy Bop Bop' which samples 'Rapper's Delight' by The Sugarhill Gang, the Fatboy Slim classic 'Everybody Needs a 303', Cut & Paste (Matt Cantor from The Freestylers and Andy Gardner from Plump DJ's) with 'Forget It' and one of the biggest anthems of the big beat era 'Keep Hope Alive' by US group The Crystal Method. The success of this compilation was followed up with *Big Beat Elite Repeat* and *Big Beat Elite Complete* in 1998. Other noteworthy big beat compilations included *Hardhop + Trypno* on Moonshine Music, *Block Bustin' Beats* released on Solid State, *Electronica (Full-On Big Beats)*, on major label Virgin Records, *This... is... Big Beat* and *Essential Big Beat* on Beechwood Music, *Chemical Reaction* on Afrodesia Music, *Blow The Whole Joint Up* on Debutante and *Big Beat Royale* on Kickin' Records.

A notable massive track of 1997 was by Danish hardcore duo ETA, with their track 'Casual Sub (Burning Spear)' - a remake of the 1971 funk ditty 'Burning Spear' by S.O.U.L. written by Richard Evens. This was originally a record in the hardstyle genre, which was initially intended to be played at 45 RPM (around drum & bass speed), but when the tune was discovered by John Stapleton (who compiled the *Dope on Plastic* series and was the mastermind behind the Bristol club night BlowPop) he slowed the tune down to 33 RPM and it became a huge big beat hit and reached No.28 in the UK singles charts.

Another big track that came out that year was the Daft Punk-esque 'Jaques Your Body (Make Me Sweat)' by Les Rythmes Digitales. This tune has a very interesting history, as it was originally released in '97 to an underground impact, and was reissued again in 1999 to a similar reception, but the tune didn't really take off properly... until 2005! The reason for this renaissance was it was picked by Citroen to advertise their C4 car in a very memorable advert featuring a dancing Transformer.

Also on Wall of Sound, Mekon released his debut album *Welcome To Tackletown*. It contained the namesake single that was released the previous year, as well as the single 'Revenge Of The Mekon', which featured one of the more unconventional collaborations in the big beat canon – famous gangster Frankie Fraiser. When I asked Mekon what it was like working with Frankie, he said "Scary - We were drinking all day. He was fun, but very scary!" Mekon was also a member of a band called Agent Provokateur, who were also signed to Wall of Sound. They were a collaboration between himself Matthew Ashman (formerly of Bow Wow Wow), Dane Pepper, Dann Saber (ex-Black Grape) and Cleo Torres on vocals. The year saw the release of their one and only album *Where The Wild Things Are*. There was a lot of confusion however, as the name of the band was the same as that of a famous lingerie company: "Agent Provocateur started around the same time as the knicker company," Mekon told me, "and the guy that came up with the name was going out with our singer, Cleo Torrez, who was also working with Joseph Corrie, whose company it was, and gave us both the name at the same time. There were loads of lawsuits flying about at the time, but I think Joseph got the better of it."

Another notable act on the underground tip that made it big in 1997 was the duo of Deeds Plus Thoughts - Robert Cains and Robert Luis (who runs Tru-Thoughts Records). "Yes. This was the first music I made and the debut single got some great support," remembers Robert

Luis. "I even got a call from John Peel saying he was going to play it on Radio 1 which was amazing."

1997 saw the return of former Beats International vocalist, Lindy Layton. Winding back the clock to 1989, she was the vocalist for Norman Cook's band Beats International, which spawned the 1990 megahit 'Dub De Good to Me' (a mashup of The S.O.S. Band's 'Just Be Good To Me' with the bassline of 'Guns of Brixton' by The Clash). It reached No.1 in both the UK singles charts and the US dance charts, though the lifestyle wasn't all glamorous. "I met Norman after searching for him as the producer of a prize white label I bought," remembers Lindy when we spoke back in September 2017. "After convincing him to work with me, we recorded 'Dub Be Good To Me'- it was just a bit of fun so was a shock to realise the attention it attracted.

"Those days felt very much like work and, as a 17 year old child, just a bore really; a van full of stinky blokes dragging me round the world was a pain, as all my friends were at raves and discovering acid house.The fun for me started when we stopped touring and Norman relaxed a bit with work after the unfortunate end to his marriage. He turned his marital home into a 24 hour party house."

After a brief solo career in 1991, she would lay low until 1997, when she joined up with house producer and DJ Steve Proctor (who ran the label Better Days) to form Hardknox. Lindy explains how Hardknox came about:

"I spent a few years with the boys touring and getting somewhat jaded with airports, I spent my time settling in London as a young adult. I bought a flat walking distance to the Record and Tape Exchange and spent most days swapping white labels for old blues and reggae records. I DJed in the evening - very late nights in a grotty Members Bar on Talbot and All Saints, playing 12 inches on one turntable, taking the record off each time. I met a record producer, who invited me to make an album for the Japanese market. I spent the next two years recording an album in Notting Hill which was supposed to be in a reggae lover's rock style. It wasn't in the end.

"As I sat with Maxi Priest writing, the studio next door to mine was sounding much more interesting. Mental Heads were in there recording 'Inner City Life' which, at the time, was a sound unheard to me, didn't take me long to investigate. My dog would walk around the studio and end up in there, and it was from that I got involved with a young programmer with an open mind. I guess from my DJing and interest in hip-hop breaks and programming, we began our contribution. I didn't want to sing anymore, I liked to cut breaks and learn to programme them. Steve Proctor taught me to use an Atari computer and sampler and that was that. I was full of energy and anxiety, and working with the loudest, most aggressive sounds suited me fine.

"That was pretty much the 90s for me."

Hardknox, who were Steve Proctor (left) and Lindy Layton (right) – Picture with kind permission from Lindy Layton.

Hardknox's style of big beat was a lot more dark and gritty, and they released four singles, 'Psychopath', 'Coz I Can', 'Come In Hard' and 'Attitude' for both Skint Records and Jive Electro. Their self-titled one and only album was released in September 1999 and contained the track 'Fire Like Dis', which was used in a Fiat Grande Punto advert. In 2010, Hardknox briefly reformed for Cut La Roc's Big Beat Reunion night at the Concorde 2 in Brighton.

One of the most fascinating big beat stories was the story of the act Deejay Punk Roc, which had similarities to the story of Milli Vanilli. The act was essentially a British white guy - Jon Paul Davies - but for some reason, for publicity photographs, press releases and live concerts, Davies' manager hired Charles Gettis, a former veteran turned DJ, a black guy from Brooklyn, USA to represent the act. His/their first release was the early electro inspired 'My Beatbox' in 1997 (which was also used in the Sony Playstation game, 'Thrasher: Skate & Destroy') on Davies' Airdog label. It was initially on a compilation called *A Collection of Speaker Poppin' Electro Beats.*

"When my British label phoned me about the tapes they'd heard I thought it was bullshit," Gettis explained in the April 1998 issue of *Jockey Slut.* "You see none of this stuff was supposed to be released. Just tapes for parties or just stuff to give to the boys. That sort of thing." [104]

The first Deejay Punk Roc album *Chickeneye* was released in 1998, and was very popular with both critics and listeners with Gettis (the man fronting the project) opening for The Prodigy and Nu-Metal band, Korn. Even at the time, there were persistent rumours that Gettis was just a hunky front for a nerdy British producer.

The project carried on until 2002, with Jon Paul Davies pursuing other projects such as Trinity Hi-Fi. In a Discogs comment page in 2012, Jon Paul Davies came out that he was the real Deejay Punk Roc.

The man who fronted the act, Charles Gettis, sadly died sometime in the 2010s.

Also in 1997, Bolshi Records signee Laidback (Jason Cohen) released his acclaimed debut album *International*, which contained previous singles, such as 'Wrecktify' and 'B-Boy Noise', as well as new material. In an interview for this book in December 2017, Jason Laidback explains what it was like to have a successful album. "The bass was big, the beats were bigger, it was a messy time of mashed up genres and the jilted generation bumpin' into each other on the dancefloor. Indie met hip-hop, we dropped some 303 psychedelia along the way, the sampling rule book got eaten up and spat out, while London clubs like Blue Note, Dogstar and Bar Rumba embraced it. The Prodigy blew minds with *Fat Of The Land* live and there was a sense of freedom to express yourself without any chin strokin' or arm folded purists getting in the way. Even Ministry Of Sound opened its doors to the scene and set up a big beat label. The buzz of Derek Dahlarge playin' my single 'Wrecktify' at their launch night and him choosing 'B-Boy

Noise' as his opening track on their FSUK compilation got me itchin' to get back into the studio and use all my early hip-hop, funk and electro knowledge on my own debut album *International*. Geekin' out in the long hazy late night experimental studio sessions, gettin' lost in dubs and edits and then doing interviews with producers I admired for America's *Rolling Stone* magazine was amazing. It's a bit of a blur now but once I heard DJ Shadow's album *Endtroducing*, it felt like a new scene was exploding and I was very proud to be a part of it."

Moving back onto the Wall of Sound Front, after a tour of Australia, DJ Regal had decided to leave The Wiseguys, but DJ Touché carried on using the Wiseguys name, and started work on the second Wiseguys album *The Antidote*. Regal, on the other hand, started a new group called Bronx Dogs, in collaboration with Richard Sen - the group that, in many ways, single-handedly started a new sub-genre, which would later be known as funky breaks - a sound not too dissimilar to big beat, but based mainly on classic funk, soul, disco and the early days of hip-hop (this side of big beat/breaks is what the Bristol scene would especially embrace). Their first release together as the Bronx Dogs, 'Tribute To Jazzy Jay' for Kontraband Records, was an obvious shout-out record to early hip-hop legend, Jazzy Jay. The following year saw the duo form their own label, Marble Bar, as well as releasing their debut album *Three Legged Funk* in 1999, which featured the Sesame Street sampling 'And The Letters Spell?' DJ Regal remembers this transitional period in an interview with me in October 2017: "The highlights for me, of my time working with Richard Sen, was working with Richard Sen! (a Graff legend and amazing DJ to me already) and then really, all the time we spent in the studio. We both came from the early 80s electro heyday, but then we brought together our different takes on hip-hop, disco, house and breakbeats... in the end, Bronx Dogs was a ruff-rugged and raw entity, and neither one of us really knew how to weld our influences together into a sustainable format. We could be bloody-minded with our remixes, always throwing curve balls and hating the status quo, but we loved our time in the studio, and we made some very interesting, strange and funky-ass music ... which has mostly remained underground!

"As an artist highlight, the two studios we used, at Alex Turner's dungeon in Exmouth Market and Craig Walsh's little bunker at Weatherall's multi-room complex on Scrutton Street, are etched in my brain, and I have very fond memories of those times. DJ Harvey's awesome review of our 'Mixed Blood' single for *MixMag* update will also go with me to my grave – a very nice man!"

The Boutique and Other Club Nights Prosper

Moving now to the DJ/Club side of things - in April 1997, it was the first anniversary of The Big Beat Boutique night in Brighton's Concorde, and as a celebration Fatboy Slim and Jon Carter did a back to back set dressed in T-shirts with their names on and a photograph of Brighton's Palace Pier. On May 24th-26th of that year, The Big Beat Boutique held a tent in Brighton's Essential Festival and each night the place was rammed with up to 2000 people, with even more outside the tent - it was a pivotal moment for the little club's history, considering that the Concorde venue only held a modest 300 people. In a 2015 interview for the BBC, Norman explains that "The Big Beat Boutique held about 300 people but we realised that if everybody who'd ever come to the Boutique turned up on the same night we'd have 2,000 people. And if we put those 2,000 people in a tent and played them the same music, they'd go more nuts than they did in a smaller place. So there was a feeling that we could take the formula bigger." [10]

The Big Beat Boutique was no longer just restricted to the Concorde in Brighton too. The night would later tour all around the UK (and eventually the world) with a regular slot at The End in London called Skint On Fridays, return visits to Brighton's Essential Festival, a residency in Amnesia in Ibiza, a tour of Asia, and the night even had its own tent at other festivals such as the Creamfields Festival in Liverpool. Later on, the Boutique would even grow to have branches in Dublin, Berlin and New York.

In a December 1997 issue of *Jockey Slut*, Gareth Hansome looks back on the massive success of the Boutique brand that year:

"The queues are starting earlier and earlier. The most amazing situation has evolved down the Boutique, a situation we have defiantly pursued since we opened a year and a half ago. The DJ can play what the fuck he wants and not to conform to any particular style or genre. Like Fatboy Slim said 'It's like DJing in the middle of a riot.'" [97]

Fatboy Slim and Jon Carter DJing at the Big Beat Boutique circa 1997-98 with kind permission from Damian Harris

The Heavenly Social's residency at Turnmills in London was still going strong, though this time it had another rebranding – The Heavenly Jukebox, which also coincided with the fact that The Chemical Brothers could no longer be residents, due to their phenomenal success. Extra features were added to the club, including a cinema room showing cult movies, and a room for record collectors to get a vinyl fix, which was a fixture for northern soul nights back in the day. The Turnmills residency ended in 1998.

1997 also saw the establishment of the big beat club night Molotov Pop, which took place in Manchester (mentioned briefly in the previous chapter). Gary Maclaran, who manages Mr. Scruff, told me a little about this night:

"Molotov Pop started in 1997 and I started it with Steve Smith. Steve was too busy to be involved after the first few months so I (Gary) carried on with it for a few years with Eric Barker (brother of Andy Barker from 808 State). It was at the Boardwalk. It was on the rest of the big beat craze, so did well for a while. We were sponsored by Levis for the first year. Aside from the usual artists from Skint etc. we did a few shows that included Afrika Bambaataa and Malcolm Maclaren. It closed in 1999. We went on to do the Music Box with Keep It Unreal (Mr Scruff) which originally started at Planet K in 1999."

"The big beat scene in Manchester was non existent as far as I remember in the 90s," said Tim Ellis, who was a promoter for Molotov Pop. "Hence us setting up Molotov Pop. Manchester has a very cool music scene and we got a fair amount of stick from DJs and promoters who were involved in similar (but musically purer in their eyes) scenes. I'm talking about jazz, funk, soul and hip-hop nights. Nevertheless we saw an opportunity to showcase big beat. We'd done a couple of one-off nights with Wall Of Sound when they were doing promo tours with their artists and could see the potential there.

The night's resident, Jane Winterbottom, who DJed under the name of Funk Boutique, had some very fond memories of playing at Molotov Pop, sharing the bill with two hip-hop legends from the Zulu Nation. "My fondest memory of being resident at Molotov Pop was playing alongside Afrika Bambaataa and Def Jam's Jazzy Jay," she told me. "Jazzy Jay is one of the most amazing DJs I have ever witnessed on the decks. They came back to my house after the gig and hung out with the Mancunians. They were the nicest guys, and I was totally inspired by meeting them.

"We had some fantastic guests on at Molotov Pop. I played with Adam Freeland one night. I liked his stuff a lot. Mark One and Stefano were fellow residents."

"My proudest moment was seeing the queue round the block of approx 1000 people waiting/trying to get in a Wall Of Sound party we hosted one night with The Wiseguys and Les Rythmes Digitales both live," remembers Tim Ellis. "That was great fun!"

Big Beat is Embraced by the Advertising World

One place where big beat thrived hard wasn't, in fact, the clubbing world, but in the world of advertising. A journalist for the *New York Times*, Simon Reynolds, pretty much sums up the advertising world's infatuation with big beat in an article from March 1999 - he says that "Big beat works well in TV ads and Hollywood films because it is good-times music, plain and simple. It's also catchy, sampling hooks and riffs from early rap, disco, raunchy arena rock and '60s frat-party sounds, like garage punk and surf music." [101]

Another attraction to big beat in advertising was its lack of lyrical content. "If you compare a band like Korn with Fatboy Slim, both are very youth-oriented," said Robert Kaplan, the Messner music supervisor, who was responsible for a late 1990s Philips CD player advert. "But Korn comes with a lot of baggage: it's very angry, sonically, vocally and lyrically. Whereas Fatboy Slim doesn't stand for anything." [102]

"Syncs were where the money was back then," remembers Wall of Sound founder, Mark Jones. "Even though it's gone down quite a bit nowadays - because they know that's where the money is. We had loads of tracks synced in."

One Wall of Sound album that was used very heavily in syncs back in the day was the Propellerheads' one and only album *Decksanddrumsandrockandroll* (which will be covered more in depth later).

"Yeah, it was crazy how many syncs we got from that album," remembers Alex Gifford from the Propellerheads. "We definitely earned more from syncs than we did from actual record sales. I think it had to do with a number of factors — many of the tunes are quite cinematic and orchestral, which is often a good fit with film, and they're all, to some extent, steeped in 60s and 70s funk and soul, which have become synonymous with action scenes and a certain kind of tongue-in-cheek glamour. You can't picture a scene from *Starsky and Hutch* without immediately hearing the soundtrack and vice versa.

"I think one thing we're pretty good at is pumping up those kinds of slightly arch, retro elements into something slightly larger than life, which I guess is the sort of thing that many movies and ads aim to do visually. Getting the request to use 'Spybreak' in the *Matrix* soundtrack was staggering though — as much as anything because it seemed so implausible that a tune which we'd put together in my spare bedroom as the soundtrack to an imaginary spy movie should have somehow found its way into a major scene of a real Hollywood blockbuster. I'm happy to say that practically all of the sync requests we've had over the years have been for the kind of movies and products that we'd have chosen ourselves, given the chance, which has made accepting them a lot easier. I couldn't believe it when I was told about *The Simpsons*, it felt like such an honour. In fact it was ages before I got to see that episode — I could never seem to find it — but it was utterly awesome when I finally did."

The aforementioned 'Spybreak' track would also get used in the movie trailers for *Dogma, Inspector Gadget, Spy Kids* and *Chicken Run*.

One notable track that the advertising world embraced was the Lunatic Calm track 'Leave You Far Behind', which was a popular staple in movies such as *The Matrix, Charlie's Angels, Spider-Man* and *Tomb Raider: The Cradle of Life* and video games during the 1990s and 2000s. Simon Shackleton reminisces on its heavy usage back in the day:

"At the time we really weren't interested in the licenses it was picking up, but we did realise that they were good for us financially, as well as sustaining us as a unit for a few years beyond that. Our goal was simply to get out on the road to play our music to people, and then get back to the studio to write some more music. The advertising side of things was a real thorn in our side actually, because it led to a lot of conflict with the record company and led to our walking away from our record deal with MCA."

Another big beat troupe whose music was embraced by the world of advertising was Bentley Rhythm Ace, most notably their signature tune 'Bentley's Gonna Sort You Out'. "It was really funny at first, but a friend of ours at the BBC got told off for constantly using our stuff on daytime makeover programmes," remembers Richard March from BRA. "Mike was renting a flat off her at the time - I think she was just making sure he'd be able to pay the rent! In 2016, I got a call from our publishers saying Audi wanted to use a track in an advert which I was really excited about, but I misheard them and was surprised to hear the track on an advert for Aldi supermarket..."

The artist who the advertising world most embraced was Fatboy Slim, and from the late 1990s-present day his tracks have been heard on many adverts for brands such as Adidas, Honda Civic, Levis 501, Gap, Nissan, Mitsubishi and many more. Another artist from the big beat ship who was also very prolific was US producer Freddy Fresh, whose music was used in several adverts for brands such as Renault, Adidas, American Express, Ribena juice and more recently Ritz crackers. Theo Keating aka DJ Touché from The Wiseguys (now Fake Blood) had his track 'Ooh La La' used in a Budweiser advert and in a snippet for an interview for Jeremy King on the website Tranzfusion in 2005 he explains the difference between getting your track on adverts as opposed to the radio: "I don't have a problem with putting music to ads, as long as you don't have any major ideological problem with the ad. Getting your songs on radio, getting any kind of exposure is very hard and getting it on an ad is just another way of getting exposure... if it was a political campaign or a product that was deeply unsound, then no, I wouldn't go for it. Hopefully with something like a beer there's no deforestation or exploitation of people of the world. But you always have to use your judgement." [22]

Not everybody was happy with the use of their music in other mediums. Fatboy Slim's seminal track 'Right Here Right Now' was used in several political campaigns including those for Tony Blair, Al Gore and the Young Conservatives - he was understandably not too happy about this.

1997 was also the year of the James Bond film *Tomorrow Never Dies*. The famous US dance music producer, Moby, was commissioned to do a very special "modernised" remix of the classic John Barry theme, and opted to go for a Propellerheads-esque big beat rendition of the iconic theme song. It was a big hit, and reached No.8 in the UK singles charts, and was an even bigger hit in America, where it was No.1 in the Billboard Hot Dance Club Play Chart. Moby would see even bigger success two years later with his album *Play*.

The video game industry was very receptive to the use of big beat music in their soundtracks at the time. Probably the most prolific use of big beat in video games would be from the breakbeats-meets-ska act, The Dub Pistols. "It was brilliant - we spent a lot of time on tour buses back then, and you sit through the tour buses playing your games," reminisces Barry Ashworth from the band. "We did so many games back then such as 'Tony Hawk's' and 'Mat Hoddmann's BMX', as well as some films - it was pretty incredible, and a hell of a lot of remixing."

The Dub Pistols would have their tunes licensed for many of the big AAA games of the time; these included 'FIFA '99', 'FreQuency', 'Mat Hoddman's Pro BMX 2', 'Tony Hawk's Pro Skater 2', 'NBA Live '08', 'Tiger Woods PGA Tour '09' and 'Dance Dance Revolution X'.

Another act on the big beat front who gained significant support from the world of advertising was Liverpool band Apollo 440, who had their tunes used in many blockbuster films of the day, including the theme tune to the 1998 movie *Lost In Space*, a track for the *Charlie's Angels* remake, and even some video games. "One thing leads to another and the ads and movie syncs just keep escalating," remembers Noko from Apollo 440. "Every track from our *Electroglide In Blue* album ended up being used in one way or another, running into the hundreds, and it's fascinating to see your music filter into the culture via all of these different delivery systems.

"Though we'd had lots of our tracks used in movies, '98's *Lost In Space* was the first time we were commissioned to do an actual movie theme, which, as a major soundtrack fan, was such a thrill (I'd spent a lot of my time in the '80s thumbing through grubby charity shops, meticulously collecting movie scores - especially John Barry, so touching base with the movie world proper was a dream-come-true).

"We were asked to do the same for the *Charlie's Angels* movie the following year. What we never got the chance to do with @440, was do a whole movie soundtrack - we came pretty close in '97, when Sony asked us to score their entire 'Rapid Race' speedboat race Playstation game.

"I had to wait till 2009 to do my own full score, when I did Éric Valette's French-language noir thriller *Une Affaire D'Etat* and his next one *La Proie*, two years later. I've just finished scoring an interesting documentary movie *Ex Dominatrix* by Darren Cavanagh, which was released in December 2017."

Skint Records Rises and the Emergence of "Intelligent" Big Beat

1997 also saw Skint Records getting major label distribution from Sony Music - a real sign of the already rising label upping their game. As well as that, Skint also formed an underground spin-off label called Under 5's. These releases were more low-key and experimental, and featured artists such as Danielsan, Wildstyle Bob Nimble, Martin and the Mint Gun Club (aka Mint Royale). This sub-label disbanded in 2001, but was revived in 2009 to (mostly) specialise in dubstep - one of the tracks in the second wave of Under 5's releases was one of my own early tunes entitled 'Put Your Money Where Your Mouth Iz' back in March 2010. In an interview for this book in October 2017, Danielsan (aka Daniel Curtis) described working with Under 5's as "Great." He added "I'd been sending Damian [Harris] tapes for about 6 months and he eventually caved in and created a label to house all the waifs and strays who weren't ready for Skint. Just having a record out, getting it mastered, designing the label and having it reviewed was amazing. I put 3 EPs out and they sold pretty well."

According to a 1998 interview in *Jockey Slut*, another attraction to signing Danielsan was because, like Damian Harris, he supported the football team Arsenal.

The year also saw them sign one of their most popular acts from that period - the Lo-Fidelity Allstars, originally based in Leeds. The lineup included Phil Ward, Andy Dickinson, Martin Whiteman, Del Vegas, Johnny Machin, Dale Malone, Dave Randall and John Stone, and they opted for Damian Harris' Skint label, despite offers from larger labels. Their first releases were the EP 'Kool Rok Bass' and the singles 'Disco Machine Gun' and 'Blisters On My Brain' - in America, their releases were distributed by Columbia Records. Another noteworthy signee of Skint Records at the time was the Middlesborough collective, The Space Raiders. They were Gary Bradford, Mike Hornby and Martin Jenkins. Their releases included 'Glam Raid', 'Monster Munch', 'Laid Back', and the very funky '(I Need The) Disco Doktor', which got a house remix, courtesy of Brighton commercial house duo, Phats & Small. They were also the support act for the Lo-Fidelity Allstars during their 1998 tour. They also released two acclaimed albums in 1999 and 2000 respectively.

One of Skint Records' more individual signings of 1997 was Indian Ropeman. Born Sanjiv Sen, he was formally a member of the hip-hop collectives Blitz Mob and First Down. Indian Ropeman's music was a very creative hybrid of big beat and traditional Indian music. His first release on Skint Records was the EP 'Money for Old Rope' in 1997. The success of this was followed up with the humorous single 'Dog In The Piano' in 1998, which samples a phone call of an angry, profane man asking Pet Rescue to get his dog out of his piano - a rather fun choice of a vocal hook, coupled with an extremely catchy Roland TB-303 melody. It encapsulates the whole big beat movement. His one and only album *Elephantsound* was released in 1999 and was very well received, but sadly ignored by the mainstream. The album also spawned a couple of singles, including a cover version of the Cream classic 'Sunshine Of Your Love'. Indian Ropeman, like The Chemical Brothers and The Prodigy, had the distinction of also being a live show, unlike most acts from the big beat era, which were mainly DJ sets (though that was to change by '98).

It wasn't just emerging big beat acts that joined the Skint roster; the West Coast breakbeat legend that formed the big beat prototype, Bassbin Twins (Pete Houser), also recorded for the label, releasing the EP

'Bassbin Twins VS Skint (Two Turntables And A Crate of Skint)', which mashed up various Skint releases. He would also work for Norman Cook's Southern Fried Records releasing the Cook co-produced track 'Out Of Hand'. When I spoke to Pete Bassbin in 2018, he told me what it was like working with two great big beat labels:

"I had been a fan of Skint by the time Damian Harris had asked if I'd like to do something, and he sent a whole batch of Skint vinyl and I dove in paying homage back to it by stitching together an EP. I still remember the fax that came after I sent my tape back: it said 'YES YES YES YES YES...' over the entire page. Both labels represented the right music and people so I couldn't be happier about them."

Behind the scenes at Skint, a man named Ste McGregor would arrive to make music videos for the company, including the video for the Midfield General single 'Midfielding' featuring spoken-word from comedian Noel Fielding. In an interview I conducted with Ste in September 2017, he (later to be known by his DJ alias Kidda) tells his story of when he made videos for Skint: "Danielsan – 'Force Tan' was the first; it was made from drawings we'd do sat in the front room, using old photos of friends or books like *Subway Art*. There wasn't any kind of work ethic involved, we were a couple of overly-creative slack fucks who interrupted our Tony Hawks and fag-smoking sessions by occasionally doing a drawing of one of our mates until it made us laugh. Then I'd take them upstairs, scan them in, and make them move. We did that 'til I had three minutes of animated footage and bingo! Moosic video! We framed some of them and showed them in our mate's mum's pub, where we used to go most Thursday nights to DJ. Made some good headaches there. Midfield General – 'Midfielding' still brings a tear to my eye for lots of reasons. It was the first thing I had ever done that made people laugh out loud - the best feeling in the world. It also kicked off my animation career, and took me around the world to various film and video conferences. Always grateful to the General for letting me have a crack at that one."

Big beat would also help inspire a new sub-movement in the genre that was dubbed by famous journalist Simon Reynolds as "intelligent big beat", something he would aptly describe as "an oxymoron-in-waiting" [73]. Probably the most well known artist in this new (and sadly short lived sub genre) would have to be Req (real name Ian Cassar). He started his career as a graffiti artist, and despite being a DJ since the 80s, didn't dabble in production work until the mid-1990s, and was signed to Skint Records. His first album, *One,* was released in 1997 and was praised by critics and got plaudits from the likes of Coldcut. In 2015, *Fact* magazine ranked it at No.14 in their '50 best trip-hop albums of all time' list. Two more acclaimed albums would emerge from Skint Records - *Frequency Jams* in 1998 and *Car Pain Scheme* in 2000. Req moved to Warp Records in 2002, where he released the album *Sketchbook* to more critical raves. Another artist that Simon Reynolds would lump into the "intelligent big beat" tag were the Lo Fidelity Allstars, and in many ways it is a good way to describe jazzier breakbeat artists like DJ Shadow, The Ballistic Brothers and Quantic.

Also on the more 'intelligent big beat' end of the spectrum, Mancunian beat master, tea drinker and fish eater, Mr. Scruff, also released his debut album which was titled… *Mr Scruff.* It contained tracks that had been featured on his previous EPs 'Frolic' parts 1 and 2 such as 'Chicken In A Box', and the EP 'Limbic Funk'. The album was released on Pleasure Music, but was reissued in 2005 on Ninja Tune under the name *Mrs. Cruff.* As a tradition in Mr. Scruff albums, it contained tunes that cut up recordings of voice-overs from documentaries and children's programmes to make a story - this is demonstrated in the opening and closing tracks 'Sea Mammal' and 'Wail'. The album was well-received, and led to four acclaimed follow-ups on Coldcut's Ninja Tune label. When I spoke to him in March 2018, he told me about the ingredients that made his unique quirky, humorous and soulful sound so special:

"To my mind, my contemporaries were people like Mark Rae, DJ Food, Vadim, The Herbaliser, Andy Votel, The Runaways, The Wiseguys, Attica Blues, The Nextmen, Mixmaster Morris and Coldcut. All people with a passion for music, roots and a magpie mentality. The soulfulness comes from the myriad of black music influences, and the humour, much of which stems from unlikely combinations of samples, is a very British thing."So overall - 1997 was a great year for big beat fans.

Beats International - Big Beat Overseas

It wasn't just the UK that was finally feeling the big beat - the movement was becoming international. In an interview for DJhistory.com in 1999, Norman Cook AKA Fatboy Slim explains why dance music (which, of course, applies to big beat) is so international:

"Less lyrics. It's more instrumental. You don't have to speak a language to get it. If there's a hookline, you can just mime along to it, you don't have to know what the story of the song is. It's like the opposite of folk music, where it's just telling you a story." [75]

Americans Embrace Big Beat

The place where big beat had its biggest following outside of the UK was in the USA.

Easily the most popular non-UK big beat act was The Crystal Method (Ken Jordan and Scott Kirkland) from Las Vegas. Their career kick-started in 1995 when a UK DJ called Justin King was interested in signing them to his label City Of Angels, which showcased US talent. Their first release was 'Now Is The Time'. They then moved to Outpost Recordings in 1996 and started work on their acclaimed debut album *Vegas,* but in the interim they released their second and most famous single on the City Of Angels label 'Keep Hope Alive', which was used in the film *The Replacement Killers,* as well as being the theme tune to the show *Third Watch.* It was also used in countless video games (like 'FIFA '98') and television commercials. September of 1997 saw the release of their aforementioned debut album *Vegas,* which was later certified platinum in 2007 and was a big success worldwide.

One of the ingredients for their crossover success was their fusion of rock music and dance. "It was natural for us," states the band in a 2004 interview for *Resident Advisor.* "Growing up in the States, rock was a very big part of our lives. I grew up listening to AC/DC and groups like

New Order, so rock guitars and electro were big influences on me." [23] This crossover success was the inevitable gateway for the American audience to finally embrace electronic dance music. Their second album *Tweekend* was released in July 2001, and featured guest spots from Tom Merello from Rage Against The Machine, Scott Weiland from Stone Temple Pilots and many others; the album sadly received mixed reviews.

As well as performing live and producing, Ken and Scott Crystal also hosted a radio show called 'Community Service', which aired every Friday Night on Californian Radio Station Indie 103.1, which closed initially, but saw a revival in 2011 and airs to this day on Sirius XM's Channel 52. January 2004 saw them release their third album *Legion of Boom* to undeservingly mixed reviews (though it was nominated for a Grammy for best electronic/dance album). Like their previous album, this record had several vocalists including *Resident Evil* actress Milla Jovovich and John Garcia from Kyluss. They also produced a movie score for the 2005 indie film *London* directed by Hunter Richards and in 2008 they remixed 'Why So Serious' by Hans Zimmer (The Joker's Theme) from the Batman movie *The Dark Knight*. 2009 saw them release their fourth album *Divided by Night* which became their most commercially successful album since their debut in 1997 and featured guest spots from Peter Hook, Justin Waterfield, LMFAO and more. In 2013, Scott Kirkland was in hospital to remove a fossa arachnoid cyst in his brain and thankfully the operation was a complete success. The following year saw them release their self-titled fifth album. The Crystal Method still perform and make music to this day.

Another notable US big beat act was Cirrus, who were Aaron Carter (not the teeny-bopper with the same name) and Stephen James Barry. Their first single 'Superstar DJ' was a hit in America, reaching No.26 in the US Billboard Dance/Club Play Charts, and the success of this resulted in their debut album, *Drop The Break* being released on Moonshine Music in 1997. Two more albums were also released – *Back On A Mission* in 1998 and *Counterfeit* in 2002. They released four more singles including the Billboard US Dance/Club Play Top 10 hit 'Boomerang'. Their tunes were also featured on several video games including 'FIFA 2002', 'Gran Turismo 3', 'Test Drive 6' and 'Supercar Street Challenge'.

One of the more notable and most successful American big beat acts was Freddy Fresh (Fred Schmid). Initially a hip-hop DJ in the 1980s,

Freddy's career shifted to rave in the 1990s then to techno, but by the mid-1990s, he embraced the rising big beat scene. "I did not realise that a movement even existed, as I live in Minnesota and here, in the 1990s, it did not exist at all," reminisces Freddy Fresh in an interview I conducted for this book in September 2017. "My first awareness into the 'scene' was when I found out Norman Cook was playing my records, and he later invited me to play at his Big Beat Boutique. It was there that I met him and things developed that would lead us to working together."

By 1998, Freddy would become one of the biggest acts in big beat, and to this day is still making anthems in the genre.

American big beat DJ, Freddy Fresh promoting his album *Surrounded By Funk*. With kind permission from the man himself, Freddy Fresh.

1997 was the year that the United States of America would finally embrace the scene, which sowed the seeds for the late 1990s "electronica" movement, which was similar to that of the 2010's "EDM" craze in many ways. Acts like the Prodigy and The Chemical Brothers would finally see mainstream success in the US, which was unusual in the grunge and hip-hop dominated world of the US charts at the time, and in many ways it was a breath of fresh air.

"There wasn't a big big beat scene per se, we certainly appreciated those sounds, but they were mixed in with everything else," remembers Rusty B. from the All Good Funk Alliance in an interview with me in September 2017. "Personally, The Chemical Brothers and Fatboy Slim's early singles really moved me in a big way, I wanted to make breakbeats after hearing that stuff, but stuff like DJ Icey and Überzone were just as exciting."

One act that the Americans really embraced, even before big beat made it big over there, were The Chemical Brothers. Tom Chemical remembers the early days of being in America in an interview for *Pitchfork* magazine in July 2015: "One of the first places we played live for a lot of people was in Orlando in 1994. We were just amazed that someone knew who we were, and got in touch and paid for a plane ticket to America to play. And then we turn up, and it's a massive, full-on rave. We had this track, 'Chemical Beats' and we'd show up with an MPC and a Juno-106 and some distortion pedals and just make it up. No one was asking us to come and play that kind of thing in England then. We'd turn up in the States and play records like 'Song To The Siren' and people would know them. It was mind-blowing, really. We'd made this record in our bedroom, and suddenly we were in America, which, for us, was an exotic place to go—even though, I must admit, Orlando is maybe not the most exotic place in the world. But for us, at that time, we couldn't believe it! And then we'd go off to San Francisco and New York.

"Someone the other day was saying they were surprised at the massive EDM-ification of American music, but we used to go there in 1994 and play these big raves that were all separated by scenes and miles. And now they're all being joined up." [24]

Rusty B from the All Good Funk Alliance remembers seeing The Chemical Brothers live, which he recalled to me. "I remember seeing The Chemical Brothers perform at Buzz in Washington D.C. and being blown away at how huge the music sounded. They played all the hits, but really mashed them up with their songs and samples from other songs on top. It was one of the first times I heard someone really remix and rework songs on the fly. It was a heady time, but I was super influenced by seeing them. The Prodigy show on the other hand seemed more like a rock show, I felt way more connected to The Chemical Brothers show."

It wasn't all sunshine and roses however, as the Fatboy himself did his first US tour in 1997 to promote the *Better Living Through Chemistry* album with Jon Paveley - the man behind Astralworks, Skint Records' US distributor - having to really encourage people to go and see him. The ticket sales were abysmal, and on some nights he barely drew crowds in their tens, let alone their hundreds - this is hilariously ironic in hindsight, as Norman today can fill 20,000 in a giant stadium with no problem and headline the main stage at major festivals. "I'm not worried about the US at the moment," stated Fatboy in an interview documented in the 2002 biography *Funk Soul Brother* by Martin James. "I do this for the experience - I get to travel, I get to see places I'd always wanted to see. It beats becoming a fireman." [27].

However, when he returned to the US in 1998 and 1999, it was a completely different story, with him selling out clubs (and eventually arenas) around the country, due to his phenomenal success worldwide. It should also be noted that in these early American shows (especially during the Fatboy-mania phase of 98/99) a lot of the less savvy people thought that the Fatboy Slim act was an actual live band rather than a DJ playing records. Many people were quite baffled when they saw him performing and demanded refunds. This all changed when they finally got the concept of a superstar DJ during subsequent visits and especially when the "EDM" craze started in the early 2010s when DJs as headliners started to sell out sports arenas there.

"I'd turn up at a gig, I'd start playing records with people standing there looking at me and going 'What time is Fatboy Slim on?'" remembers Norman Cook in an interview for *London Real* in 2017. "After half an hour, they're like 'Actually, what time IS Fatboy Slim on? When are you going to stop playing records - where's the drum kit, and where's the amps,' and actually then lean over to me and go, 'When's the band on?' - I'm like 'No - I am Fatboy Slim!' and they go '. . . .okay!'." [92]

Easily the act that made the biggest impact in the States was The Prodigy, who were an actual live act with guitars and drums. Paul McGuiness in an article for the *Electronic Telegraph* in 1997 said "You have to be prepared to put on a show, which British rock bands seem to think might detract from the authenticity of their music. The Prodigy are one of the few bands plugging into theatrical traditions." [25].

During the height of their fame in America, they even received the much-coveted prize of being parodied by comedian "Weird Al" Yankovic. Their track 'Firestarter' was parodied as 'Lousy Haircut' on his television series *The Weird Al Show*, which was broadcast in America on the 20th September 1997. Also, their track 'Smack My Bitch Up' would receive a parody version in the States from lounge crooner parodist Richard Cheese (Mark Jonathan Davis). Their fame made Ed Simons from The Chemical Brothers somewhat jealous. "The Prodigy seem to be getting all the attention," he said in an interview, "but we've already done three big tours out there, filling venues bigger than them a long time ago. We really love playing in America. It's like 1989 for them, all pretty new and it's refreshing." [3].

Frank Cueto from the All Good Funk Alliance remembers The Prodigy's early impact in the States in an interview for this book in September 2017:

"The early rave days of the 90s was such an experiment and there were a lot of styles being played at the time and the branching of styles was just in its infancy. It was then when some DJs would throw in some tracks that could be considered big beat or at least the early versions of it. Prodigy definitely was the group I remember the most."

"I first heard of Prodigy, and I ended up catching them live at a little show in Boulder, CO in the early 90s," remembers Rusty B, also from the All Good Funk Alliance. "I then moved out East where I started hearing The Dust Brothers, which was The Chemical Brothers alias, and that stuff mixed with Florida breaks. The Florida scene and big beat to me, at that time, were really exciting, I was a huge hip-hop fan, and to hear those samples and breakbeats used in electronic music felt really fresh at the time. Like Frank said, these big beat tracks were mixed in with techno, house and a real blend of styles that the U.S. East Coast DJs would play. "

One fan of the genre who would later produce big beat tracks of his own was Jason Ard, who goes by the DJ name of Old Flame. When I spoke to him in September 2017, Jason explained how he got into big beat: "I discovered big beat around 1998. I was in high school and I heard 'Dirtchamber Sessions' by Liam Howlett and the *Amp 2* compilation. After that I started digging, copying tracklists and learning about so much great music known as big beat. It was so refreshing. I obviously got into it a bit late, as it crossed over around 98/99 with artists like Fatboy Slim, The Chemical Brothers and The Prodigy. A lot of compilations were out, but there wasn't a ton of big beat shows in the Southern U.S. The Crystal Method was leading the pack in the States. Fatboy and The Brothers came to Atlanta a few times."

The Americans embracing the big beat movement was key in sowing the seeds of both the "electronica" fad of the late 1990s-early 2000s and the "EDM" craze in the 2010s. Without big beat, dance music wouldn't be the driving force in America it is today. It should also be noted that a lot of people who produce "EDM" and a lot of modern day journalists seem to be unaware that dance music (or electronica as they called it) was quite big in America in the late-1990s to around 2000-ish, and only seem to think that electronic dance music of any kind became big around 2009 when David Guetta started having hits there. In fact, the very first modern electronic dance hit there was of course 'I Feel Love' by Donna Summer back in 1977, when Guetta was only 10 years old (and don't forget that electronic music on record has existed since the 1920s!).

Canada Also Embraces Big Beat

Enter Myagi (Andrew Mavor), who would later join Freddy Fresh on his Howlin' Records label. In an interview for this book in November 2017, Myagi remembers how he discovered big beat (and later breaks) growing up in Canada.

"So I discovered big beat and then breaks through a pretty odd route. I was really into groups like Nine Inch Nails and Thrill Kill Kult in my early high school years, and the electronic elements those acts integrated really spoke to me. Around 17, I got into acts like the Crystal Method, Fatboy Slim, Hardknox, Freestylers etc. There was a lot of crossover happening between the underground and the mainstream at that point, and it was basically around the same time the internet became available. I'd find artists who were responsible for a track I'd like, then I'd look up everyone they'd ever worked with and every label who had published their music."

Myagi's roots were funnily enough not in dance music, but in the American rock music of the time - his own musical output has an equality interesting origin.

"Myagi started off as a band I was in, in high school. I had a horrible voice, but I convinced myself otherwise. It wasn't a great first move into songwriting, but I had fun taking my ideas across the finish line. For better or worse, I decided working solo and things would improve my workflow. I bought a Roland SH7, a Groovebox, Korg Poly800,

Roland Juno1, MPC2000xl, even more kit, and set about writing a massive amount of poorly conceived ideas with little or no focus. There were no people into what I was into, and there was no YouTube to learn via video. Everything was self taught and done through experimentation. I think that really helped. I found more music by people who ended up being massive influences sonically - Monkey Mafia, Soul of Man, Fuzz Townsend, Bentley Rhythm Ace etc. Eventually I developed a bit of a style, pollinated by what I heard from these guys - a sort of good times, hands up, beer sloshing mashup of rock, house, funk, hip-hop and acid."

He also remembers gatecrashing Fatboy Slim's entourage, drunk, and seeing him and Theo from The Wiseguys performing in Canada back in the day. "I was in first year university at the time, and a friend and I had some drinks and walked around Toronto before the show. At around 5pm, we saw a limo pulling up in front of a radio station and joked it might be Norman Cook... turned out it was. Half drunk, we fell into their entourage and pretended like we belonged there as he did an interview. It was the start of an awesome night. I remember Theo from The Wiseguys dropped the *Superman* theme, which I thought was fucking hilarious. I may have been a little tipsy though. It was a great show. At that point Fatboy Slim's draw had tipped the scales into full on big room stuff, but the energy in the place was awesome. Probably 5000 people or so, if I remember right. All the classics of the time got played. It was super eclectic and one hell of a lot of fun."

Song For Manumission

Ibiza in the Balearic Islands of Spain is, of course, one of the biggest homes of electronic dance music, with a rich history going back to the 1980s. Big beat, however, was a little more niche there (their tastes are generally more house orientated), but there was one big beat DJ who would later end up getting a residency there - Derek Dahlarge. When I interviewed him for this book in October 2017, Derek remembered his legendary residency at the infamous Manumission club, which was known for incorporating DJing with some very sexy theatrics and acrobatic shows, which were also quite controversial. "To go there and to play in, by far, the greatest club ever, in my opinion, was amazing," he recalls. "To play at the opening night, surrounded by 10,000 people totally having it and the most beautiful girls you've ever seen and also some hilarious characters. I sat there with Mike [McKay] from Manumission, and I jokingly said to him 'I wish I could do this every week', and he turned round to me and said 'Why don't you?' and I laughed, and he said 'No, I'm serious - why don't you stay - you can stay in the Manumission Hotel', which is like heaven on earth - it was like Disney World for adults, and I was blown away and I was like 'Fuck it - I'm not going home' - I had three amazing years there - to have a three year residency in the best club in the world was a dream come true."

Manumission was begun in 1994 by brothers Andy and Mike McKay, and in 1995 gained media attention when Mike's girlfriend Claire started performing a live sex show with another woman at one of the events, with Mike himself getting in on the action at an AIDS Benefit show in Paris in 1996. These live sex shows were an integral part of the infamy of Manumission – I don't think my mum would approve of these shenanigans! The night also had a residency in Manchester.

The Manumission Residency also made headlines. Because Derek was doing this new residency for a while, he was reported missing for over a month, with the UK clubs and Wall of Sound label getting very worried, and an appeal went out to him on the Essential Selection, though this was nothing more than a misconception - "I didn't go missing at all," said Derek on the BBC website in 1998. "I came out here to do the opening party of Manumission and they asked me to stay." [89]

When speaking to Alex Hardee from CODA agency in November 2017, he remembers a particularly humorous incident at the Derek Dahlarge residency involving Jon Carter super glueing a dildo to Derek's head - it even made the cover of *Mixmag*. Like his mate Jon Carter, Dahlarge, as you would expect, was a class-A hedonist.

A movie about the Manumission nights was made called, appropriately, *Manumission - The Movie*. A soundtrack CD was also released, which featured an early version of the Fatboy Slim song 'Love Island' from his second album *You've Come A Long Way, Baby* which was then called 'Song for Manumission'. It also contained tunes by Groove Armada, The Wiseguys, Carl Cox, Tall Paul and DJ Cam and was mixed by Les Rythmes Digitales.

Big Beat Gets Love in Australia

Another place where big beat had a good following was Australia. In the late 1990s, Wall of Sound acts were regulars at a festival called Vibes On A Summer Day, and Fatboy Slim would later headline several festivals and arena events in the country. A notable DJ from Australia who was influenced by big beat was producer Matty Blades. "Big beat was one of my biggest and earliest influences," remembers Matty when he spoke to me. "The late 90s was an exciting time for home production. Propellerhead Software had just released Rebirth in 1997, which was very exciting to any nerd into music production. With this new technology, you wouldn't need an expensive studio, which opened the door for anyone with passion. We would spend days reworking tracks from our favourite artists just in time to drop."

Matty also remembers what the Australian big beat scene was like back in the day. "I first heard the term in the mid 90s. There were two big albums which made a big impact on me: The Chemical Brothers' *Exit Planet Dust* and Prodigy's *Music for the Jilted Generation*. It really was the only new music that spoke to me and my friends at the time. We would create our own mix tapes by recording individual tracks off the radio, and create catalogues of our top tunes. I always thought growing up in Perth in the 90s felt rather isolated from the rest of the world, but the kids were extremely passionate about their music. The internet hadn't really kicked off, and for most of the kids we only had "alternative" radio stations like Triple J, or trading old cassette tapes with your mates. I was still a bit young when big beat hit Australia, so my introduction was at bush raves and the occasional illegal party. The big artists didn't always travel to Perth so when they did it was always a good party."

"There wasn't much of a 'scene' as such," remembers Australian DJ Kid Kenobi for an interview for this book. "It was more just a few different crews putting on a few different nights here and there. Some of these crews and DJs came from the house scene, some were from a hip-hop background, and some - like me - were a mix of raver and hip-hop fan.

At the time, I was in a DJ crew with two of my best mates - DJs Q45 and Ritual - who were also from Sydney. We were only just starting out and were residents at a monthly event called Green & Jazzy put on by Will Cate and Mitesh Solanki. We played a lot of big beat - myself in particular – but, like the big beat scene in the UK (from what I can gather), the night itself wasn't just about playing big beat, we played a mix of styles with everything from hip-hop to old rave, jungle, drum & bass, and house.

"There were also side rooms at some of the bigger house parties that played big beat which I was lucky enough to play. It was awesome getting to play this non-house music style to a really 'loved up' house music crowd! They loved it!"

Kid Kenobi also shared some fond memories of supporting Fatboy Slim in Australia:

"When I got to support Fatboy Slim, the gig took place in a big dome shaped building and, for some reason, the heat got trapped right up at the top where the DJ was playing (on a balcony overlooking the crowd). It was SO hot. Norman had a guy that looked like a 'Mini Me' from the Austin Powers films dipping towels into buckets of ice and throwing them onto him while he played. Norman was going off relentlessly, despite the heat. I was still a relative newbie to DJing at the time, and I'd never seen anyone DJ in that kind of heat before. It was intense! His remix of 'Renegade Master' was also massive at the time, and I'll never forget when he finally dropped it. The place erupted!"

As well as Matty Blades and Kid Kenobi, Laidback also shared some great big beat memories from the land of Oz:

"So, I'm in Australia, driving to the gig, and the promoter's saying 'the club's empty, I've lost money' - and then he cracks up when I walk into a rammed room full of big beat fans! Phew, now the DJ nerves kick in, but after a few vodkas I'm in full flow, it's goin' off, the atmosphere's electric, the set's building and I'm halfway through. I feel relaxed, so I'm showin' off and scratchin' over a string breakdown, but then I get that comedy zip sound effect loud over the system. My elbow's jogged the needle so hard on the other deck, it's skipped right off at the quietest part of the track, and now the club's in SILENCE! Nothing, nada, zilch, you can hear a pin drop! I never went to DJ school, but I doubt they really teach you what to do in those situations, so my natural reaction was to slowly, sheepishly, look up, shrug my shoulders and smile. Luckily all 2000 people smile back, cheer, and every hand in the place goes up and claps in unison. Milk the applause, scratch in the next tune and the room goes nuts! So, a mistake is my favourite moment, probably because the set was going so well I got away with it, or more to the point, Australia was the home of the biggest breaks nights and the energy of every incredible Oz crowd was with you every step of the way!"

By the end of the 1990s (and even into the early 2000s after big beat's "death") the Australians really started to embrace it.

"We got a lot of radio support in Australia as Dynamo Productions and we got to play in venues that held 1500 people," remembers Boca 45. "In the early 2000s, they were fed up with house music and wanted something different. It was still danceable, it was funky. People like us, Krafty Kuts and A-Skillz did really well in Australia at the time."

In the 2000s, DJ Regal from The Wiseguys would move to Australia and have a solo career over there. In an interview for this book in October 2017, Regal members these times. "I left for Oz in late 2001 and recorded two albums there. By the time I returned seven years later, I met and had the best times with so many of Australia's best artists, made some great music, even won an award and, in hindsight, it was my reward and swansong, all rolled into one. I made friends for life over there and it will always be a part of who I am."

Not all big beat DJs had a pleasant experience with the Australian crowd. When Freddy Fresh was booked to be the headline DJ at the Torquay Festival back in 2000, the gig was a complete disaster, with the crowd bottling him on stage. Freddy tells us about this 'show from hell'. "I was booked to play Torquay Australia - a large festival with over 60 rock bands and 60 DJs. Due to weather issues, the entire festival was moved 60 miles up the coast, and they cancelled all of the DJs except me, as I was the headliner, and they kept the rock bands. It was a very well-paying gig, because it was the millennium in the year 2000, and it was a massive festival of rock and rollers. I was opening for the Violent Femmes and Blink-182 on a back to back weekend gig.

"On my first night, I was nervous because there were over 25,000 people there, so I had quite a few beers to calm me down. When I got up on stage and started performing, within about one minute I felt something fly past my head and, as I looked on the stage, I could see it was raining down shoes, boots, pop cans, bottles etc. Everybody was just pelting me with objects, and I was literally petrified, but in my favour I did not run off the stage, I merely hid behind the DJ set up, I couldn't understand why they were hating me, when I had only been on a few minutes. This was also the year that I was voted as one of the top 50 DJs in the world, and I was quite confident in my DJ skills at this time - so it made no sense to me that they just hated me. Finally I realised that they could not hear anything I was playing, and my monitors, which were to the side of me, were making so much noise that only I could hear them and no one else. The crowd could not hear any music at all!

"As I panicked, I turned behind me to look for the sound crew to turn the sound on, and there was no sound crew to be found as they had all left to go home after the Violent Femmes performed, assuming that a mere DJ didn't need any sound support whatsoever! Finally, someone else jumped on stage and turned the sound on, and within seconds all of the people stopped throwing objects - but at this point I was irate, angry, frustrated, trembling, and nervous, and still scared from what had just happened. To make matters worse, I ran up and down the stage telling everyone to 'F' off, and giving the whole crowd the finger, while I was being filmed the entire time on Australian television!

"To my surprise, this only animated the crowd, and made them much more excited - that was not my original intent, so I pulled off - but on the next night I had another issue. The sound crew from the night before had been reprimanded heavily for what they had done, leaving me hanging, and so that night I had a whole crew of angry sound people taking care of me. I only realised this because the soundman threw down my monitors so hard on the stage that he made the record skip, and then he gave me the finger behind my back, I was later told. All in all it was a very challenging gig!"

Europe, Eastern Europe, Brazil and Japan Love Big Beat too!

Moving away from Oz, a notable act that would later see huge success was Dutch DJ, Junkie XL (aka Tom Holkenborg). In March 1997, he released his first LP *Saturday Teenage Kick*. The album received notoriety, as bootleg releases went under The Prodigy name (with the album being renamed by bootleggers as *Castfeeder*), misleading people to think it was an unreleased Prodigy album. It also contained the tracks 'Def Beat' and 'No Remorse', which were staples in video games of the time. His second album *Big Sounds Of The Drags* was released in 1999, but his real big break didn't start until 2002. When doing inroads as a film composer, he was asked to remix the then-obscure 1968 Elvis Presley song 'A Little Less Conversation' for a Nike World Cup Commercial, which will be covered in more depth later.

Another European country that had a strong big beat following was Germany. One German DJ who was influenced by big beat was producer Quincy Jointz (real name Dirk Schäfer). "I discovered the Chemical Brothers album *Exit Planet Dust* in a record-store in my hometown Freiburg," remembers Quincy. "I was fascinated about this sound - between hip-hop, sample madness and the energy of a rock band. Didn't know that it was called big beat.

"At this time I was DJ in a students-club and played all styles. The crowd loved the new sound. I can't remember if there was a real big beat scene here. Before I discovered big beat I was doing house and techno songs. Not much sample-based. Then I started to work more with samples and no longer cared about focusing on only one style or more or less one tempo."

Acts in the German big beat scene would include Surreal Madrid (best known for the track 'Girls Of The Nite') and the Torpedo Boyz, who have a strong underground following to this day.

DJ Regal from The Wiseguys remembers playing in Germany back in the day: "If ever a venue hid its potential, none comes close to Darmstadt's abandoned Science & Chemical building at the back of the local porn-supermarket car park, in the middle of fucking nowhere, Germany. Without doubt, the craziest, sweatiest, loudest and most mental crowd I've ever played to, before or since, and I include our Bondi Beach gig in Feb '97.

"We turned it on that night! But we had many a great night in two short years of gigging together."

One particular country that developed a very strong big beat following was Japan. To this day, Fatboy Slim remains very popular there (he was also big over there during the Beats International era), and in his heyday Freddy Fresh was, in his own words, "treated like royalty". When Norman played his first show in Japan as Fatboy Slim in 1998 at the 1800 capacity Garden Hall venue in Tokyo, it sold out within hours, and the pre-sales demand for *You've Come A Long Way, Baby* in Japan was astonishing for the time, with both 'Rockafeller Skank' and 'Gangster Trippin' reaching No.1 in the Japanese singles charts.

Probably the most famous Japanese big beat act was the Boom Boom Satellites - formed in 1990 in Tokyo and consisting of Michiuki Kawashima and Masayuki Nakano. Their first group release was in 1997 with the EP '4 A Moment of Silence'. They were even featured in *Mel-*

ody Maker magazine and were compared to both The Chemical Brothers and The Prodigy. They released their first album *7 Ignitions* on April Fools Day 1998, and then performed some high profile gigs, including a support slot for Moby. They were also asked to remix several big name acts, including rock band Garbage. They released a whole slew of albums between 1998-2016 and were very popular in the advertising and syncs world.

Another notable act was Captain Funk (Tatsuya Oye), who was described by Freddy Fresh in a 2008 *Discogs* review as "The Fatboy Slim of Japan" [87]. Despite putting out his records since 1995, his first solo release as Captain Funk wasn't until 1998 with the 'Roller Coaster EP' and his debut album *Encounter with. ...* He also DJed at many high-profile events, such as the famous Fuji Rock Festival, as well as overseas.

In a special interview for this book in December 2017, Captain Funk remembers what the big beat scene was like in the land of the rising sun:

"Since I was a teenager, and long before big beat burst onto the dance music scene, I had been into old school music such as electronic funk, hip-hop breaks, and rare groove. After I started my professional career as an electronic music producer in '97, I was always exploring the possibilities of incorporating that musical background more into my production and DJ style, which was an extremely peculiar thing for a techno producer in Japan to be doing.

"Thereabout I began to find several artists and record labels outside of Japan to which I could relate, in terms of how they would upgrade their eclectic, old-school vibes to the latest version of electronic/dance music. Some good examples are Jedi Knights, Bassbin Twins, Lionrock, and early releases from Skint records. A part of them ended up being classified as part of the 'big beat phenomenon' after the mainstream successes of Fatboy Slim, Chemical Brothers, and the Prodigy.

"It was striking that a large number of indie rock fans and journalists in Japan, who had not really been crazy about dance music, started paying a lot of attention to what was happening on the scene. The big beat music had such enormous potential to draw rock festival goers, mods, crate diggers, B-Boys (breakdancers), skateboarders, and techno ravers literally onto one dance floor. And it did happen at Machinegun, a party I had organised for almost four years from '97 to '01 at Maniac Love, Tokyo. I invited every conceivable guest DJ who could resonate with the open-minded audience coming together at the party. As long as the music fitted the vibe of the party (which was essential), the crowd welcomed these DJs, who were spinning tunes ranging from The Bar-Kays to Iggy Pop, not to mention the latest big beat, drum & bass, and remixes of J-Pop music.

"The big beat scene, in and out of Japan, significantly contributed to getting rid of boundaries and narrow-minded sectionalism with which we music lovers quickly tend to get caught up. In that sense, I would consider the word big beat as a new attitude or movement of 'party music,' rather than just a musical formula/genre."

1999 saw the release of his 'Bustin' Loose EP', which was massive with the big beat crowd. Famous fans included Coldcut, Si Begg, Ken Ishii, Carl Cox, Freddy Fresh and Fatboy Slim. A notable tune off the EP was the rock & roll inspired track 'Twist and Shout' (not a cover of the classic rock & roll standard). "This may sound funny, but at first, I didn't intend to include 'Twist & Shout' on the EP," Tatsuya remembers. "My concern was that the extremely uplifting, vintage-soul-music-influenced track could mislead, or turn off, the existing fans of Sublime records, my then-label, which was strictly focused on techno music in Japan. But, unexpectedly, the label director strongly suggested I feature the track in the EP, as it should stand out in the international dance music scene. I was afraid that the Captain Funk project might be easily pigeonholed as a big beat artist, and end up being 'consumed' in the short-term. However, at the same time, we strongly felt the necessity to give a decisive impact to the music scene across the globe (where Japanese people/DJs were still very susceptible to the dance music coming from the UK/EU/US, whose people/DJs were not particularly interested in what Japanese musicians/DJs were doing, barring a couple of exceptions).

"While I accepted his opinion, I had him keep the release title 'Bustin' Loose', a breakbeat disco/funk track which I expected could more easily resonate with the audience. My hunch was half right. Some dogmatic journalists and DJs would snub the release as 'kitschy' or even 'silly.' However, the chance came out of the blue. We began to receive a lot of great feedback and appreciation from outside the bounds of the pure techno realm. Fatboy Slim (Norman Cook) and Freddy Fresh were two big examples of them. Norman sent a fax to our office, saying 'What a fucking insane record. I love it. Can I have two more copies so I can play A1, B1, B2 without forgetting? Will road test tonight at The End.' That was a huge honour for me. Freddy chose the track at the top of his playlist. Krafty Kuts included it in his DJ mix CD *Slam the Breaks On*. Also, some influential Shibuya-kei DJs were spinning the disc everywhere in Japan.

"Those supports and voices encouraged me tremendously and made us feel that our risk-taking was paying off. The moral of the story would be that it is far more impressive when others discover your good qualities without you telling them what they are."

During this time, Captain Funk toured with US big beat DJ Freddy Fresh and also another Japanese big beat DJ, Fantastic Plastic Machine. "If memory serves me correctly, I played with them as part of the national tour promoting my DJ mix album called *Style #08 Captain Funk* (Toshiba EMI)," he recalls. "I invited Freddy to the parties in Tokyo (at Liquidroom) and Osaka (at Grand Cafe). As Japanese guest DJs, Fantastic Plastic Machine and Yasuharu Konishi (from Pizzicato Five) joined us. Throughout the journey, I talked a lot with Freddy about our favourite soul and funk discs, music production tips, and music scenes around the world. In Tokyo, I remember taking him to Akihabara, the famous electric city, to check old Japanese gadgets. Years later, we got together again at a DJ party in Munich. The good news is that we're still friends."

One other notable Japanese act was the aforementioned Fantastic Plastic Machine (Tomouki Tanaka). Originally the bassist in the rock band Margarine Strikes Back, he became a DJ in the early 1990s, mainly playing in the Kansai area, and was part of a DJ team called Sound Impossible. In 1997, he started recording as Fantastic Plastic Machine for Readymade Records (a sub-label of major label Columbia). The first two albums *The Fantastic Plastic Machine* released in 1997 and *Luxury* in 1998 were critical successes and his music was used in quite a few high-profile films such as *The Girl Next Door* and *Austin Powers 2: The Spy Who Shagged Me*.

Japanese video game soundtracks from the time also had a big beat vibe. Probably the most prolific Japanese composer in the big beat style for video games was Hideki Naganuma. In 1998, he sent a demo tape to the video game giant, Sega. "I found Sega's job advertisement for sound creators on a *Sound & Recording* magazine," he recalls. "Then I sent a demo tape and a resume to Sega. That was the start of everything." The company hired him, and he did the music for the Sega Dreamcast game 'Sega Rally 2' as well as the music for 'Hip Jog Jog' and also did voice editing work for the Japan only Sega Saturn game with a very complicated name – 'Shōjo Kakumei Utena: Itsuka Kakumeisareru Monogatari' (try saying it!). In 2000, he composed the soundtrack to the acclaimed skating game, 'Jet Set Radio' (Or 'Jet Grind Radio' in North America), which was initially released on the Sega Dreamcast console, but was later ported to other consoles down the road. In an interview for this book, Hideki remembers composing the game's acclaimed soundtrack, and how it was influenced by the big beat scene.

"In 1999, when I couldn't decide which type of music I should make for 'Jet Set Radio', one of my senpais, Mr. Tomonori Sawada, who did the sound effects on 'Jet Set Radio', recommended me to listen to Fatboy Slim and Captain Funk. And I thought 'This is it!' I think this was the first time I listened to big beat style music. I knew Norman Cook and I liked his early music like Beats International from before, but I didn't realise that he had started Fatboy Slim until about that time. In Japan, J-Pop/Rock is always in the mainstream charts. Club music like 'Block Rockin' Beats' never appears on top hit charts. I think only electronic dance music fans knew about big beat at the time."

His soundtrack was described by *Vice* magazine as "energetic, rhythm-heavy and defiant... an eclectic mixture of hip-hop, dance pop, ska, and Japanese rock, a multicultural melange of youth culture and an irrepressible, joyful sense of revolution. Every moment thrums to its soundtrack, which is, on the default settings, emphasised almost more than the in-game sounds, positioning it as a central consideration of play." [26] Naganuma would also compose the music to the game's sequel 'Jet Set Radio Future' for Microsoft's Xbox console. Probably his best-known soundtrack would have to be for the 2005 Nintendo DS Game 'Sonic Rush' - a handheld entry in the insanely popular Sonic The Hedgehog series.

After the fall of communism at the start of the 1990s and Western music was finally legalised there, Russia became a very popular market for big beat music. In an interview for the BBC, Fatboy Slim remembers a gig he did in Gorky Park in Moscow back in 2001.

"We didn't expect people in Moscow to have understood or embraced rave culture. But it was a beautiful sunny day, and there were tons of raving Russians. Somebody felt excited enough to encapsulate the day by writing all over himself in biro!" [10]

Russia had (and still has to this day) a very strong big beat scene with its own homegrown big beat acts. One of these acts was Spiralli, who were very well-known in their day. They were heavily influenced by The Prodigy, and even tried to imitate them in appearance, as well as musically. In 1999 they opened for The Prodigy on their Russian tour. When chatting to St. Petersburg producer Exploynk in October 2017 he said that "Liam [Howlett] wanted to buy a Soviet Synth RITM-2 when he saw how they played on it and how it sounds." So in many mays a band that The Prodigy influenced ended up influencing The Prodigy themselves!

It should also be noted also that in the 1990s, Russia (as well as Eastern Europe in general) was going through some very difficult economic times, so big beat was something of a saviour (especially The Prodigy). Alex Hornet, who runs the big beat label Criminal Tribe Records in Russia, remembers when he discovered big beat in an interview for this book in November 2017:

"My acquaintance with big beat music began, like that of many, in the nineties. I was quite young. At that time, our country was on the verge of total collapse, after the dissolution of the Soviet Union. From the West, everything that represented foreign content and product, including music, poured into our market. As now, I remember, in our yard, everyone wore different sweaters, t-shirts, caps, with names such as Nirvana, Onyx, Metallica, and of course, The Prodigy. I heard more than once their main hits at the time. As that time, my friends and I sat and discussed the meaning of the phrase 'Smack My Bitch Up'. But at that time, my soul was closer to rock/metal music and its sub-genres, such as Nirvana and Korn, and many others. To return again to big beat music, I started getting more into it around 2004-2005, especially after I discovered an artist named Illian Ils."

Alex also remembers what the scene was like in Russia.

"In the CIS countries (Commonwealth of Independent States), representatives of which are on our team, such genres as big beat began to be formed only in the late nineties. The first artists, the first albums in this style, began to appear only since 1998. There is no point in denying that in terms of modern electronic music or rock music, we have since been a catching up country. Now the situation has radically changed, but it took many years."

Russia wasn't the only country in Eastern Europe to have a big beat following. As well as a strong following in Ukraine, big beat however was more niche in the country of Belarus. Den, who's part of the Belarusian big beat group the Funky Boogie Brothers, told me in November

2017: "My first memories of big beat are from 1997-1999. This was a turning point in our musical tastes, influenced by Fatboy Slim, Chemical Brothers, Wiseguys and others. Also this musical flow and a number of video clips with B-Boys pushed us to create the breakdance team Da Swimmers. In those days the big beat scene in Belarus was small. A little later it became more known, with Belarusian bands such as Stone People, Access Denied. The impact was significant, because in 1999 we started our first attempts to write tracks in a broken style."

Another country in Eastern Europe to have a strong big beat scene was Hungary. When I spoke to DJ and Hungarian *Playboy* journalist, Zenit Incompatible, in April 2018, he told me about the large following big beat had in Hungary back in the 1990s and 2000s: "There was a huge big beat boom in the late '90s here in Hungary, which still remains in some places. Several DJs have played with the greats; also, our beloved, game-changer pirate radio station, Tilos Radio, and their DJs, jumped on the bandwagon as well.

"Then in 2000 another radio station called Est FM was set up. There were some DJs who dedicated themselves to many genres, but the usual daytime rotation also included lots of big beat or similar tunes, usually the happy ones. Because it was a commercial station, it had a bigger audience, and when nu skool breaks came along, the older, heavier records were usually popped on the turntables as well - because big beat served basically everyone - including rock and punk music fans - the parties were outstanding, just very happy!

"Some of the veteran DJs in Hungary to name a few: Palotai, Titusz, Rob, Superman, Marvin, TB Gon, Grasshop, InfraGandhi, Reza, Izil, Feaky D... all of them played in a small, underground club (it was actually in a Metro Station) called Cha-Cha-Cha in the early 2000s. Still played big beat, mixed with literally everything. The scene evolved from the open air acid parties, then went to the smaller stadiums, then to the clubs - Kultiplex, Merlin, etc. - sadly all of them are closed now."

Zenit also added a favourite memory of performing as a big beat DJ in Hungary:

"I could tell stories till dawn about watching Fatboy Slim, The Chemical Brothers, The Prodigy, Lo Fidelity Allstars (that was a huge night, by the way), Bushwacka, Freq Nasty, Basement Jaxx, Dub Pistols, The Freestylers or Groove Armada several times - but for me, it was at a festival I played back in 2007.

"I managed a stage there and all of the Saturday line up cancelled, so I played an 8 or 9 hour set till sunrise, and it was just beautiful. Hundreds and hundreds of people dancing their asses off, while the sun rose behind them at the beach of Lake Balaton."

One of the most famous Hungarian big beat acts back in the day was a band called Neo. Originally formed in the early 1990s under the name of Self Destroy, Neo's line-up includes Eniko Hodosi (sadly one of the very few female big beat artists), Matyas Milkovics and formally Mark Moldvai and Peter Kovary. Their debut release was on EMI Records with a remix of the theme tune to 'The Pink Panther' in 1998, which was followed up a year later with the single 'Persuaders', and their debut album *Eklektogram*. In 2002, they moved to the Hungarian indie label Magneoton where they would release three albums, *Lo-Tech Man, Hi Tech World* in 2002, *Kontroll (A Filmzene)* in 2003 and *Maps For A Voyage* in 2006, though by this stage they moved to a more electro pop sound. Their latest album was 2011's *The Picture* on Neoworld Records.

In 1997, big beat DJs Derek Dahlarge and Jon Carter became the very first international DJs to tour Brazil. When I spoke to Derek for this book in October 2017, he remembered these groundbreaking times: "They were brilliant days. To get to travel the world. Unbeknown to us, we were the first ever DJs to tour Brazil. We did all the major cities, Rio, San Palo, Porta Regla etc. We were young at the time as well, it was all pretty new and exciting and it was a real honour and a privilege to get to go and play in these beautiful, amazing places, these electrifying cities you know, and basically turn up and play our favourite records. Working with Jon was great - he was hilarious and we were inseparable - we were like Batman and Robin."

"I just played a carnival in Salador, and that was amazing," Jon Carter told 7 magazine in May 2000. "We were on this float, the biggest lorry you'd ever seen. The whole lorry was just a sound system. There was this girl (Daniella Mercia) singing on top, the Brazilians call her Madonna. She's huge out there, and there was this 13-piece percussion band drumming. I played for about two hours, driving passed about a million people. It was bizarre." [106]

In 2000, Fatboy Slim would later land on Brazilian turf, and after the massive success of his Big Beach Boutique 2 event in 2002, he would put on some gigantic, open-air shows there, including the biggest one of his entire career in 2004, where he played to a record-breaking

360,000 people, which, at the time, was the biggest audience *ever* for a DJ concert. Fatboy still continues to sell out stadia and festivals in Brazil to this day, which is pretty much his most successful market outside of the UK.

Italy was another region where big beat had a very strong following in the 1990s. "I first came across big beat in the late nineties, through my older brother Roberto, who was my main music mentor at the time, and arguably the best DJ in Sicily," remembers producer and DJ, Fab Samperi, who sometimes goes by the name of The Captain. "Big beat was a big part of his DJ sets, and I can safely say he made a major contribution to the city's music scene. Big beat was in its glory days when I was about 20.

"In 1998 Rob, together with a few more DJs, started a monthly club night in Catania named Piatto Forte. Within a few months, it became one of the most popular events the city has ever seen, and the only large event in Southern Italy where you could dance to that kind of music.

"As the scene was growing strong, many big beat acts started touring Sicily over the following few years, and Catania became one of the most important cities in Italy for the new alternative music scene, which would include, besides big beat, more genres such as dub, jungle, acid jazz, and nu-funk.

"Other Italian cities with an active big beat scene were notably Bologna, Milan, Naples, and Rome. Due to my musical background, I would say I had no choice but get heavily influenced by the style.

"As a kid, I grew up mainly with rock, soul, blues, hip-hop, and electronic.

"Big beat was the magic glue that would bind it all together! It would combine all of those familiar genres into a new energetic one. it was the answer to the demanding needs of a changing society, and it had a great impact on the Italian dance culture. I feel big beat was a blessing for DJs like me, who couldn't find their musical identity in the old genres, and without a doubt, it became a great inspiration for my music production style."

Despite not strictly being a big beat act, Fab also remembers catching Asian Dub Foundation doing a rather unconventional gig on Italian turf:

"Summer 1999, Asian Dub Foundation were touring Sicily, and the only scheduled show on the east coast (which is where I live) was not in a cool venue of the main city, as expected. Instead, they ended up performing in a small square of a ten-thousand-inhabitants town, located by the sea, about an hour drive from Catania. To make things worse, it wasn't even promoted well, so besides me and a few of my friends, nobody was really aware of it.

"When we got there, basically it was all old people and a bunch of local children. Too funny! It was the right thing in the wrong place!

"But as Andy Warhol once said, 'Being the right thing in the wrong place is worth it, because something interesting always happens.' As a matter of fact, it turned out to be a great concert, we loved it and the band had fun too. After the show, I had a nice chat with the boys. Nice memories."

Sweden - home of the Swedish House Mafia (obviously), Avicii (RIP)… and some quartet known as Abba, became the home of the big beat producer Rasmus (though he currently resides in London). He was signed to Boshi Records in 1997, where he released his first EP 'Mass Hysteria', which was followed up with an album of the same name a year later. A second album *Serious Pranks* was released in 2000 and in 2001 he collaborated with the Sneaker Pimps on the techno tracks 'Men of the 303' and 'Clean N Green'. He has also remixed fellow big beat artists such as Bentley Rhythm Ace and Deejay Punk Roc.

"I heard 'Big Beat Souffle' by Fatboy Slim played on the radio in 96/97 by Swedish DJ Calle Dernulf and was sold," Rasmus told me back in December 2017. "Something about the anarchic freedom of chopping up drums and dirt, I also was a huge drum and bass fan at the time. Now I've gone all prog psy, funny how things change. I don't think there was a scene in Sweden at the time, lots of hype but no scene. Stockholm 20 years ago, I don't even think they had traffic lights then, could not see any red signs anyway."

Rasmus is still making records today. He also goes by the names of Dub Dayor, Randy Gardell and Homer.

One of the biggest international big beat successes was Pepe Deluxé, who are based in Finland. They were formed in 1996 by DJ Slow, JA-Jazz and James Spectrum. "Like pretty much everything else about us, our beginning was also a bit unusual," remembers Jari aka James Spectrum from the band. "David Paul of Bomb Hip-Hop Records wanted DJ Slow to produce a track for the second *Return of the DJ* compilation. Slow asked my friend, DJ and record collector JA-Jazz, if he knew someone with production skills. We three got together, created the tune 'Call Me Goldfinger', and realised it was so much fun working together that we should start a band. So we had first a record deal, then the music, then the name (that was designed to annoy all those 'DJ supercool this and badass that' hip-hop guys), and then the band."

Jari also remembers what the big beat scene was like in Finland at that time:

"The scene was great and very active - but unfortunately it was located about 2000 miles southwest from Helsinki. To be honest I can't recall of ever hearing about a big beat party here. And the big record companies were totally clueless – for example when Bomfunk MC's A&R guy presented their album at Sony Finland, saying it could sell 'even 10,000 copies!', he was laughed at by everyone: 'Never!' Then Sony Sweden took over and little later 'Freestyler' from the same album became the biggest selling single in Europe that year."

Their first EP 'Three Times A Prayer' was on their own Tiger Records, but was signed to Catskills Records in 1999. There, they released their first album, *Super Sound*, which featured the track 'Woman In Blue' (also known as 'Before You Leave (Twisted)'), which was featured in a Levi's Jeans advert from 2002 and reached No.20 in the UK singles charts. Because of sample clearance issues, they had to do a new version with alternate samples. "We had very little idea that it was a big hit," Jari told me. "You have to remember that this was before social media, before internet got big – and Catskills Records guys made a wise decision to inform us on a 'need-to-know basis.' So, for example, we never knew that Sony and EMI were asking £500,000 for the samples in 'Before You Leave' when the song was chosen for the Levi's ad. Also we didn't really tour; we just took the Sony licensing deal money that helped us to build our studios, launch our careers, make records, and also to break up the original lineup. A really great thing about 'Before You Leave' is the fact that it didn't really go away – it's been synced to many ads, TV-shows etc. ... even the French Presidential elections!"

They also got involved in some big name remixes including Eminem and Sir Tom Jones. "Of course it was quite crazy, but this was a very unusual era in the music business," remembers Jari. "The last and biggest wave of selling records, the rules kept changing, and especially in the UK, rock and traditional pop stuff were considered zombies. I remember that our Sony A&R representative was laughingly telling about one of her bands, how they were desperately trying to do something cool: 'They should just enjoy a retirement.' This band she was referring to was Toto. The only thing I regret is that we didn't get to work with Beck. At that time he was super duper creative."

Pepé Deluxe have released many subsequent albums since, and they are still going strong to this day. In February 2018, Jari remembers some of the highlights of being a member of Pepé Deluxe: "Oh we are hoping that's yet to come! Actually, we took all the key elements of big beat - that is big funky drums, catchy sounds and hooks and the 'hodge-podge collage' approach to ideas - and applied that to working with musicians and recording traditional and historical instruments. It's still an essential part of our sound. Another thing is the big beat's 'larger than life' approach to making music, and that led us to compose the first ever tune using The Great Stalacpipe Organ, the largest musical instrument in the world, located deep down underground in Luray, Virginia. To us, music's never been about reaching goals; it's about opening new doors to new adventures."

Big beat even had a cult following in Denmark. One of the genre's biggest names over there is a DJ and producer who goes by the name of Wiccatron (real name Kim Sø), who tells us what the big beat scene was like on Danish turf:

"Denmark is a small country, with a whole lot of mainstream music on the radio, but plenty of the trendy UK sampled music and EU dance and breakbeat techno made its way to the dancefloors. I remember tracks from the *Leftism* album by Leftfield, Meat Beat Manifesto, Fluke and The Grid and remember how I would sneak into the mixes a mind blowing 'hard to come by' remix or build up to a special big beat or house, electro remix of some loved tunes by the crowd. I was putting in artists like The Prodigy into my mainstream mixing at this time, giving the crowd and the breakers, including me, peak time on the dancefloor."

When big beat arrived in Poland, however, there was a lot of confusion. As stated previously in the book (see 'The Many Origins of the Name Big Beat'), there was already a Polish style of rock & roll (which was sometimes known as 'big bit') that shared the same name (talk about an identity crisis!). It didn't stop big beat from developing a small following there. One of the most well-known big beat crews in Poland was the XLNT Crew formed in 2003 by Michal Borczon. "XLNT Crew was born on 1st January 2003 and it was set up by a group of DJing friends," Michal told me in February 2018. "We played different kinds of electronic music at that time. Throughout the years, there have been quite a few changes to the original squad. There was a time when the

Crew consisted of seven DJs (two of whom were also music producers), a VJ, two graphics artists and a party promoter. In the busier days, we used to organise parties every week in different parts of the country. There were also times, however, when virtually nothing happened. In 2014 we decided to turn XLNT Crew into XLNT Records, and started releasing our music. The crew consists right now of five people: three from the original squad (Ane, BMD, Fazi), producer max.sugar and Bob, a guy responsible for graphics."

He also set up the club night, and successful indie record label, Tru-Funk, in 2010, which revitalised the big beat sound long after the genre's heyday. "Our first party was on Halloween. There were five DJs (BMD, Cez14, Chudy, Silo da Funk and DJ OJJ) and a VJ Olek. The party was really great, and so we started our 'residency'. A month later, another DJ, Warson, joined us. That party was also a success, so I decided to think of something bigger, especially now the budget was raised a bit. At the start of 2011, Tru:Funk crew was born in its original squad, consisting of five DJs (BMD, Cez14, Chudy, Silo da Funk and Warson), a beatboxer Faroth and a VJ Olek. In January 2011 we launched Tru:Funk officially, inviting Lebrosk from the UK to headline the night. In February we invited Jayl Funk from Germany. In March, the star of our show was Slim (from GoodGroove Records). In April we invited BadBoE and after that party we decided to take a short break.

"However, in the meantime, another idea was born. At the beginning of 2011, I had two edits made ('Bangerwall' and 'Your Thing') and thought of releasing the tunes on Polish based label Rebel Scream. However, the whole releasing process seemed to drag on for too long, so I started looking into options of releasing music as Tru:Funk. Warson had two tunes made as well, and after meeting Jayl Funk and hearing that he would have a track for us also, I thought that it was time to start something new.

"And so, in April that year, Tru:Funk was born as a digital label, releasing music exclusively on Juno Download. Along with Chudy (who's been running TF as a label with me since then) we've decided there were three main rules undermining the label: 1. All music must be FUNKY and we should like it. 2. All tracks must be professionally mastered. 3. The releases should be coming out every month. And it worked fine until it stopped... There was a moment when the parties did not attract as many people as we'd hoped. As for the label, we realised that there were actually more people supporting us in, let's say, Germany, than in our native Poland. That was sad... We lost a bit of interest in releases, apart from the fact that many artists decided throughout the years to change their musical tastes, so much that it wouldn't make much sense to be releasing the music under the funk genre. TF as a label still exists and – from time to time – you may expect a release from us, but, on the whole, I personally think it's a thing of the past."

France Has Yet to Discover Big Beat

One place, however, where big beat was a much more niche genre was France. During the "French Touch" era, which included artists such as Daft Punk, Stardust, Bob Sinclair, Cassius, Air, DJ Cam etc. the French didn't really have much time for the big beat genre (and in many ways, who could really blame them, as French Touch was their big movement at the time). That was, except for Romain Coolen aka DJ Prosper. In a special interview for this book in September 2017, Prosper remembers the moment he discovered big beat: "I think at the time I was into trip-hop from Bristol (Massive Attack, Earthling etc.) I heard new guys like The Dust Brothers (The Chemical Brothers), Fatboy Slim, Metro LA and Bassbin Twins on trip-hop compilations, but their tracks where much faster than the Mo' Wax stuff. I remember two specific compilations - one was English : *This Ain't Trip-Hop* (1994) and the other was American: *Trip-Hop Acid Phunk* (1995). Of course *Music for the Jilted Generation* by The Prodigy was also a revelation! From that point, I went every weekend to record shops to find stuff (UK and US) from that new scene... I wanted to be a DJ without mixing trance."

He also recalls how it was very difficult getting gigs at the time.

"The only record shop in Paris to find proper stuff was Rough Trade. There I saw Skint, Wall Of Sound, FC Kahuna, Moonshine Rec, etc. But after the first Chemical Brothers album and Fatboy Slim's second album, this music was seen in mainstream shops. As for the DJs around me, every one played techno or hip-hop... I was very atypical, my music was appreciated but it was hard to find gigs, so it was most of the time private parties."

Big beat however did develop a small cult following over there, though he had to travel all the way to Rennes to perform.

"The first big beat party I went to was in a small club in Paris. A customer from Rough Trade gave me a flyer, cause he knew I was into this music. I promoted a party with Midfield General and Ivan Smagghe (who was a seller at Rough Trade at the time) for a breakbeat set. It was nice, but there were no more that 300 people; this guy lost money I think... he never did another big beat party. The same year I heard that the Transmusicales of Rennes (brilliant festival in Brittany) was booking artists like Propellerheads, Bassbin Twins, Lionrock, Death in Vegas, Freestylers and Fatboy Slim. So I said 'Fuck Paris, let's go to Rennes.' And after that, I saw Monkey Mafia and Cut La Roc at Elysée Montmartre (1000 people) and the first live show of The Chemical Brothers in Paris (La Cigale) - 500 people. So everyone loved that music, but there was no party or gigs, only records in shops."

Prosper's eclectic producing and DJing style was very much influenced by big beat, and to this day he remains one of France's most successful and prolific underground producers. "Yes, cause this music made me want to be a DJ; I used to listen to rock, funk, hip-hop, reggae and house - this music was also influenced by that too, but it was more energetic! I remember I was obsessed by *Check Your Head* (Beastie Boys) - the only album I could listen to from the beginning to the end, and *Exit Planet Dust* (Chemical Brothers) was the second. That was exactly the open state of mind I was looking for all my life! This music made me feel good."

DJ Prosper's favourite act in the genre was the Bassbin Twins (Pete Houser), and he also shares fun memories of the generosity of Pete Bassbin as well as some memories of befriending US big beat DJ, Freddy Fresh.

"I was a very big fan of Bassbin Twins - I think I have nearly all their records! One of the best remixes they've done was 'Chupacabbra' for Freddy Fresh.

"So one day, I decided to buy all the Bassbin Twins records I had missed in record shops. I found their website and sent an e-mail: 'I'm French and probably the only DJ here who's playing your music. I have money and I want to buy all the records I don't have yet.' One week later, Peter Tall answered me: 'I don't have everything you want, but I can try to get some of them for you.' Another week later, I received a package for free with all the funny sketches drawn on the package - that was such a great day for me!

"More than 25 records from the Bassbin Twins arrived - I said to Pete: 'I don't know how to thank you - I made a track with a friend, that's my first tune, I can give it to you and I hope you'll like it, as it was influenced by you.' That was 'D'all"Ass.' Pete liked it a lot, made an edit, and used it as an intro for his gigs in 1999!

"He sent me a recording live from Dallas, every time I hear it - it's cheap thrills. I was supposed to release an EP on Bassbin Twins' label, but it never went out and I lost contact with Pete. As for Freddy Fresh, I had the occasion to meet him in the South of France and Paris. He's such a nice guy, I wish I had more time to spend to make music with him. He's got so many exciting stories to tell, I could listen to him for hours, I truly love this guy and I'll always consider him my friend."

France is also home to probably one of Fatboy Slim's biggest fans - François Deman, who has run the website fatboyslim.org (formally normancook.info) since 2004, the biggest and most well-known Fatboy Slim fan site on the internet, and is approved by none other than Norman Cook himself. "I discovered Fatboy Slim with the video for 'Right Here, Right Now' in 1998," remembers François in an interview for this book in October 2017. "Broadcast on MTV France, I wanted to know more about the album and the big guy at the end of the video clip. I remember first listening to the album *You've Come A Long Way, Baby*: the shock... I loved the whole album. In 1998, I was a student, listening to The Chemical Brothers, Prodigy, and of course the phenomenal Daft Punk, but I liked Fatboy Slim more. Very few people in my entourage listened to Fatboy Slim; there was no internet at home. Then I discovered in 1999, the first album of Fatboy Slim from 1996 (*Better Living Through Chemistry*) in the discount trays of a record store. It was excellent. Paradoxically, I became more addicted in 2004, because that corresponds to my debut on the internet (I was just starting to master a computer!) By searching and exchanging messages with fans of Fatboy Slim, I realised that Norman Cook was not only the DJ Fatboy Slim, but also a producer / composer / sampler. Then there was the release of the long awaited album, *Palookaville*. I started to find collectors on eBay. Fatboy Slim has helped me in the discovery of samples, music, vinyl... people do not realise how difficult it was at the time to find info on Fatboy Slim (YouTube starting, MySpace boom...), everything was new."

François in the interview also gave a little bit of information about the history of his fan site.

"Normancook.info was created in Dec 2004. I had completely missed out on earlier fansites. At the time, I was actively participating

140

in the official forum of Fatboy Slim, as a moderator. NCI (norman-cook.info) has become a learning curve in web mastering for me; I learned to blog like a journalist, to seek information, to gather elements; exchanges on Napster / Soulseek quickly allowed me to archive all the live recorded DJ and radio sets known at the time. NCI had a golden age between 2007 – 2008.

"Facebook then took over, which was much easier and quick to manage, meaning in 2012 normancook.info became a little abandoned. Norman switched to EDM. Strangely there was also a problem with the web host that had stolen the domain name normancook.info. I felt it would be a shame to lose all the work of a small community (playlists, forum, information etc.) I found that the fatboyslim.org domain name was free. I booked it for a few years, because I always had the idea to create an online encyclopaedia on Norman. Since 2015, I've done some renovation work and I've uploaded all of Norman's sets on Mixcloud. Little by little, although it's a painstaking exercise, I think I can make available the most complete fan site for 2018 to celebrate the 20th anniversary of *You've Come a Long Way, Baby*."

Surely, François must be Norman Cook's most dedicated fan!

Despite the low popularity of big beat in France, Apollo 440 were invited to perform at a very prestigious show in Paris in 1998 opening for French electronic music pioneer, Jean Michell Jarre, for his 'Nuit Electonique' show. Noko from the band remembers when we spoke in 2017: "It was Bastille Day and France had won the World Cup two days before. The mayor had asked JMJ to put together a huge free concert, and as we'd just remixed his 'Oxygene 10' track and collaborated on the 'Rendezvous '98' World Cup Theme, we performed both in front of 600,000 people who'd been up for two days celebrating. I remember turning round onstage, as a million pounds worth of fireworks went off on the Eiffel Tower immediately behind us, whilst Jean Michel went apeshit on his theremin, thinking 'there are worse ways of making a living!'

"We were playing in Paris, and I came down to the hotel breakfast bar only to find our drummer Kodish having breakfast with Bobby Charlton (Manchester United football legend) and his wife - 'Noko, come and meet Bobby and Norma' he shouted - of course!"

Another place where big beat was considered more "niche" was New Zealand. One producer who was influenced heavily by big beat in that region is Tim Adam, who sometimes DJs under the name of Timmy Schumacher. In an interview for this book in September 2017, I asked him how he got to discover big beat. "Really really hard to pin. I think it was when my local record store clerk handed me Midfield General 'Worlds/'Bung' or when I heard Propellerheads 'Dive'. In reality though, when not DJing, I was out clubbing most weekends at my local haunt The Box in Auckland. The DJ there was dropping tracks like 'Chemical Beats', 'Everybody Needs a 303' and 'Higher State Of Consciousness' to jazz up the usual 4/4 carry on. The big beat sound was like some kind of glorious train smash of everything I was into."

Unfortunately, nights such as the Social and the Boutique weren't happening over there.

"I read various music magazines and fantasised about attending gigs like the Social and BBB. I had the mixes, I followed the music. I wished I could be in the thick of it. We saw all the internationals passing through Australia - Fatboy Slim, The Wall Of Sound guys - and no one brought them over to NZ. Finally we started getting guys down like Laidback and eventually Cut La Roc and Deadly Avenger came over on the festival circuit. It was pretty amazing to meet these guys. "

Despite the lack of big beat in New Zealand, it did influence Tim's music greatly. "The ethos behind the movement has stayed with me. I keep it pretty close to my heart when I'm in the studio or out playing tunes. Just the idea that music is a gigantic, big, fun, stupid collision of cross pollination of styles. It's kept me incredibly open, it's kept music incredibly enjoyable and it's always a reminder to be true to your musical roots. Fronting is not an option."

A place where big beat had a smaller (but a very strong cult) following was Switzerland. One notable name is Terance Thoeny aka Pulp-Fusion. "Well... to be honest: the big beat scene back in the 90s in Switzerland was in my own room at my apartment, and on my discman," he remembers. "I never attended a big beat party or anything like that, never... of course we would have done, if there had been one... maybe in the underground of Zurich, but that never was my first choice for a party weekend area..." Despite big beat's lesser popularity there (like the DJ Prosper story), it didn't stop Terance from discovering, and eventually making, big beat music. "Well, I had the luck of growing up with a jukebox full of real great rock 45s at my parents' house... so my love for rocking music (heavy drums and cool riffs) started early. I remember that I could write the name Kiss in that original font/logo even before I learned to write my name. I always collected and played guitars and let my hair grow real damn long. Then the day came when I heard about the street parade in Zurich, Switzerland... 100,000's of people dancing in the streets to techno music... couldn't understand that, so I decided to go and check this out with my friend. I never saw anything like that before; also I never really listened to techno music, but I was totally blown away by the scene. From that day I was fascinated by electronic music; I think I heard The Prodigy, and after *Jilted Generation* came out, I was blown away again with 'Poison' and 'Their Law'... that was the first time I heard heavy rock drums and guitars mixed up in a electronic way - it had such a dirtiness (and it still has!) I never lost the love for big beat and in 1995, when *Exit Planet Dust* came out from The Chemical Brothers, it changed the way I saw music... "

Another notable big beat act from Zurich, Switzerland, where there was, in fact, a bit more of a scene, was Bee&See, who is only one person – Thomas Binzegger. In an interview for this book in January 2018, Thomas remembers the big beat scene in Switzerland:

"At the time, it was pretty challenging to get your hands on the newest international releases in Swiss record stores. I spent some time in the UK in 1995 and seized the opportunity to stock up on records. I remember that the sound I discovered there, eventually to be known as big beat, made a great impression on me for sounding 'different', fun, but equally punchy. Mind you, I was previously interested in hip-hop, but found the sound increasingly dull and the scene too restrictive. So, I was looking for something else. Trip-hop was nice, but not sufficiently danceable.

"When I came back from the UK, I felt ready to make a tape with the sound that I loved, not knowing whether anyone would be either interested or knew about this music. All five tracks were on records I found in UK stores back then, and they made it onto my first big beat mixtape, which eventually got me involved in the emerging Swiss big beat scene.

"I was approached by a guy named DJ Muri, who was starting to establish big beat in Switzerland through dedicated parties; he told me that he loved my big beat tape - to be frank, this is the first time I really

143

ever heard the term. Muri set up big beat parties in Zürich's club X-Tra on the second floor, which held only a few hundred people, but always used to be pretty crowded. I was resident DJ for some 2-3 years from 1997 onwards. Multiple times, these big beat events featured bands and guest DJs like the Dub Pistols, Freestylers, Les Rythmes Digitales, Cut La Roc, Catskills, Kings of the Wild Frontier (and many more). It was then relocated to the main hall, which fits around 1500 people. X-tra also had a label on which I released a single in 1998, a second one in 1999, as well as two official compilations called *Big Beatz Session 1 and 2*.

"Besides X-Tra in Zürich, which attracted mostly a student crowd, the Swiss big beat scene developed mainly around freestyle sports, especially snowboarding. I was spinning, for instance, at Freestyle.ch, an international festival for the promotion of freestyle sports (similar to the US X-Games) or the Snowboard World Cup, as well as writing the soundtrack for the snowboard documentary *Primevil* (2002). The freestyle scene attracted a lot of attention and provided a local context for this sound. At a freestyle event one skater, for instance, insisted on me playing Prodigy before going on the ramp, providing the appropriate dynamic for him. The close link between freestyle sports and the big beat sound is, to my mind, a peculiarity of big beat in Switzerland.

"It also gave it a fairly rural and decentralised fan base, since it was developing around (snowboard) events that took place in smaller resort towns in the mountains. Interestingly, it was frequently clubs in those places that were interested in progressive music, rather than the major Swiss cities. For me personally, the pick-up of the big beat sound by the freestyle scene provided a momentum, creating more possibilities for spinning and visibility around and even outside of Switzerland (in the French-speaking part of Switzerland, I was affectionately called "notre Fatboy Slim hélvétique").

"More long term, I feel that big beat slackened the Swiss club scene, which was pretty much dominated by house and hip-hop in the first half of the 1990s, inasmuch as it provided a liberating party atmosphere, compared to most other sounds that were around at the time.

"What remained challenging was getting your hands on the newest records, if you were digging in Swiss record stores. We rarely had any promos, white-labels were almost impossible to get, even more new releases were only available upon request or through contacts. Our disconnectedness was exemplified when I congratulated the Freestylers on their newest release, which, as they told me to my embarrassment, was 'already released quite a while back'. Also, it seemed that many record stores weren't fond of the music. In 1996, I discovered some big beat records tucked away in the corner of a Zürich record store, one of them being The Chemical Brothers (then Dust Brothers) remix of 'Feet' by the Sandals. The owner appeared somewhat surprised seeing me purchasing these records: 'Are you really playing this stuff to your audience? I pity them!' "

Switzerland also became home to a popular internet radio station dedicated to solely playing big beat - bigbeat.ch (later to be known as bigbeatradio.com), which was set up in 1999. It was run by Ramon Ott (who produces under the name of Rams Le Prince), and in an interview for this book in November 2017, he told me how it came to be. "I discovered big beat when I was still a kid - it was about 1998 - just after the release of *You've Come A Long Way, Baby* (Fatboy Slim's second album), when I was at my friend's place.

"He said that I should lay down on the sofa - he told me that the music he will play me will change my life forever. What followed was the 'Rockafeller Skank' - I was instantly hooked and bought tons of records. It was a great time, where big beat was available at the record stores in Switzerland if you were motivated enough to dig through a lot of records.

"In 1999 I started bigbeat.ch with two friends after a night out where we heard some very bad music. It was something nobody would have ever expected - two years later we had our first attempt to run a big beat internet radio station with no idea that it would last for over 10 years. At that time I was writing a lot of music, and I also played in a punk band. I tried to start writing music that sounded like Fatboy Slim. Sadly, I wasn't able to reproduce such fat sounds with my limited equipment and - most of all - limited skill set. However, I never gave up, and over the years, had a little tiny bit of success with it after all."

Despite its longevity over the years, bigbeatradio.com unfortunately closed in November 2017 due to legal issues.

Leon Fijalkowski, who was bass guitarist for the bands Parallax and Hoodwink, who were signed to Mute Records in 1997, remembers opening for The Prodigy on their Swiss tour in the mid 1990s:

"I was in a techno thrash big beat band back in the 1990s called Parallax, and we had done quite a lot of touring in Switzerland. We got invited to support The Prodigy in Zurich in a big concert hall. They were quite big at the time, and this was before *The Fat Of The Land*, where they adopted the punk look with the spiky hair and all that sort of stuff. We were very excited about supporting them, but they still looked like quite normal guys. I remember setting our gear up, and they hadn't arrived yet, and there was this guy wandering around the stage messing about with my amplifier, and I said to him 'Look mate, don't mess with my amplifier - we're trying to do a soundcheck. Bugger off, please!' and he was really apologetic and he was like 'Sorry mate, sorry mate!'"... and he scooted off. My friend pointed out it was Keith Flint from the Prodigy - so I've been really rude to this guy, who I was invited to support. It was a great gig - we had a good time, it was a big crowd, and The Prodigy were awesome."

Another big beat act who would share the bill with The Prodigy in Switzerland was PulpFusion, at the Open Air St. Galen Festival in 2008. "That was definitely one of the biggest festivals in Switzerland... Open Air St. Gallen 2008!" he recalls. "I played at the Bacardi Dome... it was funny as hell: I started with my set, the 'Tent' (something like 2000 people) was full - before I came on, it was normal electronic music playing... I started with my heavyweight beats and breaks and with my big beat stuff, and five minutes later the crowd was gone, and I played in an empty Dome! I was like: 'Damn!' - but I decided to just carry on what I'd been playing... five minutes later the Dome was full again... so I had a lot of luck and just changed the whole crowd in ten minutes. Well... and what has this to do with a big beat related memory? The thing is: after we finished our set, we just moved to the Main Stage, where The Prodigy started their amazing show just as we arrived... and THAT feeling was amazing! I think then I saw The Prodigy for the first time in my life. It felt (for me!) like I'd done the warm up for them..."

So overall - the big beat scene had a healthy life in all corners of the world!

You've Come A Long Way, Baby - Mainstream Success Peaks (1998)

If there was one album that defined 1998 it would be Fatboy Slim's second studio album *You've Come A Long Way, Baby* – more about that later - but there were also a lot of other big releases coming out that year.

The Big Tunes of '98

To open the year on the 26th January, the Propellerheads released their one and only album *Decksanddrumsandrockandroll* on Wall of Sound Records - an album allmusic.com described as "close to rock & roll as big beat techno is going to get" [67]. Despite getting somewhat of a critical panning at the time (though reviews from the fans and over time have been much more generous), the album was very successful on its release, and its tunes would see second lives in the advertising world, most notably 'Take California' (the vocal hook is rather humorously based off a sample of controversial US President, Richard Nixon). It would get used in the very first iPod advert back in November 2001, and the track was also nominated for a Grammy for 'Best Rock Instrumental'.

Alex Gifford in an interview for this book told me how the album's rather explosive cover was created:

"We actually did that explosion - it wasn't photoshopped. We got a special effects guy that apparently used to do *Dad's Army*, and we rented an old airship hanger to do it. Because I learnt that the stunts in James Bond were real and not CGI, I thought - why not do the same thing? We said 'Let's do a shot that's marginally dangerous,' with a slogan on the back of our album cover saying 'PROPELLERHEADS DO THEIR OWN STUNTS', which eventually was sadly never used. It cost half as much as our whole album budget! To begin with, the explosion wouldn't go off, and we were so bruised by the end of it - I think we did about ten takes to varying degrees of success."

147

Another notable track on the album was the John Barry influenced 'History Repeating' featuring the vocals of the legendary diva, Dame Shirley Bassey, which reached No.19 in the UK singles chart, and was also a hit in America, reaching No.10 in the US dance chart, making it Bassey's biggest hit in the US since 1973. The tune was used in a Panten Pro V shampoo commercial and also on a Jaguar S-Type commercial, as well as being the theme music to the UK chat show *So Graham Norton*. Alex Gifford remembers how the tune came about:

"The Shirley Bassey episode came after a long stream of crazy-but-true events. Things were happening insanely fast — we were travelling all over the world doing shows and press and the rest of the time working flat-out to finish an album — so fast that our disbelief threshold had got pretty high. The band and the label were on such a collective roll that things that would normally be totally astonishing were beginning to feel almost normal. We'd recorded an instrumental based around a loop we'd sampled from the soundtrack of a Russ Meyer movie, and it sounded like the kind of tune that you'd expect to hear Shirley Bassey sing on — something a bit swanky and Barry-esque from the late 60s. We hadn't seriously considered taking it any further than that, but anything seemed possible at the time, and one day when we were joking with Jonesy (Mark Jones - Founder of Wall of Sound Records) about it he said, 'Let's ask her then!' So we did.

"I wrote the lyrics to 'History Repeating' overnight, recorded a rough guide vocal and we sent it off to Shirley Bassey's management the next day. Initially they came back to us to say that she wasn't looking at new material, which, to be honest, came as a bit of a relief to me, but a month or so later they contacted us again to say that she was up for it, so after we'd picked ourselves up off the floor, a deal was worked out and a date set for recording her vocal.

"None of us in the band or at the label had ever worked with a legend of such truly epic proportions before, so prepping for the actual recording session required a fair bit of bluffing and hand-waving on our part to try to give the impression that we were, in fact, an experienced, competent production team and not in any sense a bunch of chancers quaking at our respective knees. To be fair to ourselves, we did know pretty much what we were doing — there was just something about that name SHIRLEY BASSEY which kept making it pop into your head in massive, blinding lights and reduce you to jelly. The recording session was surprisingly easy - we got a bit nervous beforehand, as she's such a big, epic name. She arrived with a small entourage and she had a musical director with her, who notated the demo vocals I'd done, and she said 'How do you want me to sing?' I replied 'Well... like Shirley Bassey!' She was really up for it, and she was so professional. It was kinda intimidating for us, as we were unknown in her circles."

"I was very involved in the Props' album release and was present at the Shirley Bassey recording session for 'History Repeating'," remembers former Wall of Sound Label Manager, Jemma Kennedy. "That was pretty memorable. She was and is a legend."

The American release of the album was heavily revised when it was released on Dreamworks Records (they are the same Dreamworks who make CGI Movies like *Shrek* - for a short time, they also released records) and the US version featured a couple of new tracks, such as '360 Degrees (Oh Yeah?)' with golden age hip-hop artists De La Soul and 'You Want It Back' featuring The Jungle Brothers. As previously stated, this was their one-and-only album. Mark Jones' (Wall of Sound Founder) most frequently asked question is "When is the next Propellerheads album coming out?" Whether it will remains to be seen (fingers crossed, eh?).

When I spoke to Alex from the Propellerheads, he told me how he felt about the album's wild success at the time:

"Astonished and really stoked, naturally. More than anything it was the fact that we — the band, label and everybody else involved — had together somehow made it happen on a ludicrously low budget and without really knowing how we were supposed to do it. It felt like proof that anything is possible when you have a Good Thing and run like hell with it. Over the years I've been lucky enough to work with various people who themselves have gone about their careers in non-obvious ways, and if I've learned anything from them it's that you should never feel obliged to do something a certain way just because that's the way it's usually done. It's all about self-confidence, I think, and total commitment to whatever it is you do well. And I can honestly say that we didn't make any compromises along the way, which made the unexpected success of that record extra gratifying.

"We also had a theory that it might have had something to do with a comet. After the release of the 'Take California' EP, we decided to spend some time in a proper, grown-up studio where we could record live rhythm section parts, because it was impossible to record Will's drum kit or really crank up my bass and keyboard amps in our tiny home studios. We booked a week in a place called Chapel Studios out in the wilds of rural Lincolnshire and together with engineer and co-conspirator Chris Lawson piled all our gear into a couple of cars and headed north.

"Some weeks earlier I'd made an impulse purchase from a discount fireworks shop of a crate of ten large skyrockets, the kind suitable for large public firework displays and the storming of small embassies. I'd discovered that the well-timed release of even just one of these things was a highly satisfactory way of adding emphasis to any noteworthy event, so towards the end of our drive to Lincolnshire we pulled into an isolated lay-by and launched a ceremonial rocket into a vast, tranquil and perfectly clear night sky. It's surprising how loud a decent-sized firework is when heard against a background of near-total silence — the whoosh of the ascending rocket sounded like a passing jet fighter and the deafening crackle of the starburst had us practically diving for cover as it ricocheted off distant, unseen objects, scattering colonies of outraged crows.

"Somebody then remembered that a comet was supposed to be passing so close to the Earth that it was going to be visible to the naked eye from places where there wasn't too much light pollution and, sure enough, following a brief period of vigorous and wildly divergent pointing, we found it: a bloody great comet hanging low in the midnight sky like some kind of spectral, cosmic hairpin, its tail sweeping upwards to one side and its head pointing down towards — I kid you not — our final destination. It was more than averagely spooky, and when we eventually arrived at the studio and started unloading our gear, it came as a relief to find a complete absence of holy families, donkeys, shepherds and wise men, though Will said he'd spotted some sheep hanging around a sort of stable thing. Comet Hale-Bopp remained in the sky all week, helping us find our way down the dark, narrow lane which lay between the studio and the local pub as we stumbled home each night.

"We marked the end of our stay in Lincolnshire with a final ceremonial rocket launch from the studio car park and set off back to Bath, happily hugging the master tapes of the live jams which would go on to form the basis of 'Spybreak', 'History Repeating', 'Velvet Pants', 'Bang On!' and 'Bigger'. So, the secret to the success of *Decksandrumsandrockandroll*? Two rockets and a comet, mate.

"When the album went gold in the UK I remember trying to visualise what a hundred thousand records would look like if you spread them all

150

out on the ground. I worked out that if you laid them end to end in a line, it would be nineteen miles long! Nineteen miles of the same record, it's nuts! I mean, where WERE they all? Where do they all GO?"

On February 1st of that year, US big beat DJ Freddy Fresh's acclaimed Essential Mix for BBC Radio 1 was broadcast, where in the two hour time slot he mixed 105 tunes ranging from big beat, 1980s electro, quirky spoken word, pumping techno, early hip-hop and more. Freddy reminisces about this mix in an interview I conducted with him in September 2017: "To be honest, I was told by the record label in London (Eye Q Records) that I had the option to do a special mastermix for BBC Radio. I worked a few days on one, and as I was walking to the post office to drop the CD off in the mailbox (I was a late bloomer to modern technology, internet etc.) I had an incoming phone call from London (Eye Q Records). They mentioned to me in passing that several MILLION people would hear my mix. Luckily I had not yet reached the post office. I tossed my mix in the garbage and went back in the studio to 'do it again'. The result was the mastermix that you heard on BBC." Pete Tong, during the show's broadcast, described it at the time as "The cleverest mix we've ever had for the show." [100] Other big beat themed essential mixes on the show that year included the Freestylers and Norman Cook (Fatboy Slim), which was a recording of a show from his sell-out tour of Japan.

On the singles front, there was an overload of popular big beat tracks that came out that year. Adam Gillison, who is manager in the long established and legendary independent record shop Jumbo Records in Leeds, reminisced with me back in November 2017 about what it was like during the peak of big beat's popularity: "At the height of the craze for big beat, there seemed to be a new variant on the sound every week, and boxes of records arrived daily in Jumbo from various enterprising distributors, who successfully navigated this fast-moving scene. This eclecticism drew in fans from across the dance and rock spectrum, in a similar way to how acid house had done ten years previously, and as electroclash would do in the years to come. A prime example was Norman Cook's remix of Cornershop's 'Brimful Of Asha' - a minor hit from a relatively underground band at the time, that went on to become a massive crossover smash."

A face from Norman Cook's past, Ashley Slater (from their Freak Power project), also joined the big beat camp, this time signed to Skint Records under the name of Dr. Bone. His debut release as Dr. Bone was

151

the 4-track EP 'Everybody Thinks I'm Paranoid'. The most famous release under the Dr. Bone name would have to be the 1999 track, 'Coma Cop' (From the EP, 'Cop In A Coma') as the music video featured Flat Eric (the puppet from the Mr. Oizo track 'Flat Beat') having an autopsy followed by the Dr (Ash) topping himself graphically. Slater also recorded on Norman Cook's Southern Fried Records under the name Elmo (in tribute to the *Sesame Street* character), with his one-and-only self-titled track being released a year prior.

As well as Dr. Bone, Tzant (a collective consisting of Jamie White, Ian Shipley Lil'Rich Henderson, Marcus Thomas and Moussa Clarke) released the funky big beat anthem 'Sounds Of Wickedness' (it reached No.11 in the UK charts) - "We are currently record of the week on Zoe Ball's morning show on Radio One, priority playlist on Kiss FM, and we seem to be on MTV and *The Box* all the time," stated Jamie White from Tzant, on his now defunct website, popstar.demon.co.uk. "As you can see, it took a long time getting it right, but we are all very pleased with the end result. We have started work on a follow up Tzant single and an album, which will be in the style of 'Sounds of the Wickedness' (hip-hop influenced house)" [76]. This track was also heavily touted by the then-popular website of the time Mackie's World (which actually still exists, despite not being updated since 2000 or so - visiting the site really is like travelling back in time), which, like Jamie's website, documents that a Tzant album was in the works, but never came to fruition. The follow-up single 'Bounce With The Massive', reached a more modest No.39 in the charts.

Sheffield band, All Seeing I (Dean Honer, Jason Buckle and DJ Parrot), would also have a hit with a cover of the Sony Bono song 'Beat Goes On', which was, in fact, based on the version by Buddy Rich. The tune reached No.11 in the UK singles charts, and the success of this led to them producing another cover version of the same song for teen idol Britney Spears' debut album *Baby One More Time* in November of that year.

As well as that, an even bigger track emerged. While not a big beat record (it's a hip-house remix) it was very influential in the movement. This was Jason Nevins' hip-house remix of classic hip-hop act Run-DMC's 'It's Like That', which was a gigantic hit worldwide and reached No.1, and was a million seller. It led to many inferior mediocre copycat records being made that reworked classic hip-hop tracks and added breakbeats or house beats over the top of them, to mixed results.

Interestingly, the remix was initially offered to Fatboy Slim, but he turned it down. "You know what the best move I ever made was? Turning down the chance to remix Run DMC's 'It's Like That'," claimed Fatboy in an interview for *Muzik* magazine in July 1998. "It would've been 'Renegade Master' at Number Two, then Cornershop at Number One only for Run DMC to knock it off the top slot, and 'Rockafeller Skank' coming out straight after. I'd have seemed like a megalomaniac." [28]

1998 in many ways was big beat's biggest year...

"I was delighted when acts like Fatboy, The Chems and The Prodigy got huge," remembers Carl Logan, who was a journalist for *Melody Maker*, and now works for *DJ Mag*. "The Prodge were a bit different, as they were on the hardcore continuum, but even they were probably influenced by the band side to big beat. Even though there may only have been one or two of them, big beat acts began to be treated like bands — especially the Lo-Fi Allstars. The music press would write about Underworld (not big beat, but they were a dance act who had the audacity to use a guitar!) as if they were an indie band, even though - shock! horror! - they didn't have a drummer. Photoshoots, interviews, good quotes, broad influences... A lot of dance acts had been faceless, anonymous or just more bald men, but big beat acts talked a good talk and would invariably large it, too. There wasn't a character in big beat called Derek Dahlarge for nothing!"

Major labels were also capitalising on the big beat craze. One notable track was a mashup of Britpop band Blur's enormous grunge parody hit 'Song 2' and 'Smack My Bitch Up' by The Prodigy. The track was called 'S.M.D.U (Smack my Dick Up)' by Brock Landars (trance producer Dave Seaman and DJ megastar Paul Oakenfold), signed to Parlophone records. It had a very tacky looking cover, which looks like a really naff disco compilation rather than an epic big beat record. Another 'Song 2' remix which was popular at the time was a bootleg by Flatback 4 (Phil Jones and Steve Edwards) entitled 'Song 3'.

Fatboy Slim Becomes the Biggest DJ on the Planet

Norman Cook released two of the biggest remixes of his career in 1998 - the most famous one being the aforementioned 'Brimful Of Asha' by indie band Cornershop, which was a gigantic hit in the UK charts, reaching No.1 on the strength of his remix alone (the original track only reached a modest No.60 when originally released in 1997) and the tune also reached No.16 in the US Billboard Modern Rock Tracks Chart.

The song is, in part, a tribute to Bollywood Actress Asha Bhosle and the word "asha" also means "hope" in the Hindi language. The song is also a reflection of the political and social turmoil in India, with lyrics such as "She's the one that keeps the dream alive, From the morning, past the evening, till the end of the light." The song's chorus of "Everybody needs a bosom for a pillow, mine's on the 45" sums up the entire song, as a story of somebody listening to Bollywood to find hope and a place to rest their head.

The original track was a lot slower and laid-back, while Norman's remix was more funky and uptempo. Interestingly, he was so enthusiastic about doing the remix, that he did it… for free!

Norman's northern soul tinged remix was already a big hit at the Big Beat Boutique and received massive pre-release buzz from Annie Nightingale and Steve Lamacq on BBC Radio 1 in its days as a white label, but unfortunately, it did weaken Cornershop's career, as every subsequent release from them was compared to Norman Cook's remix. The *NME* magazine ranked it at number 2 in their list of 'The 50 Best Remixes Ever' saying that it "does what the truly great remixes do – render you unable to enjoy the original." [85]

In an interview for *Songfacts* in 2017, the lead vocalist for Cornershop, Tjinder Singh, felt that the remix was, in some ways, responsible for the band's decline. "It's a lovely song to be remembered by," said Singh. "But the way it brought success falling from the skies, also meant that it changed focus on to the remix, so it took the carpet away from underneath us, as an album artist. We've never been able to fully recover." [84]

As well as the Cornershop remix, another big remix came from Norman Cook (this time, as Fatboy Slim) in the form of Wildchild's (Roger McKenzie) 1995 hip-house anthem 'Renegade Master', done in tribute, as Wildchild had unfortunately passed away a couple of years prior to this. It got to No.3 in the UK Hit Parade and is probably the de-facto track in the entire big beat genre. The back-to-back successes of these two remixes lead to Norman being asked to remix all sorts of people, such as The Beastie Boys ('Body Movin''), Stretch & Vern ('Get Up, Go Insane'), Groove Armada ('I See You Baby Shaking That Ass'), Underworld ('King Of Snake') and Phats & Small ('Turn Around').

Most infamously, Norman turned down the offer to remix Madonna's single 'Ray Of Light', despite being asked personally by Madonna herself on the phone while he was halfway though an interview - all because it wasn't his cup of tea - a decision that Norman would later regret (but the remix went to Sasha instead). He also turned down remixes for Paula Abdul, Aerosmith, Britney Spears and even Meatloaf (who wanted him to co-produce his next album.) Overall, it is estimated that Norman turned down about 130 remix opportunities that year.

Norman didn't turn down everything however - his friend Robert Luis, who was part of the duo Deeds Plus Thoughts, released their EP 'Wig Shaker' that year, containing one of big beat's biggest anthems - the Fatboy Slim remix of their track 'The World Is Made Up Of This And That', and that would become an iconic tune in the genre. "Norman had been playing the track from our debut single," remembers Robert when we spoke in 2017. "He called me up one day and said that it had been going down well in his sets, and would we be up for a Fatboy Slim remix. At this time his Wildchild and Cornershop remixes were out, which were massive, so I said yes, but also I had to say I could not afford to pay him (I was putting every penny I had into pressing up vinyl) and he said he did not want payment. So it was pretty crazy to suddenly be getting a remix from an artist who was so big. For me it showed the really generous side of Norman.

"A few months after the release, the remix got interest for an advert and I called up Norman and said 'It looks like we might be getting the track on an advert', so I could send him some money, as it was in my mind I had not paid him, and he said to keep the money I got for it, as he was fine. It was a very kind gesture. I learnt a lot about the music industry from that remix as well as benefitting from Norman's generosity. I also saw the other side of the music industry, and got conned a few times from the licensing of the remix, but learnt some valuable lessons on how the music industry works. The money I got from the advert helped me invest money to start up Tru-Thoughts so I did not have to get a loan out from the bank, so it is an important remix for me away from just the music itself."

As stated by Luis, the success of this remix helped him fund the acclaimed indie label Tru-Thoughts in 1999 - a label that is still going strong to this day.

As well as all the remix work, since late 1997 Fatboy had also been messing about with a track called 'The Rockefeller Skank' (working title 'Funk Soul Brother') based off the Just Brothers' northern soul anthem 'Sliced Tomatoes' and a sample of rapper Lord Finesse saying "Right About Now, The Funk Soul Brother, Check It Out Now, The Funk Soul Brother". This tune was a huge hit when it was a White Label Dub Plate at the Big Beat Boutique residency, and it was an even bigger hit when it entered No.6 in the UK Charts in June 1998 (as well as No.21 in the US Billboard Mainstream Top-40) and the cult 1990s indie magazine *Select* described it as "A record of immense stupidity and genius." [68]

In an interview for this book in September 2017, DJ Rehab remembers the first time Norman played 'The Rockefeller Skank' in New York at the Twilo Club. "The club was packed and he played 'Rockefeller Skank' for the first time in New York. The dance floor completely erupted when the breakdown and build up happened. I have never seen that sort of reaction from so many people for a song they didn't know. I ran over to the booth and asked Norman what song it was, and he just said it was his new song and would be out in a few months."

"It's the one and only record out of all the zillions I've made," remembers Fatboy Slim for an interview for XFM Radio in 2007, "when me and Simon [his engineer] looked at each other and said 'This sounds like a hit'." [11]

Clearing the many samples for the track was a nightmare, and Norman had to release 100% of the track's royalties, 25% to each artist, meaning that he doesn't receive any royalties for the track himself. A special white label remix of the tune also exists, mashed with 'Satisfaction' by the Rolling Stones, that was (and still is) very popular to this day with DJs, including myself.

"He always had a magic touch and he absolutely inspired me," muses Jon Carter in the liner notes for the 20th Anniversary edition of Fatboy Slim's *You've Come A Long Way, Baby* album in 2018. "I thought I had a fast rise as a DJ, but he had an insane speed! It was all off the back of this one anthem. It was the start of the software based audio FX units. Each record he released had a new style, and he could marry samples he knew without being cynical." [105]

By the end of 1998, Fatboy Slim would end up being the biggest DJ in the world.

Everybody Wants a Slice of the Big Beat Pie

It was also at this time, because of the success of Jason Nevin's Run DMC remix, that early hip-hop music was experiencing a renaissance. To capitalise on this, several classic hip-hop artists embraced the big beat scene. Grandmaster Flash released a (now very obscure) album called *Flash Is Back*, co-produced by Arthur Baker (producer of the groundbreaking Afrika Bambaataa track, 'Planet Rock'), and an uncredited Freddy Fresh, and it also featured remixes from Midfield General, Danielsan and Stretch & Vern. The hip-hop pioneer who was most infatuated with the big beat movement was Afrika Bambaataa, who also had his classic track 'Planet Rock' remixed, big beat style, by GrooveMan, and Bambaataa also lent guest vocals on a few tracks from the period - most famously, the big hit by Leftfield 'Afrika Shox', which went to No.7 in the UK charts in 1999, as well as 'Mind Control' in collaboration with Nebula Funk; he also collaborated with Überzone, Fort Knox Five and Loop Da Loop. Bam also played in several big beat nights at the time, such as The Boutique and BlowPop.

It wasn't just hip-hop pioneers who were hopping on the big beat bandwagon - the influence of the genre could even be heard in mainstream pop records. The William Orbit produced Madonna track 'Beautiful Stranger' (from her 'Ray Of Light' album) took several cues from Norman Cook's production style (notably his northern soul-tinged remix of 'Brimful of Asha'), as well as Beck's hit record 'Sexx Laws'. Even 'Overload' by the girlband Sugababes has a very big beat vibe in its production, and the mid-2000s Black Eyed Peas album *Monkey Business* has big beat influences, notably the *Pulp Fiction* inspired track 'Pump It'. One honourable mention would have to be the 1997 song, 'Ready To Go' by alternative rock band, Republica, which was used extensively in adverts and trailers (especially football ones). The influence of big beat on this tune was outstanding. Another track that was influenced heavily by big beat was the theme tune to the hit movie *Kill Bill* produced by RZA from legendary hip-hop band, Wu Tang Clan.

Major labels also wanted remixes of their artists done big beat style. The aforementioned 'Overload' by The Sugababes had a remix done in 2000 by big beat producer Nick Faber – this is what he had to say when we spoke in 2017: "[It was] fun at first, then less fun, as you realise the record companies are asking you to remix something because of how your last remix sounded. I had a great time remixing 'Overload'; funnily enough the track came on MTV before I was asked to remix it, and I thought 'wow, cool pop tune', then I got the call from London Records. I was stoked. I recorded live guitar, bass guitar and percussion in the studio in one day, and then mixed it the next day. It turned out really well."

The success of this led him to do a remix for one of the biggest pop stars in the world - Kylie Minogue, with her seminal song 'Can't Get You Out Of My Head'. While he agreed to do it, unfortunately it meant having to copy the style of his Sugababes remix, which, by then, he wasn't happy about.

"When I was asked to remix 'Can't Get You Out Of My Head', I already had a cool Missy Elliot-style idea for what I wanted to do with it. Then the record company said 'We loved what you did with the Sugababes, can you do that?' Which is essentially the kiss of death, because you have to do what they want or they won't release it.

"After that I decided to do no more remixes and focus on writing and producing."

"We did quite a lot of remixes during the late '90s," remembers DJ Spatts from Environmental Science, who were signed to Skint Records. "Mostly indie bands and vocal led trip-hop acts that wanted us to mess with their music. In hindsight, we wasted a lot of good ideas on other people's music. There are, however, some that were a real pleasure to work on. Usually, back then, they would send you the parts on a DAT. When we remixed a track for Megadeth, they couriered a package containing 12 DATs! Just for one track! We had to trawl through hundreds of takes; vocals, guitars, mandolins, gong solos etc. That was (and probably still is) the decadence of heavy rock."

More Classics, Well-Known or Not, That Shaped '98

One of the big albums of that year was *We Rock Hard* by The Freestylers, released on Freskanova Records. The track on the album 'B-Boy Stance', featuring the vocals of Tenor Fly, was a big hit in the underground, and was successful in the UK charts (No.15). Originally released as a single in 1997 under the name of 'Mr. Badman (Revenge Of The B-Boy)', when it was reissued as 'B-Boy Stance', the hook of the track had to be changed before going overground, as it was based off 'Wonderwall' by Oasis and the Gallaghers didn't approve.

"I had always wanted to do a track using the Stalag Riddim," recalls Freestyler Aston Harvey in November 2017, "so I built a track using it in a hip-hop way which was different, as it had only been used in early jungle tracks or in a traditional reggae way. I knew Tenor Fly from working with Rebel MC aka Congo Natty, and I thought he'd be perfect for it. When we first made the track he sang the verse melody of 'Wonderwall' by Oasis for our chorus, but changed the lyrics, and when we started to promote the record, this caught the attention of a certain few Radio 1 DJs on their specialist shows; before we knew it, we were faced with legal injunctions, so had to go back in the studio and come up with another chorus. Fly delivered the goods again by coming up with an original idea, and history was made. As we caused a bit of controversy the first time around, the track got hyped up, which was a massive boost to us and helped change our musical career."

The album featured some big guests, such as London band Definition of Sound, and the title track also featured Afrika Bambaataa's band, Soul Sonic Force, who were the rappers on Bambaataa's 1982 breakthrough track 'Planet Rock'. My personal favourite on this record would be 'Breaker Beats' - a big beat-tastic re-working of the classic (but sadly oversampled) soul track 'Amen Brother' by the Winstons for the dancefloor crowd. The album was in the UK charts for 33 weeks, and did very well on a commercial level.

Like The Prodigy, The Freestylers were not immune to celebrity fans, notable ones being rock star Lenny Kravitz, Hollywood actress and pin-up Natalie Portman and Frodo Baggins himself, Elijah Wood. "Natalie Portman was at one of our band gigs once in the States," remembers Matt Cantor in an interview for *Breakspoll* in 2011. "At the after party I offered to buy her a beer. She blew me out naturally." [29]

"It was Matt that met Natalie," recalls Aston from The Freestylers when he spoke to me. "The label boss brought her to one of our shows in New York at the Irving Plaza. During '99, we spent quite a lot of time touring around the USA and gathering celebrity fans, which was great fun. I met Elijah Wood just before he starred in *The Lord Of Rings* movies - turned out he was dating a girl that booked the talent at the Viper Rooms in L.A. and really liked our music. I guess Lenny Kravitz was a fan too, as we were invited to come on his *American Woman* tour for a few of the dates."

Jon Carter, under the Monkey Mafia name, would release his one and only album as Monkey Mafia *Shoot The Boss* on May 4th that year, which contained previous Monkey Mafia hits, such as 'Blow The Whole Joint Up' and 'Work Mi Body'. This time, he formed a proper live band that would tour with him on the road, which included Dan Peppe (formally of Agent Provocateur), Paul Smith and Steve White.

As a live act, they would do some major gigs, including Glastonbury Festival. One person who went to see Monkey Mafia live when they toured Scotland was Christopher (Toph) Lang, who was events manager at the legendary Arches venue in Glasgow. In an interview for this book in September 2017, Toph remembers what it was like at his first ever big beat concert: "So it would have been '97 or '98 - it was so long ago, I can't remember - twenty years ago. It was the first time I'd seen a big beat act. I knew Jon Carter from his mixtapes at the time, and I had just bought the album - it was fantastic and I think he played at Carlton Studios in Edinburgh. I was only 18 or 19 - it was one of the first club gigs I've ever been to - it wasn't a proper club, and it was fantastic - it was really, really good. It was a mixture of big beat, and he also covered 'I See The Light' by Creedence Clearwater Revival, which was fantastic and he played some reggae beats as well."

Big Beat Goes Live

It wasn't just Monkey Mafia who adopted the live show format - Wall of Sound act, Dirty Beatniks, was also a proper band. "It went through a few incarnations," remembers Rory Carlile from the band. "The first phase was myself, Neil Higgins, Justin Underhill and Steve Ashmore playing drums. We had beats and sequences on an Adat machine, an SH-101 synth, decks, drumpad sample triggers, live drums, bass and electric guitar. We were pretty rough round the edges - we wanted to play club music with a rock & roll attitude, and, by and large, we succeeded - there wasn't much else like that out there. We were a long way from an acid jazz act, and we were definitely more than a DJ duo with percussion. In my head we were a rock & roll band, but the others might see it differently."

Another act that also opted to go the live route was Lionrock (Justin Robertson), though he didn't enjoy it at times. Justin remembers in January 2018 the touring days of Lionrock. "I hated touring to be honest!

We grew up as a live band as we went along, and by the end of it we got pretty good, I think, especially the stripped down sound system vibe. Our early shows were chaotic, but there was something exciting about trying something new. I love all the members of the group, and we became very close, especially on our American tour - that was quite hectic and we were living hand to mouth. Despite having a top twenty record at the time, I was close to bankrupt! I have some great memories, but wouldn't do it again!"

Other big beat acts who also adopted the live format included The Prodigy, Death In Vegas, Bentley Rhythm Ace, Propellerheads, Apollo 440, The Wiseguys and of course The Chemical Brothers.

Massive Success for The Wiseguys

Another major release of 1998 would have to be the second album by The Wiseguys (though this time in name only, as DJ Regal left the group in 1997 making it, in essence, just The Wiseguy) which was titled *The Antidote*. In a 2002 interview for Inthemix, DJ Touché explains that "The album *The Antidote* and 'Ooh La La' and all the rest of it – I did all that by myself. But there was still confusion. People thought that there was still two of us. And that kind of got a bit annoying to always have to explain." The album went on to sell over 500,000 copies world-wide, and carried on the sounds formed on the previous album (*Executive Suite*) of chilled, jazzy hip-hop awesomeness, but also capitalised on the big beat sound with two massive anthems of the genre, 'Ooh La La' and 'Start The Commotion'.

While they were big underground hits ('Ooh La La' going initially in at a modest No.55 in the UK singles charts) in 1998, they didn't really start to become massive until they received a second life in the world of advertising. In 1999, 'Ooh La La' was used in a Budweiser beer campaign, and because of this, the single went to No.2 in the UK charts of that year. "It was very accidental," reflects Touché. "I only expected it to be played by a handful of clubs by a handful of DJs. So when it did all blow up, it was pretty wild." [31] Two years later, 'Start The Commotion' would become a big hit in America, thanks to being used in a Mitsubishi car commercial, entering the Billboard Top-40 - a fantastic feat for a big beat track in the US. Aston Harvey from The Freestylers describes 'Ooh La La's' impact for an interview he did for *NPR* magazine in 2011:

"The big beat thing was kind of seen as happy, uplifting music; it was non-house, using samples from funk tunes or hip-hop tunes. Obviously, house music was really big, and then this was something completely different that wasn't drum & bass or house. This music came along, which was this fun music. And this track was a big commercial record, because it had hooky samples on it like Fatboy Slim's 'Rockafeller Skank' Those two tunes definitely stand out as the biggest tunes of that genre." [2]

Sample-wise, it is based off the Lalo Schiffin song 'Jim On The Move' from the soundtrack to the TV series *Mission Impossible*, which inspired the movie series of the same name. The tune's hook ("Ooh La La, Sassoon" - constantly misinterpreted as "Ooh La La Say Zoom") comes from a recording of a GrandWizzard Theodore Block party, reciting the tagline of a US commercial for Sassoon Jeans, which was made available legally in 1991 on the compilation *Afrika Bambaataa presents Hip-Hop Dance Classics Vol.1*, which is out on the Music Of Life label.

Two music videos were made for 'Ooh la La' - the first one was video footage of drag racing, while the second was filmed in an airport (where the cover of the *Antidote* album was shot) and featured go-go dancers in skimpy outfits, predating every commercial hunky house music video from the mid-2000s.

"Oh, it was a desire to find the full 'Ooh La La' track from The Wiseguys," remembers Den from Belarusian big beat act, The Funky Boogie Brothers, "a fragment of which we heard in the video of a B-Boy battle."

"I was really into hip-hop back then, but hearing tunes like Wiseguys 'Ooh La La' at nights like BlowPop suddenly opened up new possibilities," states Bristol Producer, Ewan Hoozami. "It was like hip-hop but faster and made everyone dance like crazy."

"New Years Eve 1998 I went to an event at the Brighton Centre," remembers DJ Dave RMX. "DJ Touché from The Wiseguys was doing the midnight slot and there was a queue to get into the back room that he was playing in.

"At midnight, Touché played 'Ooh La La', and the crowd went nuts, and that's possibly an understatement! From the middle breakdown onwards, I could hear him trying to mix out of it, but the crowd kept on singing. Eventually Touché gave up mixing, and let the record play all the way through. Once it finished there was a massive cheer from the crowd, the New Year had definitely started now!"

To promote the Wiseguys' *Antidote* album, Touché formed a proper live band for touring, which consisted of Bronx rappers from the DJMC Crew, Sense Live and Season Love and drummer Tall Tom. The *Antidote* tour lasted for 10 dates, stopping at venues such as Glasgow's famous (and sadly gone) Arches club, a stop off at Molotov Pop in Manchester, LA2 in London and The Beach in Brighton, where Big Beat Boutique was being held at the time. This format of The Wiseguys also appeared on BBC Radio 1's Breezeblock. A third Wiseguys album was announced in 2000 in several articles at the time, but was never released (though it could be referring to an album Touché produced for rapper Jerry Beeks, that did come out in 2001). Touché stopped using the Wiseguys name in 2002, and became a successful underground house producer for Fatboy Slim's Southern Fried Recordings, as well as becoming the Boutique's most prolific resident DJ from 2004. He also formed another duo with Simon Lord from Simian called The Black Ghosts in 2006 before having a career renaissance making house music under the name Fake Blood.

Former Wiseguy DJ Regal also formed his own short-lived record label called Marble Bar. In an interview for this book in October 2017, Regal remembers the rise and fall of one of the most overlooked labels in the genre. "I formed Marble Bar records in Sept '98, when Joe Stanley from Distance Records asked me to start up an imprint to cater for breaks and stuff. I played him '212 (The Weya Funk),' and he was sold… Distance then bankrolled the first six 12" singles and the compilation album *Marbles Vol.1*, over the next 9 months, in which short time, Marble Bar had garnered a nice little buzz for itself. Then, I made the stupidest, dumbest mistake of my life, by believing I didn't need Distance's help anymore and that we could succeed as an entirely independent outfit… Lesson #1: NEVER LET YOUR EGO MAKE YOUR BUSINESS DECISIONS!

"I'm forever grateful to Joe that he gave me the opportunity and support for that first year, and it pains me that I threw the game away so soon after, biting off far more than I could chew. Debts to distributors does not a successful label make. Marble Bar was folded in late 2001. If there were highlights after leaving Distance's nurturing embrace, it was probably our label night takeover at Fabric in 2000. Otherwise a period for me that's very much a bunch of stressful memories."

The Big Albums of 1998

Skint Records signees The Lo-Fidellity Allstars released a massive album in 1998 with *How To Operate With A Blown Mind* to sales success, which contained the hit single 'Battleflag' with Pigeonhead. While only moderately successful in the UK (No.36) it was a big hit in America, reaching No.6 in the Billboard Modern Rock Charts. One hurdle the album had to face was the enormous costs for sample clearance. "When we released 'Disco Machine Gun', we sampled a song by the Breeders," stated Johnny Machin from the band in an interview for *Atomic Duster* magazine, "and Kim Deal was none too chuffed about it. We had to withdraw it after three days. That's why it's called 'Blisters on my Brain' on the first album." Their big hit, 'Battleflag' wasn't immune to this either: "Yeah, that was [featuring] a band called Pigeonhead, which is a real funky outfit made up of members of Pearl Jam. They asked us to remix it, so we stripped the whole song bare, and I mean the WHOLE song, and put what we wanted in there. They refused to pay us at the time, but since it got in the charts, they started crawling out of the woodwork. So we thought bollocks to them." [32]

The band were even rumoured to have been asked to open for former Take That star, Robbie Williams, and remix for him. They declined the remix offer, and when asked about the possibility of supporting him, Johnny, in an issue of *Atomic Duster*, gave an extremely comprehensive reply - "No".

The Lo-Fi's, like Jon Carter, were also known for their crazy antics on stage - one gig involved them burning all their decks. "Yep. That was just a publicity stunt really. It was good fun that," recalls Johnny for the website, *Atomic Duster*. "We had this really, really old deck that was worth nothing and just about falling apart, so we covered it in lighter fuel and set light to it after our last tune. It was all a bit of a scam really, but it got us into all the music papers. Anything for a bit of publicity." [32]

November saw the release of the Dub Pistols' debut album *Point Blank* – they were one of the biggest acts of the big beat era. They are, in fact, not a Sex Pistols tribute band done in the style of dub reggae, but a ska and dub influenced breakbeat act, that, as stated previously, was formed in 1996 by Barry Ashworth. Other members include(d) producer and bassist Jason O'Bryan (1997-2010), producer and MC T.K. Lawrence, guitarist John King and DJ Stix (Steve Hunt), though their sound wasn't initially ska style. "It wasn't like that initially," remembers Barry Ashworth. 'Me and Jon Carter did the first Monkey Mafia Single ('Blow The Whole Joint Up'), and Jon signed to Heavenly, and I went my own way. The first singles weren't ska like at all - it was kind of like more electronic, noisy stuff. I went into SabreSonic Studios with Keith Tenniswood - took a load of pills, and worked into the night and the first Dub Pistols single 'There's Gonna Be A Riot' came about."

The album received favourable reviews, with many of its tunes appearing in various films, TV shows and most notably video games. One track on the album, the ska influenced 'Cyclone', was featured in the very popular video game 'Tony Hawk's Pro Skater 2', which came out on the Sony Playstation, Nintendo 64, Sega Dreamcast and the original Xbox. Despite its prolific usage in the world of syncs, the tune only reached a paltry No.63 in the UK singles charts.

Justin Robertson's Lionrock project would also see the release of their second, (and final to date) album, *City Delirious*, which featured the hit song 'Rude Boy Rock'. The track was No.20 in the UK singles chart and was featured in the video game 'FIFA '99' and the soundtrack to the 1999 Rodman Flender stoner comedy *Idle Hands*. The tune would receive a second life when it would be sampled by Damian "Junior Gong" Marley (Bob Marley's Son) for the song 'All Night'.

The Rise of BlowPop

As previously mentioned, one place where big beat was really big was Bristol, and probably the most well-known big beat night in that area was BlowPop at the Blue Mountain Club, set up by John Stapleton, best known for compiling the *Dope On Plastic* series of compilations. "I think I was the original resident at BlowPop," remembers Boca 45. "They were pretty raucous nights. I also played at the original Concorde too in Brighton. They were quite happy to play anything, even stuff like the Kinks and the Who. They welcomed all genres and they were very energetic too - It did get a little more like house music, when it evolved into [nu-skool] breaks."

Another resident DJ was Doc Moody and in an interview I conducted with him in September 2017, Doc remembers the genesis of BlowPop: "During the late 90s, having already worked as a club DJ, I fell in love with the *Dope On Plastic* compilation series, and through a series of fortunate events became resident DJ with the legendary John Stapleton at his club night called BlowPop in Bristol. I always say if James Brown is the Godfather of Funk then John Stapleton is the fuckin' Daddy!

"We had no competition, in terms of music policy, across the whole of the city for many years, and we quickly appealed to the cooler kids who wanted a bit more depth to the music they danced to. It was all beats, breaks, funk, hip-hop and anything else that was cool. Sometimes I even got to play D&B at the end of the night. Our only music policy was 'is it any good?'

"With an awesome music policy and the arrival of Stereo 8 helping run the ship, the night went off the scale. We toured the UK and most of the world and filled every venue for 15 years. Our last ever gig was a capacity filled Motion, back in 2013 I think. The night gained such a good reputation that we would regularly have a queue that stretched from the world famous Blue Mountain club all the way up to Lakota. We ended up turning away hundreds of people who got there late, for months on end. I remember a gig sometime around 2010 at the Thekla that had an over capacity queue even before we opened the doors. It was, and still is, the only club night I have played at where the warm up DJ gets a dance floor as full as the headline act.

"We hold the world record for the number of people in the Blue Mountain Club at an Ashton Court after party - the door clickers all showed just over 900! There is no way you would get away with that today. This prompted a move to the Academy nightclub, which we filled to capacity every month for over 6 years. The move to a big club and a huge stage opened up the possibilities of more live acts.

"The collective of DJs still get together for one-off events - John Stapleton and I DJed at the Harbourside on NYE. I was recently lucky enough to play samples on stage with the mighty Freestylers earlier this year (2017) at an event organised by Blowpop kingpin Julian from Stereo 8.

"The club night ran for over 15 years, and at the height we were doing two shows a month and several festivals a year, with the Scratch Perverts and the Fingerlicken Crew joining us as quarterly resident DJs. Over the 15 years we have featured most of the big names in the scene."

Live Memories - Good and Bad - and the Start of the Backlash

It wasn't all fun and joy in big beat's peak year - after three years of several successful nights in the London area, The Big Kahuna Burger club night closed its doors, as the night's appeal was wearing thin. In an interview for *Resident Advisor*, Jon Nowell said "It was like a long weekend, really. Getting twatted all the time and not having much quality control," while Dan Ormodroyd stated "Kahuna was very decadent, out of its mind, like a lunatic asylum. But we got bored, so we withdrew to find out what we wanted to do. Just as we did when we started the club." [93]

On a more positive note, Rory Carlile from The Dirty Beatniks remembers some golden events as a DJ from this period in an interview I did with him in December 2017:

"Alexandra Palace on New Years Eve 1998 was fun. DJing somewhere in Cannes, looking up to see Roger Sanchez and Arthur Baker sitting 20 feet away. DJing in Cannes was weird enough, when we were living pretty much hand to mouth in a squat at the time, let alone having two total legends in front of me. These people only existed as names on records I loved, I never thought I'd be in the same room as them. Surrounded by yachts... It was ridiculous. Playing at The End, in fancy dress, very very high, dressed as one of the Beatles in the *Sgt Pepper* dayglo military gear, and Bianca Jagger shouting at me. She wanted to put her coat behind me in the tiny, tiny DJ booth, not that I was in any condition to understand that. I was deeply confused - off my head, dressed as a Beatle, shouted at by a Jagger.

"At the time these kinds of things seemed normal... Jon Carter stage diving at some club we were playing in Europe, when the whole crowd parts. I'm sitting on a plane beside him the next day, and he shows me a lump the size of a tennis ball coming out of his thigh. Pretty much anything to do with Carter and Dahlarge round that time was comedy gold. And hearing Theo from The Wiseguys, Derek Dahlarge, and Jon Carter DJ on a regular basis - that was a real privilege."

Also in 1998 was The Prodigy's infamous appearance at the Reading Music Festival, where they ended up having a good ole hip-hop beef with the legendary act The Beastie Boys. The reason - a certain song - 'Smack My Bitch Up'. It should also be noted that during the *Licensed to Ill* era, The Beastie Boys were known for their misogynistic and sexist lyrics, though this all changed with the *Paul's Boutique* era, when they went from being trolling frat boys to the more creative, socially conscious and intelligent group that they would be best known for. The older, wiser Beastie Boys were not happy when The Prodigy played their most controversial tune.

One of the punters at the concert was Mako, who now runs the Music Review Site and blog Monkey Boxing. He remembers this event, as told to me in November 2017: "I hate staying overnight at festivals - all that bloody music and people keeping you awake. Anyway, when I saw Prodigy and the Beasties were one and two on the bill respectively, tickets for that particular day were bought. Prodigy came on second to last I think and said the Beasties had told them not to play 'Smack My Bitch Up' because it could be construed as a little bit offensive by at least half the population. In typical Prodigy fashion, they played it anyway - presumably having sensed that the Beasties might have been calling the kettle black somewhat, given their *Licensed To Ill*-era antics. After that, the Beasties came on and had a quiet word with the crowd about it all, and then sarcastically played the super-mellow 'Song For The Man' off *Hello Nasty*, dedicating it to Liam and the boys. It's quite a well-documented incident, but while people seem to remember what the Beasties asked Prodigy not to do and how Prodigy reacted, they don't seem to remember how the post-*Licensed To Ill* and now much older and wiser Beasties responded."

Thankfully the Prodigy/Beastie Boys beef would later be resolved, and they patched things up in the end.

On the mix CD side, probably the most revered that came out that year was the first volume of Skint Records' *On The Floor At The Boutique* series (similar to Heavenly's *Live at the Social* series) mixed by Fatboy Slim. Contrary to various articles, this is, in fact, not an actual live set at the Big Beat Boutique, but a studio mix done in celebration of the Big Beat Boutique moving, in September 1998, from the original Concorde venue to a club called The Beach, and then in 1999 to the Concorde 2 venue in the West Pier Brighton. "They were the favourites from three years from the Boutique that we could get permission to use," remembers Fatboy Slim for an interview for *House Of Blues* in 2000. When the interviewer asked whether it was recorded on one of the nights, Fatboy stated that it "wasn't done live - I can't lie and say it was me on two decks. There was a little bit of computer jiggery pokery going on. But it was one night - but one very long night. There's a few overdubs [laughs]." [34].

168

While it was sad to see the old grotty venue go, it was a sign that big beat was getting bigger and better. In fact, the last day of the Concorde 1 was documented in the Fatboy music video for 'Build It Up, Tear It Down' (on an interesting note - the last tune of the night was supposed to be 'We'll Meet Again' by Vera Lynn, but ended up being 'Bye Bye Baby' by the Bay City Rollers as Norman couldn't find a copy of 'We'll Meet Again', but it did get a good laugh from the crowd).

"Basically it's a collection of Big Beat Boutique favourites mixed together and sort of coincides with the club moving from The Concorde to a new place called The Beach," recalls the Skint Records newsletter from May 1998. "You see The Concorde is being knocked down this summer, so we had to find a new home. It is very sad to be leaving, as it suited the night so perfectly, but on the positive side, The Beach holds twice as many people and has two rooms, something we've always wanted, so that's enough justifying the move. The compilation is out on the 6th of July." [35]

On The Floor... was probably the perfect documentation of what the people who went to a Boutique Club Night were all about - mashing up classic funk with acid house, The Jungle Brothers at 45 RPM instead of 33 RPM making them sound like the Chipmunks, a Roland TB303 going off for five minutes straight and of course - big beat. The success of this mix CD led to two subsequent *On The Floor At The Boutique* mix CDs being made - one mixed by the Lo-Fidelity Allstars in 1999 and one by Midfield General in 2000.

Unfortunately in 1998 a backlash to the genre was emerging (more of that in the next chapter). "I remember some of the dance purists at the time mocking the scene and calling it 'student music', as if that was somehow disparaging," remembers Eddy Temple Morris in his essay for *Complete Music Update* magazine in 2011 - Big Beat: There's Nothing To Be Ashamed Of. "They missed the point totally. Of course it was student music – i.e. young people's music. This was music for all the students, not just the few doing an advanced degree in Electronic Music Production. It was happy music, drinking music, good times music, and people like myself and Alex Metric were drinking it in!"

Eddy also adds "Purists tend to hate anything vaguely enjoyable, but while they disapproved, we danced and we drank and we laughed." [36]

The Show's Not Over Until The Fatboy Sings!

The biggest event big beat-wise would happen on October 19th 1998, when the genre reached its zenith with the release of the Fatboy Slim album *You've Come A Long Way, Baby*. The title, like *Better Living Through Chemistry*, came from an advertising slogan, this time for Virginia Slim cigarettes, though it was called 'Let's Hear It For The Little Guy' and 'Viva La Underachiever' during production; the title was changed after the success of the Cornershop and Wildchild Remixes and 'The Rockafeller Skank'. It was a gigantic hit, selling 8 million copies worldwide, going platinum in the UK, USA and Australia, and won a Brit Award in 1999, but unfortunately, because of its astronomical success, it was a sign that the bubble was about to burst. The album was (and still is) very well received, in fact allmusic.com described it as "a seamless record, filled with great imagination, unexpected twists and turns, huge hooks, and great beats. It's the kind of record that gives big beat a good name." [37]

"On vacation down in Florida, I was in a CD store in a mall. I picked up Fatboy Slim's *You've Come a Long Way, Baby*, from the shelf, looking at the artwork. A worker —or maybe just a passer-by—saw me looking at the CD and said something along the lines of 'that album is sick'," remembers American DJ, Josh Gaudioso. "I didn't buy it right then and there, but—later that year on a business trip with my father—I bought it at Walmart. I have never been more excited about discovering music than I was that day. I remember playing it for my dad and uncle on my uncle's stereo in his living room, who both were supportive of my newfound passion. I would continue buying as many big beat albums as I could (Freestylers, The Chemical Brothers, anything on Skint records, etc.)."

Production on the album started in February of that year and ended in September, with some days Norman working from 9pm-6am for three nights at a time. There were apparently no creative blocks: the problem was finding time to do it, because of his increasingly hectic schedule. The album opens with the now iconic 'Right Here Right Now' (arguably his most famous track). This tune of epic grandiose is based on a now-famous string section of a folk-rock tune by The James Gang called 'Ashes, The Rain and I'. In order to clear the loop legally, Norman had to buy The James Gang's entire back catalogue! The vocal hook was taken from a 1996 Katheryn Bigelow film called *Strange*

Days with those famous words provided by actress Angela Bassett. To promote his headline set at the Homelands Festival, it would later be released as a single in 1999, where it reached No.2 in the UK charts (though it was prevented from reaching the top spot by MOR boyband, Westlife, with their song 'Say It Again').

The album also contained his previous singles 'The Rockafeller Skank' and the hip-hop inspired 'Gangster Tripping' (spelled 'Gangster Trippin' for the single release), and some new material such as the Archies sampling, 'Build It Up Tear It Down', the midtempo 'You're Not From Brighton' (where the vocoder hook was taken from a mondegreen of the vocoder from the Minimal Funk track 'Groovy Thang' which went "Everybody, Everybody" which Norman mis-heard as "You're Not From Brighton, You're Not From Brighton"), the proto-electro house banger 'Love Island' (a tribute to Ibiza that was originally in a more prototypical form on the soundtrack to the Manumission film) and most controversially, 'Fucking In Heaven' featuring guest vocals from fellow big beat producer Freddy Fresh (which was cut up from a DAT Tape during the making of the Freddy Fresh track, 'Badder Badder Schwing') saying the phrase 'Fatboy Slim is Fucking In Heaven' 108 times - in fact, a rare clean version exists called 'Illin In Heaven' for the more conservative areas of the US, which refused to stock albums with explicit lyrics. In an interview for MTV in 1998, Norman explains "Freddy sent this DAT and it had this spoken intro-duction where he said something like, 'This is a track from the new album. If you could do a remix of this, if I could have a Fatboy Slim remix, I would be fucking in heaven.'" [38]

The infamy of 'Fucking In Heaven' even inspired a club night of the same name in New York, USA run by DJ Rehab and his colleague, DJ Under. Undeniably, people were not too happy to see that on a flyer. This is the reason there is a 'Parental Advisory' warning on the bottom left of the cover, not to mention the following track 'Gangster Trip-ping', which contains the phase "We Gotta Kick 'Dat Gangster Shit" 57 times - tallying to 165 profanities on the entire album.

The album's most famous track (other than the aforementioned opener 'Right Here Right Now') would have to be 'Praise You' – a catchy, soul-inspired track with its famous hook taken from 'Take Yo Praise' by singer Camille Yarbrough. When it was released as a single in 1999, it reached No.1 in the UK singles charts as well as being a Top 40 hit worldwide, including his only appearance in the US Billboard

Mainstream Top 40 as Fatboy Slim. The tune would even see many cover versions including, more recently, one by singer Hannah Grace for a Lloyd's Bank advert in 2017. Interestingly, 'Praise You' actually preceded Fatboy Slim by a few years, and was originally an ambient track for another project he did called Yum Yum Head Food (his later track 'Sunset (Bird Of Prey)' also had its origins from this period), and despite the recognisable vocals, is drastically different from the more familiar version of the track – the original take was eventually released in 1999 as the B-side to the 'Right Here Right Now' single.

The album made Fatboy Slim a huge star, so much so that, apparently, during the album's heyday, promoters took his name off the bill of posters and flyers for their events in fear of over attendance. You've come a long way, baby indeed - such an apt title. "He [Fatboy Slim] was the first 'superstar' DJ at the club with singles in the charts, so there was always a great buzz around him playing," remembers Claudia Nicolson, who used to work for Norman Cook's manager, Gary Blackburn, and was the booker for Skint On Fridays events at the End. "The DJ booth was central to the main floor allowing clubbers to be up close with him. Always queues around the block, and so much fun." By this stage, he wasn't just playing in modest clubs, but selling out sports arenas to tens of thousands of people and headlining major music festivals. His album led him to win a Brit Award in 1999, and all of a sudden he was mingling with the likes of Hollywood actress Nicole Kidman at Cannes, and actors such as Brad Pitt (who wanted to get DJ lessons from him), *Friends* star Jennifer Aniston, Agent Sully herself Gillian Anderson and even Bill Murray were all becoming fans of the Fatboy! By this stage, his next-door neighbour was none other than the Beatle legend himself – Sir Paul McCartney (talk about a missed collaboration opportunity, Norm! Maybe it didn't pan out as he once fed Macca's vegetarian dog pork sausages?).

Another aspect to Fatboy Slim's mega-popularity was his very creative music videos. Fatboy's videos were amusing and original, and were just as famous as the music that went with them. Notable ones included the aforementioned 'Praise You' directed by Spike Jonze, which was a so-bad-it's-good home movie of some hilariously awful street dancers outside a cinema queue. Another very famous one was for 'Right Here Right Now' directed by Hammer & Tongs, which showed the evolution of man with the climax showing the large kid that's on the cover of the *You've Come A Long Way, Baby* album and 'Gangster Trippin'' which

172

was basically a lot of stuff blowing up (Michael Bay would be proud!). Another Spike Jonze directed video was for his 2000 single, 'Weapon Of Choice', which featured Hollywood actor Christopher Walken dancing outside a hotel lobby. All these videos won many awards such as 'Praise You', which won the 1999 MTV VMA Award and was voted the 'Best Music Video Of All Time' in an MTV poll in 2001. 'Weapon Of Choice' won six awards at the 2001 MTV WMAs and in 2002 it was voted the 'Best Music Video Of All Time' in a VH1 poll and won a Grammy also that year.

When I spoke to Damian Harris about what he thinks is the secret to the huge success of his record label, Skint, he said: "Have one ridiculously successful artist to pay for everything else!" That artist – Fatboy Slim!

In a nutshell - 1998 was the year of Fatboy Slim and this is where big beat's popularity peaks. The year ended with Mr. Slim doing four massive New Year's Eve parties at the the Cream club in Liverpool, the Manchester Arena, the Newcastle Telewest Arena (now the Metro Radio Arena) and London Arena - in the one day (December 31st)! This was part of the club night Cream's New Years celebrations alongside Paul Oakenfold and Todd Terry and they travelled to each venue by private helicopter. A hectic end to a hectic year for the Fatboy (and big beat as a whole!).

Stop The Rock – Big Beat's 'Death' . . . Or Was It? (1999)

"Big Beat started as a breath of fresh air and ended up like a loud, annoying drunken bloke you really wish would leave the party. Success meant that we moved from small sweaty clubs to huge arenas, and DJ sets got too predictable. So people went off in their different directions [and] big beat became a dirty term."

Damian Harris/Midfield General for the *Guardian* newspaper, 2008
[39]

By the start of 1999, the scene had become overexposed - it seemed like big beat was everywhere, and because of this, the only way was down. One of the unfortunate trends of dance music culture is that when a sub-genre or artist finally makes it overground, they are automatically pushed aside by elitists, regardless of the quality of the output.

By this stage it was: turn on the television - you hear big beat; turn on the radio - you hear big beat; go to the cinema - you hear big beat… big beat was everywhere, and sadly a downward slope seemed the only way to go.

Having said this, there were still massive success stories from many of the big players that year - but the backlash had already begun.

Big Beat Sucks!

During 1999, other music genres started to get their time in the spotlight. The infectious French house scene was getting big (Daft Punk, Bob Sinclair, Stardust etc.) not to mention the rise of trance music from the Netherlands (such as Tiësto) and the 2 step garage sound from Urban London (Dubstep was born during this period, though it didn't really take off until a decade later).

Because of the genre's over-saturation and downward quality, people seemed to have had enough of it (which wasn't helped by its association with boozy hedonism, and the poor-quality wannabe producers/DJs and trend-hoppers that were starting to emerge).

In a 2017 interview for *Resident Adviser*, Norman Cook remembers how he pulled the plug on the increasingly more formulaic big beat sound:

"The whole basis of big beat was - there's no formula, there's no rules. You could just break any rule. And the only thing really that it has in common is a big beat. What happened was, when we became popular, there was all this copycat stuff that established a sound called 'big beat', which actually became formulaic, which was exactly what we were trying to destroy. So there was literally a day when me, Tom and Ed [Chemical Brothers] went away on holiday together, and we had discussions about all these horrible big beat records - we don't want to be associated with that anymore and it's 'What's your next album going to be like?' - and it's 'Nothing like big beat'." [41]

"I remember saying at the time that big beat was the hip-hop equivalent of handbag house," Mr Scruff told me in March 2018. "Quite brash and cheesy, and not really to my taste. For longevity, I think that a style of music needs to cover different moods. With big beat it was like a party on steroids, all the time. Party music is cool, but it sounds best in the context of a mixed bag of moods, to give it more of a sense of occasion and celebration. I was, and still am, too much of a geeky anorak for that kind of carry-on!"

"It was not so much about the music, but more about the energy and the movement," recalls Alex Hardee from CODA Agency when we spoke in November 2017. "It was quite obvious why it built up so quickly, and that was why it went down so quickly as well."

As the person who canonised the term 'big beat', I asked Ben Willmott how he felt when big beat became a dirty term in an interview for this book in September 2017, and whether he was bothered by this:

"Not at all. I always joke that a genre isn't a proper genre until people are disassociating themselves from it in interviews! So nothing lasts forever. I can't think of anything worse than a type of music that didn't expand, re-invent itself or split in two at some point - it would end up like northern soul, with no new blood coming in at all.

"I think that big beat had really achieved its goal by 1999, which was to challenge house music's dominance of clubbing, and bring some of those original rave elements back into the mix. The massive gig where Norman Cook and Armand Van Helden played in a boxing ring in the middle of Brixton Academy kind of epitomised that - it was challenging at the very highest level. Someone like Van Helden or Josh Wink is a great example of someone who came through in the house/techno world, but was also clearly shaped by the influences of big beat, as well as jungle, hip-hop, speed garage etc. Something like the Jason Nevins mix of Run DMC's 'It's Like That', which was a massive no.1, or the Junkie XL refit of Elvis, again a massive chart topper, weren't big beat records, but could never have happened without it.

"In any case, the labels like Skint and Wall of Sound were releasing very different records by then, to the kind that were around at the beginning. Req's stuff on Skint, for example, which I was always really into. Wall of Sound released a Shirley Bassey record for fuck's sake - a great one too, and that made sense, because her version of 'Light My Fire' was something you'd hear around. The move to bands rather than producer, like Reverend and the Makers and the Lo Fi Allstars, turned out to be sensible, considering what the internet was about to do to the recorded music market."

"I only really started to notice its decline in about 2003-ish," remembers Cut La Roc. "1997-1999 were seminal years for music really, The Chemical Brothers, Propellerheads, Fatboy Slim, Roni Size, The Prodigy etc, let loose some incredible music, but also at this time a lot of wishy-washy music was released, particularly in the big beat genre - lots of people putting stuff out because it was the latest thing or whatever. Having a recording studio at home became a 'thing', with the advent of Logic and Cubase etc making it possible to create anywhere, which was good and also a bad thing, as it led to a tidal-wave of digital music, which definitely contributed to the demise of big beat. Shame really, but music needs to keep moving."

Big beat was, by 1999, a very dirty word in the dance scene (it was also at this time that the Big Beat Boutique night's name was shortened to simply The Boutique). Also, Fatboy increasingly stopped dropping big beat records in his sets, and went for a more all-out house sound (as well as many other artists jumping on other bandwagons such as the nu-skool breaks sound – more later).

While it wasn't a bad thing that things were calming down, the way big beat was cast off was like being caught listening to the boy or girl band of the day. Also during this period, the general quality of some of the big beat output was becoming less than desirable, and combined with the over-saturation, not to mention the very crass, boozy and boorish undertone that went with it, in many ways, the backlash and persecution of the genre was pretty inevitable.

"The big beat movement started to wane (I think 1999) probably due to key messages in the music media just stating it was OVER!" recalls the promoter for the Leeds big beat night D:Funked, Tony Green. "It was declared as deeply unfashionable to like it anymore. *Mixmag* and *DJ Mag* were big influencers then. The DJs switched to house (or started to experiment with nu skool breaks) or back to hip-hop/trip-hop funk. Big beat DJs switched their game, the producers stopped making it for fear they would be left behind (and some were) and overnight it just DIED!"

In an interview for this book in September 2017 Simon Shackleton (Elite Force, Lunatic Calm) pretty much nailed the reason for the genre's downfall: "I think it became formulaic very quickly, and was a victim of its own success. Most people making music that fell under the big beat banner were underground producers, and I suspect they didn't feel comfortable with pursuing an overtly commercial agenda with their music… not to mention the fact that the music press went from lauding it to berating it almost overnight. With its huge commercial successes, most producers and small labels were priced out of the market when it came to licensing samples, so they shifted into other music areas."

Freddy Fresh also remembers the "big beat sucks" movement that was going on at the time when we spoke in September 2017: "It waned because things evolve and change and many people used cheesy samples in big beat. To get that cool big beat sound, you need authentic 1960s sounding killer riffs (the more unknown the better) and, quite frankly, it is difficult to find those riffs unless you are a serious beat digger. This, coupled with the fact that many talented producers like Krafty Kuts, Deadly Avenger, Wiseguys, Fatboy jumped ship and went safely into house territory this same year, sort of guaranteed that this music would not be as widespread. Some gifted producers stayed true to the genre like yourself, Skeewiff, Andy 'Ictus', Mick & Marc, and a host of new talented Russian and Eastern European and also Japanese producers like the up and coming Unchant in Japan.

"In fact these same producers today do often make big beat music. Bear in mind, the unsuspecting public will lose their minds to a well produced big beat tune, and I promise you they will not stop dancing at a massive outdoor festival to a big beat set, if someone announces beforehand that a 'big beat' set is about to be played. No, if it is funky, they will dance. Period. Again this is why it is absolutely ridiculous and absurd to declare the death of any genre of music, or visual art for that matter. (Just imagine going into an art gallery and falling in love with an oil painting then to have some dork come up behind you, tap you on the shoulder and say 'Oil painting?' You're admiring an 'Oil' painting? That is so last year man... don't you know it's all about 'watercolours' now!' Big beat has its place, drum and bass has its place, techno has its place. Electro has its place. Period. A good DJ rocks a crowd by any selection necessary. A bad DJ doesn't rock the crowd."

"It was mad how acts like Fatboy and The Chems got so big, but it wasn't overnight, and partially happened after the big beat backlash," recalls Carl Loben, who works for *DJ Mag*. "When the media decided it was a dirty word all of a sudden, the biggest acts managed to swerve the backlash, but a lot of really good combos got adversely affected - which was a shame. There was plenty more mileage in big beat, I thought. It was as much an attitude as anything. An umbrella term for anything beatsy-with-attitude, which could include anyone from the electro-poppin' Freddy Fresh to soundtrack don David Holmes..."

"This whole genre had a DIY ethic as it was born from sampling and this to me is more organic," states Lee Mathias aka Stepping Tones in a 2018 essay. "I associate hip-hop and the funky breaks movement with punk, it has that smash and grab attitude. I've always enjoyed the samples at beginning of records regardless of what genre the music is; it is a sort of welcome message that sets the tone. There is always the mystery of 'where is that from?' left with the listener, especially if you are pick-pocketing from cult films and old disco records. The Manic Street Preachers *Holy Bible* album is littered with iconic vocal samples and for me it really completes and complements the songs. I wouldn't cherish that album as a piece of musical genius without the samples. Sampling might be considered a 'dark art' but I would argue 'Talent borrows, genius steals'.

"This style also endorsed a plethora of DJs who can't mix for toffee but somehow managed to squeeze a DJ or production career out of winging it with a basic cut and paste method. This just added to its eventual unpopular categorisation. I don't think big beat was for music snobs and thus why it appealed to more rebellious souls and underground urbanites. This is probably why the purists were so happy to stamp it into a musical rubbish bin and dropkick it over the nearest goal posts, desperately hoping that nobody would return the shot anytime soon. As much as I like reminiscing and discussing big beat, I'm equally amused by all the criticisms it provokes.

"To generalise, the UK music scene and perhaps this island in general, we seem to have this monstrous appetite for creating and devouring musical styles in both a positive and negative way. Perhaps this goes back to our ancestral roots where we had to 'do things' to survive, you couldn't just sit about like you can in countries and continents where you have nice weather. This island has been a battleground for moving forward in many aspects of life, maybe this grafting attitude plays weight on our creative juices? Build It Up, Tear It Down as someone once said. Still I don't personally understand this insatiable desire to declare something creative as 'dead' and then rapidly moving onto the next thing. In the UK, we are often the first to invent a new style and then are always the first to pass it out of play and substitute it for something else. Our musical cousins on the continent and in the U.S.A. seem far more delicate when it comes to music evolution and have a more natural and laid-back approach."

Not everybody jumped on a different bandwagon (most former big beat artists went either "nu skool" breaks, or straight-up house), but instead stuck to their guns with the big beat sound (like Freddy Fresh) or went off in their own unique direction (Death In Vegas for example, went retro-psychedelic rock) - one of these who formed their own original sound was Laidback, whose second album *Frequency Delinquency* was released in 2002, and was more electronically bass-driven breaks with funk elements; in many ways, a prototype of the emerging electro house scene of the time, but with breakbeats.

"Doing my own thing, not following the darker more serious nu skool breaks sound of the Friction nights, and keeping my *Frequency Delinquency* second album funky, helped longevity," recalls Jason Laidback. "That stood me in good stead for when I signed with 12Tree, under the name Slyde, to the brilliant Finger Lickin Records, and to be on that pioneering roster in the golden era of breakbeat was unbelievable. Label boss Justin Rushmore took chances, and Slyde made a diverse bass driven album, yet it still felt like it was a natural progression from my solo stuff. We tried to push boundaries with DJ sets full of our own edits, tracks like 'Vibrate To This,' 'Krunk,' 'We Love It,' 'Kiss Kiss Bang Bang' had more layers than most, and Jem Panufnik's crazy

179

puppet rockstar video for 'Sex & Drugs' was superb. I hope it all resonated with people, and judging by the way everyone speaks to me at gigs today, it makes me smile and think that it probably did."

The Big Beat Class of '99

The Chemical Brothers' third album *Surrender* came out that year, and while there were still some big beat moments, and it was still a massive hit both critically and commercially, *Surrender* did have more of a psychedelic house/trance/acid influenced vibe, in comparison to their first and second albums. "We really loved *Surrender*," stated Tom Rowlands for *Pulse* magazine in 2002. "For me, it was almost perfect." [42] The album also featured another collaboration with Noel Gallagher from Oasis called 'Let Forever Be' - a track that Noel would have preferred, if it was instrumental and, like 'Setting Sun', Noel was disappointed he wasn't in the now legendary video directed by Michael Gondy, which Pitchfork Media listed as No.7 in their 'Top 50 Music Videos of the 1990s'. The video featured actress and dancer Stephanie Landwehr depicting a woman's nightmares.

The most well-known track from that album is the now seminal anthem 'Hey Boy Hey Girl', which samples the early hip-hop track 'The Roof Is On Fire' by Rock Master Scott and the Dynamic Three. This acid house influenced banger was originally made in 1997, and first appeared on their 'Radio 1 Anti Nazi' mix, but didn't get a proper release until two years later. The tune was commercially very successful, where it reached No.3 in the UK singles charts, and went Top 10 in Ireland and Switzerland. The track also had an acclaimed video directed by Dom and Nic, which features dancing skeletons in a nightclub via the eyes of a woman's x-ray vision - it also featured cameos from Tom and Ed themselves.

The tune was very influential, and inspired a short-lived movement that *Mixmag* would call at the time 'Smash House' or to be later known as 'Hooligan House', which, in many ways, was basically very much like big beat, but with a straight 4/4 house beat, rather than syncopated breakbeats. This scene lasted until around 2004, and acts who were put into this camp included the Audio Bullys, Who Da Funk, and some of DJ Touché's output post-Wiseguys and pre-Fake Blood.

Another notable release from that year was *The Last True Family Man* by Minnesota producer/DJ, Freddy Fresh. A very creative release from Eye-Q Recordings, it also featured guest spots from The Freestylers, Grandmaster Flash and most notably Fatboy Slim on the track 'Badder Badder Schwing', which was a minor hit in the UK charts, reaching No. 34, and saw a second life after being used in the 2002 comedy movie *Austin Powers 3 – Goldmember* and most recently in 2014 for a Ritz crackers advert.

Freddy Fresh remembers working on the track when I spoke to him in September 2017. "It was an honour to work with Norman Cook (not to mention fun, as he took me to cool record stores, and we just had a lot in common, what with collecting breakbeats, records, analogue gear etc.) I greatly respect him, as he is one of the minority of UK producers that actually does most everything himself. (In Minnesota I have no choice but to make the music, mix the music, master the music etc. myself.) It was a great feeling to then hear the actual finished tune on the radio of course. (I do realise that this NEVER would have happened had it not been for Fozia Shah, Dean, Heinz and the Eye-Q Records crew.) You must remember that this was before Fatboy's landmark album hit the shelves. The song just kind of took off, as it is a very fun tune. It was a great joy to hear it played in so many commercials etc. and it holds great memories for me as a fun time in my life."

Freddy Fresh's *Last True Family Man* album was a real high for the big beat genre. It opens with the stomping 'Peter Gunn'-inspired banger 'Smokin' Gun', before going into the hip-hop madness of 'La Lyrica'. Other highlights include the funky disco house stomper 'It's About The Groove', the comedic 'Da Missus' and 'Norbert's Working', a very funky collaboration with the Freestylers 'What It Is' (another track that was in the UK charts), the downtempo 'Flashback', with a scratch solo from the pioneering Grandmaster Flash, before closing with the laidback 'It's A Latin Thing'. This was a record that showed all the layers and facets that big beat had to offer.

While not as talked about as some other big beat releases, *Family Man* is just one of those records that will give you an enormous smile and is a gem worth checking out.

The year also saw Freddy Fresh forming a 7 inch singles label called Howlin' Records with the first release being the Freddy Fresh track 'We Badd!' (which was later used in the Jackie Chan movie *Tuxedo*). The following release included a special re-edit of 'Badder Badder

181

Schwing' (with Fatboy Slim) and the label also hosted releases from Krafty Kuts, Kelly Reverb, Dyamno Productions, Ictus, All Good Funk Alliance, Mike Gates, Azaxx, Lord 69 and… yours truly - Rory Hoy (including my very first album release *Cosmic Child* and four subsequent albums, *Standing on Dust*, *Baby Likes it Phat*, *Hands in the Sky* and *Sketching Shadows*).

The label continued until 2015, with the final release being the criminally underrated and very ambitious Freddy Fresh solo album *Play The Music*. In September 2017, Freddy Fresh told me "Basically, I had just done the *Family Man* LP in 1999 and I just completed my *Music For Swingers* LP for a label in the USA. Annie Nightingale adored this new release and thought it would be well received. My career was really taking off, but, at that same month, the DJ magazines claimed big beat had died. I had just started my Howlin' label and many of my UK producer pals were halting big beat productions and going for a house vibe. I was actually warned by some close UK pals to stop producing big beat. Well of course I did NOT and only a few producers continued to make this style.

"I basically got loads of love with Howlin', selling over 5,000 7" copies on the first two releases that same year and during the year 2000. Few people were still doing big beat outside of Kingsize and a small group of other labels. Howlin' took off for me, despite the press having claimed it was a dead genre. I have always believed that, as a musician, we should make what we feel, instead of what we feel will sell. This can be a blessing and also a curse of course. And the proof that big beat will never die can be seen in the faces of the crowds when they go insane dancing to an amazing big beat style song."

One of Howlin's most popular artists was Leeds based DJ Andy Harlstead, who went by the name of Ictus (later extended to Andy Ictus). In an interview with me in October 2017, Andy remembers how he was signed to Howlin' Records:

"I actually met Freddy with my twin brother in Crash Records basement in Leeds when he was promoting his *Last True Family Man* album. He heard a track of mine that was playing in the basement already as he walked in, and he wanted to know what the track was - it was an unreleased track of mine called 'Funny Song' (now lost) and he liked it, so we got talking and he asked if we were signed up (my brother doesn't do the producing with me, but has supplied me with tons of original vinyl samples for my edits which I have done in the past). I

182

ended up emailing Freddy and told him I wanted to send him a CD (yes, CD... not MP3 haha) and he was cool with that. He basically phoned me up at work, and said he liked some of my tracks and asked if I was interested in getting some pressed onto his Howlin' Records label. Of course I said yes, and that's how that happened. It was around 2002 from what I remember... the first single was 'Soul Meeting' I think."

Ictus would end up during the 2000s becoming a regular in the local DJ circuit – it did however lead to one particularly amusing incident. "I remember once playing a B-Boy battle warm up at Stylus in Leeds and it was great," Ictus told me. "I was on my laptop, had finished my set and was getting ready to hand over to the Korean DJ who was on the other side of the room. The room was packed with B-Boys and Girls from all over UK and also Korea and I put my thumb up to the Korean DJ so he could start his set. As I came out of Ableton and started to turn my laptop off, I forgot that my channel fader was up and the Windows log off tune blasted out over the speakers... Definitely the most embarrassing DJ experience. I forgot to say that everyone in the room laughed aloud as the Windows log off tune blasted out... I laughed too and waved at the crowd... So embarrassing it was."

Another signee was Canadian breaks producer, Myagi, already mentioned in the chapter 'Beats International - Big Beat Overseas'. "I produced some funky breaks bits and got in touch with a fledgling Canadian label called 2wars who signed my first release... my second one went to Freddy Fresh's Howlin' Records," remembers Myagi. "For the life of me, I still can't remember how I got his contact, though it may have been as simple as seeing an email address at the bottom of a 45 he'd put out. I sent him over a piece of music called 'I Got Beat Up By a 303,' which he signed and released. John Peel opened his BBC radio show with it a number of times. A pretty cool thing to have happened for me.

"To say I wrote that tune on basic equipment was an understatement. An MPC2000XL, Fender P bass, a cheap acoustic guitar and samples coming off my Discman. Also a copy of Rebirth, the closest I could get to an actual TB [303]. Getting signed to Howlin' was awesome. It was a nod from a great. Also, when you're starting out in a career, especially as physically distant from a major musical hub as I was, trying to limit the number of degrees of separation between your work and those of people you admired was pretty much the name of the game."

Whilst not strictly a big beat release, one of the biggest albums of that year was *Play* by US artist Moby (aka the soundtrack album to every second advert on the TV from 1999-2004) which was released on May 17th. It is (as of writing) the biggest selling dance album of all time, with an extraordinary 12 million copies sold worldwide, but the reason why this is worth a mention is the album does have one of big beat's finest moments on it – 'Bodyrock'. Based off a sample from 'Love Rap' by Spoonie Gee, the tune was a hit in both the UK and US charts, and had a hilarious video featuring some really bad dancers auditioning for Moby (possibly inspired by Fatboy Slim's infamous 'Praise You' Video?).

Around this time, the big beat camp also made way for two new music genres as a getaway from the now "shameful" tag - funky breaks and nu-skool breaks (later to be abbreviated as breaks after it wasn't 'new' anymore). Funky breaks (which was pioneered by the Bronx Dogs, and was influenced by Bristol's more B-Boy-centric take of the genre as well as the proto-big beat sounds from the West Coast breakbeat scene from America) was almost identical to big beat, but its sample library was mainly limited to funk, soul, disco and early rap sounds rather than rock, pop, acid house etc. - artists in this style included Jadell, Max Sedgley and Soul of Man.

This also sowed the seeds for the nu-funk scene (which was basically funky breaks under a different name, and usually at slower tempo (around 110 BPM), and later the ghetto funk scene (named after the label Ghetto Funk), which was more synthetic and featured "wub-wub" basslines not too dissimilar to those used by brostep artists such as Skrillex. One of the biggest acts of the funky breaks and nu-funk scenes is the All Good Funk Alliance from the USA (Frank Cueto and Rusty Belicek), who were not shy to mention big beat's impact on those genres. Frank from the band explains in an interview for this book in September 2017: "We started around 1996 and were influenced by a lot of music at the time including some big beat. More specifically, breaks and funk. Bronx Dogs was a huge influence at the time. But Prodigy, Fatboy Slim, Propellerheads, Wiseguys, etc. all were influential."

Rusty from the band also adds: "The idea of taking breakbeat samples and adding an even louder snare and kick to it was a direct influence from big beat, but yeah just the idea of doing something other than straight house was really exciting. The whole big beat era was cool, we thought we could use some of those ideas in our whole midtempo movement."

Nu-skool breaks, however, was a lot more dark and moody (initially) and was more electronic sounding, with many of big beat's artists moving to this sound. The kingpins of this genre included Plump DJs, Stanton Warriors and Evil Nine. This scene was big until around 2008, as it started to sound almost identical to electro house, except without a 4/4 kick (this style was initially nicknamed plod, as the percussion sounded like a horse trotting), but the genre started to slowly have something of a turnaround in the mid 2010s, thanks to some fantastic works on the Stanton Warriors' label Punx Music.

"A little known fact is that, for a short time, the more electronic club orientated 'big beat' that grew into nu-skool breaks was called 'speed funk'," remembers Doc Moody, BlowPop's resident DJ in an interview with me in September 2017. "Although abbreviations of this phrase meant it didn't last long. The transition of big beat into nu-skool breaks was a natural evolution - it came about two fold. The first was a brief craze of playing instrumental D&B at 33 RPM instead of 45, the tightly produced pitched up D&B beats sounds amazing slowed down to 135 BPM and the huge sub just gets lower.

"The second came from producers crafting their own sounds, rather than the cutting and pasting of samples that gave big beat its defining flavour. The old funk breaks at the front of big beat were now filtered down, and backed up by much heavier and tighter produced kicks and snares. With the BPM going from 120 odd to the mid 130s, this was a perfect sound to a dance floor wanting a fatter sound come 2am. With the energy climbing as the tempo went up, and the pills went down, nu-skool breaks took over, and spread out, being a bigger melting pot for musical ideas."

It should also be noted that, at the same time, the old school hip-hop revival was in full swing (thanks to the Jason Nevins remix of Run DMC mentioned in the previous chapter), with a new wave of turntablists (DJs who scratch a lot) entering the arena. These included artists such as DJ Format, DJ Woody and DJ Yoda. One thing that these acts had in common was big beat's irreverent sense of humour (especially with DJ Yoda, who even incorporates flat-out comedy into his sets) and its vast and eclectic approach to sampling and crate digging (DJ Format's 'Here Comes The Fuzz' samples an obscure Elvis track, but you wouldn't think so by listening to it). These acts (as well as the funky breaks and nu-skool breaks, and nu-funk and ghetto funk later on) would, in a sense, carry on a lot of the ethos that was set in stone by big beat.

Heavenly Records - the people behind the Heavenly Social and Heavenly Jukebox nights, where the Chemical Brothers, Jon Carter, Richard Fearless, David Holmes, and many more got their start - opened its first bar in central London near Oxford Circus, The Social, which is still in operation to this day. Other bars would later open up in Islington, Bristol and Nottingham, though those bars nowadays don't use the Heavenly name. Despite this, the Social brand is still going strong, and in an interview for this book in November 2017, I spoke to the co-founder of the Heavenly Social, Robin Turner, to ask what was the secret to the Social brand's longevity. "Hard to say. Hopefully people trust us. We've consciously never tried to be cool, we're just people who love music, who all work in the music industry and enjoy turning people on to new sounds. Hopefully that comes across – we've made a lot of brilliant friends through the club nights and through the bar and we continue to do so."

On the singles side, big beat wasn't quite dead yet. Fatboy Slim released two singles from his *You've Come A Long Way, Baby* album 'Praise You' and 'Right Here Right Now', which were gigantic hits worldwide and had very memetic music videos. 'Ooh La La' by The Wiseguys was reissued to massive success, where it would sell 500,000 copies because of the track's renaissance with its usage in a Budweiser advert (it was also a hit in Mexico, where it featured on the Ingles Airplay Chart). To promote the reissue, Touché appeared on *CD:UK* and *Top Of The Pops*, with cult underground hip-hop band Ugly Ducking fronting him, to make The Wiseguys seem like a proper "band". In his blog 'Ear to the track' Andy Cooper from Ugly Duckling remembers being a temporary "Wiseguy":

"We met Touché to create a show routine for his track that had now climbed to number two on the BBC Top 20, and later in the afternoon we were taken to a nearby TV studio to film a performance of 'Ooh La La' for a music show called *CD:UK* which was largely viewed by children. It was new and fairly intimidating being around all of those lights, cameras and assistants, but once the music started, we basically jumped around while rapping excitedly. Our *CD:UK* performance aired the following Saturday, but we never saw the broadcast because, that same

morning, me and the guys were in a cramped Vauxhall mini-van travelling to Twickenham film studios in West London where we'd be appearing on the most famous music show in Europe: *Top of the Pops.*

"When the van arrived at Twickenham, we were escorted to a modest
dressing room. I couldn't help but see the absurdity in a scenario where
a totally inexperienced idiot like me was pretending to be in a hugely
successful group as the lead-singer/rapper of a song I'd only just recently heard for a European television audience of millions. Next thing
I knew, the director called for 'The Wiseguys' and we were briskly
rushed to the famous *TOTP* stage where we took our place under the
lights as host Jamie Theakston introduced us, and the music began to
play. Luckily, we didn't mess up and the tune was so popular that the
crowd was easy to please. As a completely unseasoned entertainer, it
was incredibly odd to watch an audience go nuts during a performance
in which I was participating. It felt like I was acting in a movie that,
somehow, I was also watching; if that's possible. As I was being swal-
lowed by the crowd, I remember catching a glimpse of Mark Jones
standing off to the side smiling with delight; I have to imagine the
money was rolling in for Wall of Sound." [77]

The Wiseguys would also support The Beastie Boys on their UK
Tour in May of that year on the 3rd-8th of that month, including two
nights at the legendary Wembley Arena.

You could compare favourably both Wiseguys (and also the Bronx
Dogs) albums with the musical output of Jadell (real name James Hatt.)
In 1999, he released his acclaimed debut album *Gentleman of Leisure,*
which was followed up with *How Do I Do?* in 2002 - two gems in the
big beat catalogue (despite the diminishing returns on the second album). "I really enjoyed it, and still do," Jadell told me in December
2017, regarding producing music. "If you really enjoy it, then it's a bit
like painting or any other art form, you get better and better at it. I had
been listening to so much music all my life as my mum was massively
into soul, so I had a bit of a kickstart with things. By the time I started
doing my own producing, I think I knew what sounded shit and what
would work in a club. Sometimes things get done quick, sometimes they
take fucking AGES. Always an enjoyable learning process though.

"My first LP came out in 1999, and I was very proud of it. I'd started
to work with all-live instruments on a few tracks, and that was amazing.
Layering up a string quartet, and working with Jimbo 'Raw Deal' Rob-
bins and a three piece horn section, man that was incredible. I felt like

Brian Wilson sometimes. I toured the first LP *Gentleman of Leisure* in France and a lot of Scandinavia, where I seemed to be doing pretty good, as well as most of the UK.

"We hired out these nutty kids to go and plaster shit-tons of JADELL stickers in all the trendy areas of the main UK towns, I remember. One night I was walking home with a bottle of Jack Daniels in my hand and I walked past one of those crazy van guys that fly poster at four in the morning - he was putting up my posters along Golbourne Rd bridge. I thought 'FUCK YES, THIS IS REALLY HAPPENING!'

"I also began to get remixes, which I totally loved doing. My first ones were for Grand Unified, The Jungle Brothers, The Aloof, Emiliana Torrini, Jacknife Lee and Deadly Avenger. I also collaborated with James Lavelle on his 'Nigo' project with Kudo from Major Force. Tony Vegas (who I had a flat with for a year) and I did two tunes with them. Theo Wiseguy co-produced a few things with me, as did Nick Faber.

"By the time I started my second LP, things at Ultimate Dilemma were drawing to a close. Max had moved on to working at Mushroom/Infected records, and was running the UK wing of Rawkus records. I'd go in for meetings to play him tunes I was working on for the album, and he could barely give me two minutes of his time, he was so busy on other stuff. So, I jumped ship and went to Illicit recordings, which was Deadly Avenger's label (who I got on really well with). During that LP, I was out getting fucked up ALL the time. I always felt ill and had a hangover in the studio. But I did work hard on it, and was extremely pleased with it. Unfortunately, unbeknown to me, the record label was in huge debt and hardly any promotion at all was done for it, so it went nowhere."

On the Wall of Sound front, Les Rythmes Digitales (Stuart Price) released his second album *Darkdancer*. Despite backlash at the time because of its retro sound, the album was very well received with its neo-1980s revival style being considered ahead of its time, and was the forerunner to the electroclash sound of the 2000s. It was included in the book *1001 Albums You Must Hear Before You Die*, and the album featured guest vocals from classic Hi-NRG singer Shannon and Nik Kershaw. Price was also having success as a member of the 1980s themed band Zoot Woman (with brothers Andy and Johnny Plake), and like Les Rythmes Digitales they were forerunners to the electroclash sound. "Zoot Woman worked with cutting edge video director, Dawn Shadforth, with stylist Fee Doran and photographer Rankin - it was amazing working with the best creatives," remembers Price's former manager, Claudia Nicolson. "A memorable night with them was supporting The Human League in Amsterdam; they were lovely guys and a real pleasure to work with. They were doing promo in France when Stuart got a call from Madonna's camp to ask if he would go to LA to meet her and the band. I was very excited for him, knowing what it meant being an 80s icon of his, and what an opportunity for such a talented young artist." The band would later become Madonna's opening act in 2001, and Zoot Woman would release five albums to date (two being on Wall of Sound), countless singles and (under the name of Paper Faces) work with the likes of Kylie Minogue, Scissor Sisters, Armand Van Helden, Chromeo, Frankmusik and of course, Madonna. Claudia Nicholson also remembers a particularly nightmare-inducing image of Les Rythmes Digitales: "My favourite memory was Les Rythmes Digitales playing live in fancy dress as Ronald McDonald." Scary!

Other notable singles of the big beat class of 1999 included Ashton Harvey from the Freestylers recording under the name of Nu Generation for a remake of Fontella Bass' soul classic 'Rescue Me', which went to No.8 in the UK charts. Another similar remix around this time was for the classic rock & roll track by the Kingsmen 'Louie Louie', by the Three Amigos (Dylan Amlot, Marc Williams and Milroy Nadarajah) which went to No.15 in the charts - a little on the cheesy side, but a very fun track none the less (though their 2001 reworking of Edwin Starr's '25 Miles' is also worth listening to).

Another big hit in 1999 was 'Stop The Rock' by Liverpool group Apollo 440 (who previously had hits with 'Ain't Nothin''Bout Dub', 'Krupa' and 'Lost In Space'.) Hailed by critics as their breakout single, this Status Quo sampling banger reached No.10 in the UK charts, and was included in the soundtracks to the films *Gone in 60 Seconds*, *Boys and Girls* and *Bedazzled*, as well as the video games 'FIFA 2000', 'Gran Turismo 3: A-Spec' and 'Pixar's Cars: Mater-National Championship'.

"'Stop The Rock' is probably the most 'big beat' thing we've ever done - we just seemed to hit the zeitgeist with that one," remembers Noko from the band when we spoke in 2017. "It's the @440 party tune with a whole bunch of layers to it, that just keeps on giving! I always think analysing these things slightly demystifies the magic alchemy: it all came together very quickly. I had the basic track already grooving around and the whole 'Stop The Rock' vocal idea was the very first idea that popped into Mary Byker's (real name Ian Garfield Hoxley) head as soon as he bounded up the stairs to our old Camden Parkway studio - Job's a good 'un.

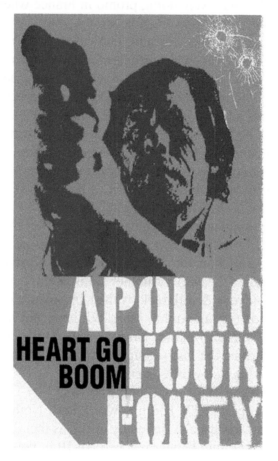

Flyer for Apollo 440 Single 'Heart Go Boom' – the follow-up to 'Stop The Rock' courtesy of Lee Mathias

"We'd been doing a promo tour of radio stations in Germany a few weeks before and a DJ on one of the local stations was using this little orange Boss VT-1 FX unit to create different characters from his own voice. I immediately saw the potential, bought a VT-1 there and then in Köln, and the 'voice' of 'STR' was born - we called the character The Digital Midget due to the extreme formant shift effects. Things came full circle when we did the rounds of radio promo for that single and Byker and I conducted the interviews 'in character' with him speaking and me manipulating the pitch and formant live: it could be absolutely hilarious - the radio DJs loved it. Silly times.

"One of my favourite things about that song is the lyric 'We shape the rock like Henry Moore - Aphrodite At The Waterhole, come on' with its reference to the Tony Hancock film *The Rebel* - immaculately non-linear!"

The classic music video featured a dog on the run from the law. The year also saw them release their third album *Getting High On Your Own Supply*, which was well received by critics at the time. The band would later work with some very big names, including guitarist legend Jeff Beck. "We produced and co-wrote some tracks for Jeff Beck's *Jeff* LP a few years later, and having him playing the most incendiary and lyrical electric guitar in our Cally Road studio for two weeks was pretty priceless too," remembers Noko. "He has so many great rock & roll anecdotes too."

Another massive Fatboy Slim remix came out that year. This time, it was for Groove Armada's (Andy Cato and Tom Findlay) 'I See You Baby (Shakin' That Ass)' featuring the vocals of New York MC Gramma Funk, who the duo met in Manumission in Ibiza - she was wearing nothing more than a skimpy nightie and feathers (it was Manumission after all!). In February 2018, she sent me the story of how she lent those famous memetic vocals to the iconic track:

"When Gramma Funk met Groove Armada… she was the 'The Mistress of Oral Communications' on the mic during their weekly DJ stint at Manumission Ibiza, they invited her to record a track with them in a studio in London, she gave them her New York phone number and said 'call me after the season'. Well, it appears that Groove Armada was serious about their invitation, and called Gramma Funk in New York inviting her to, once again, come to London to record with them. She travelled to London to write and record her vocals for one track.

"At that time she brought on the acts with her funk hosting, but was not accustomed to recording music, so when she recorded her vocals, the lyrics were never written down, but instead free flowed from her…

"Groove Armada played an instrumental track, which wasn't the actual track used for the single, and she told them to just let the music run, no pauses, and no breaks… When Gramma Funk left the studio that night she had no idea how her lyrics and vocal performance produced with Groove Armada's music would manifest in the music world.

"While in a London cab with her twin sister Koi Sojer, they heard 'I See You Baby' on the radio for the first time, and broke out into a scream and began shouting to the cab driver to turn it up, because it was her on the radio. She says it was truly an amazing feeling, and so great to share the moment with her twin sister.

"With the release of the remixed version of 'I See You Baby' by Fatboy Slim, music critics in the U.S. and in Europe were buzzing about Groove Armada's hit single, 'I See You Baby', which became so hot in the U.K. that it contributed towards Groove Armada's new album, *Vertigo* (on Pepper/Jive) reaching gold status (100,000 units sold) and, since its U.S. release, 'I See You Baby' has gained international acclaim and climbed the national record charts, making it a classic hit and one of the stand out tracks on the album."

The author (Rory Hoy) with Gramma Funk in London. Photograph by Tom Hoy

While a minor hit initially reaching No.17 in the UK singles charts, the tune would get a massive resurgence for its usage in a famous and very popular Renault Megane advert in 2003, which caused 139 complaints from media watchdogs because of the tune's usage of the word "ass" and the commercial's provocative rump shaking, meaning that the ad couldn't air until 7:30pm. Because of the success (and controversy) of the advert, the tune was reissued again in 2004, where it reached No.11 in the UK singles charts.

In April 9th of that year, the Boutique's Skint On Fridays events at London's The End club came to an end. "We've had some wonderful times at The End," [43] quoted Gareth Hansome for *NME* magazine in 1999. The final night included sets from Deejay Punk Roc and Bronx Dogs. During this time, Gareth was also considering doing a regular Boutique slot in London, but this never came to fruition.

Big Beat Embraces Festivals and Arenas

One of the most famous gigs of that year was when Gareth Hansome organised two massive Big Beat Boutique shows at Trentham Gardens in Stoke-on-Trent and at the Brixton Academy in London, on the 10th and 11th June with the first set being broadcast on BBC Radio 1 on the 'Essential Mix' show. The headliners were Fatboy Slim and US house legend Armand Van Helden duking it out back to back in a boxing ring – it was billed as 'A Date With Destiny'. "I wanted to put on an event which included Norman DJing being the focal point, and being a lot more visual as a DJ when playing records," explained Gareth in the BBC2 documentary series *Acetate*, broadcast in 1999. "Norman's always up for a laugh, and Armand surprisingly was up for it more than we expected." [44] Support came from Cut La Roc, Jon Carter and Lo-Fidellity Allstars. The now defunct website Mackie's World gave a comprehensive review of this now legendary event:

"The camera crews at the door indicate that something very special is happening tonight, as you walk up to Brixton Academy past hundreds of fans desperate to get their hands on the last few tickets for a 'once in a lifetime' opportunity to see two of the world's biggest DJs in action. To much applause and cheering, Armand Van Helden enters the ring from one side, accompanied by an understandably large group of security men, and a geezer wielding the star-spangled banner. The unexpectedly short Van Helden drops his silk gown and removes his boxing gloves to reveal he's dressed up for the part - customised basketball top, loads of jewellery - everything about him says 'I'm trendy, me'.

"On the giant video screens, we now see Norman Cook entering the ring from the other side of the arena. The crowd goes radio rental (mental)! Norman disrobes to reveal... a Hawaiian shirt and jeans... and no-one bats an eye-lid.

"Norm and Armand start the theatrics at the front of the ring - forehead against forehead they stare each other out during the coin-toss to decide who will attempt to win over the crowd for an hour with their DJing skills first. Armand wins the toss and elects to go first, and immediately sets about playing an impressive hour-long set of New York house and garage, starting with his forthcoming single 'The Boogie Monster'. However impressed the crowd is with Armand's DJ antics, they don't really get going until he plays his number one hit single 'You Don't Know Me', then die down again until Brixton boys Basement Jaxx' 'Rendez-vu' is dropped as a set closer.

"To yet more applause Norman Cook arrives, and thrusts a litre bottle of vodka in the air - the crowd respond to every action he makes. On the dancefloor, a whole different mood has been created just by Norman's appearance - everyone spent the whole hour jumping up and down like an extremely happy yo-yo. Tracks incorporated included that Des Lynam cover of 'Rockafeller Skank', 'Fucking In Heaven', Chemical Brothers' 'Hey Boy, Hey Girl', Leftfield's 'Phat Planet', 'Everybody Needs A 303', 'Right Here Right Now', 'Fatboy Eminem (Hi My Name Is The Funk Soul Brother)', 'Satisfaction Skank (I Can't Get No Funk Soul Brother)', 'Kung Fu Fighting', and even the Kinks made a much welcomed appearance towards the end of the set.

"After four hours, what we'd all been waiting for began - Ambidextrous - Armand Van Helden on the right deck, Fatboy Slim on the left deck for two hours, non-stop tunes from the likes of Bob Marley, plus many other peculiar choices including TLC – 'No Scrubs', Jungle Brothers – 'I'll House You '98', Tori Amos – 'Professional Widow', Wildchild – 'Renegade Master (Original)', 'You Don't Know Me' (again), and 'Praise You' as a very fitting finish to the event of the year. Although most people considered it to be Norman's night, it wouldn't have been half as fun without Armand (with his endless supply of tricks, including slowing down one record to about 10 BPM, then speeding it back up to 300 BPM or so, whilst mixing it with another top track) - as there was effectively two hours of Fatboy Slim, we didn't get bored for one minute." [45]

More massive shows also happened in 1999 - both The Chemical Brothers and Fatboy Slim did headline sets at the Homelands Festival in Winchester, a gigantic joint-headline show at the Red Rocks outdoor arena in Colorado, America, which was also documented on television, and - most infamously - the disaster that was Woodstock 1999. While the Chemical Brothers' set went without a hitch, Fatboy's set on the other hand was a different story. At the beginning of his set, some stupid idiot drove a giant van into the middle of the crowd, though thankfully nobody was killed and, after the show, Fatboy's dressing room was set on fire. As previously documented by many others, Woodstock 1999 was an absolute shambles of an event and that's why they haven't done it since. During this period, Norman was earning massive sums in America, which were a record at the time.

The year also saw The Freestylers doing a legendary set at the famous Glastonbury Festival on the Jazz World stage – a set that was considered the best of their whole career [46]. "We spent a lot of 1999 in the USA and had only got back a few days previous to the show, so we were all pretty jet lagged," Aston Harvey told me. "We played the previous year in the dance music tent and were upgraded to the Jazz World stage this time. About five minutes before we went on, I had a quick check to see if anyone had turned up to see us play, and was a bit upset as there weren't many people there plus it was a big field so looked extra empty. Anyway, we've always had a set intro to get the crowd hyped before we actually come on stage, and as soon as that went on, the masses started filling up the field, and within about five minutes of us actually coming on stage it was just a sea of people. It felt like a culmination of a year of touring and hard work had actually paid off, and I think we were still all buzzing from it weeks later."

By this time, popular Bristol big beat night, BlowPop, would even have its own tent at the famous Glastonbury Festival – not a bad feat, considering the "death" of big beat. Doc Moody remembers the times when they hosted this special big beat tent when he spoke to me in September 2017. "One of the stand out moments for me has to be with BlowPop at Glastonbury. During the late 90s/early 2000s, BlowPop was in charge of the backstage entertainment at Glastonbury.

"This consisted of a modest size PA, a little stage, two sets of decks, with a sound engineer, a bar and a coffee stall. It was amazing; basically, if you had an Artist Pass, you could get in, and, as we were the only music once the stages shut, all the artists would come and hang out. We were treated to many of the stars warming up, or doing an impromptu set after their gigs. I think we did four years in total, it was very special.

"So picture the scene... the night sets in and all the stages shut down and silence falls among the gentle hills of the countryside, then across the fields the not-so-faint thud of our backstage PA, pumping some ridiculously good music, drifts out across the whole festival.

"Like a zombie apocalypse they come, one or two at first, gathering around the now decidedly nervous looking security guards standing next to a single piece of waist high barrier across the yellow brick road, leading to the fattest music known to mankind. Once the crowd reached a hundred or so, people started walking past the security guards and flooded our marquee. It was fucking great - we rolled the sides of the marquee up so everyone could get in on the music. A hundred quickly turned into thousands, and it was like magic. The true majesty of the power of music to unite shone down on me, like a message from the gods in that single moment - either that or I timed it just right with the pills I had just dropped. It's probably the best gig I've ever played, as it wasn't planned, it just happened. I have played a few 20k festivals, and been in awe at the dance floor, but this had a feel of an old school illegal warehouse - so much fun. Eventually, the whole of the security team was summoned to usher back the revellers, now lumbering on the 'whole of Glastonbury', to their respective sleeping bags. Due to the overwhelming breaches of all known health and safety laws, we were consequently banned from Glastonbury."

One very well known club night began in June 1999, and it's one that continues to this day - Keep It Unreal, hosted by Manchester DJ, Mr. Scruff (Andy Carthy). He was inspired to do this night because of the frustrations of having to restrict his music to a mono sub-genre during most club nights, similar to the reasoning behind the starting up of The Heavenly Social, Big Beat Boutique etc. While not a big beat night per se, it is similar in its vibe, as it pulls from such a broad range of musical sources like jazz, soul, funk, disco, house, reggae, ska, drum & bass, electro, hip-hop, breakbeat etc. "I think that my own wide ranging approach to music, and the music that I played at my own nights, were

196

inspired by learning my craft in the 1980s, when most DJs played across the board, and had a good working knowledge of many genres," Andy explained to me in March 2018. "People like John Peel, Stu Allan, Greg Wilson, Steve Barker, Hewan Clarke, Colin Curtis, Gilles Peterson, Coldcut etc."

In many ways Keep It Unreal is like a more soulful and sophisticated spiritual successor to the classic Social and Boutique nights. As well as its regular haunt at Manchester's Band on The Wall venue (though in its first 10 years, the night took place at Planet K, then followed on at the venue Music Book) the night has toured all around the UK and has even toured around Europe and the USA, making it, in a spiritual way, the most successful big beat night of all time (in the sense that he plays a BIG range of BEATs, rather than playing endless Fatboy Slim-esque records).

The author (Rory Hoy) with Mr. Scuff. Photograph by Tom Hoy

Keep it Unreal is also the name of Mr. Scruff's second album, which was released on Coldcut's label Ninja Tune on the 7th June coinciding with the opening of the club night of the same name. *Keep It Unreal* the album contained what has become his signature tune 'Get A Move On!' - a jazzy house number based on 'Bird's Lament (In Memory Of Charlie Parker)' by Moondog, with the vocals coming from T-Bone Walker's 'Hypin' Woman Blues'. The tune would end up being used in countless adverts and TV shows in years to come, and was a prototype of the genre that would later be christened electro swing.

The LP also contained guest vocals from UK Rapper Roots Manuva (who would later return for Andy's fourth album *Ninja Tuna*), soul singer Fi, and BBC Radio DJ (and big beat lover) Mary-Anne Hobbs. It got warm and receptive reviews and sold over 500,000 copies world-wide. As per tradition with Mr. Scruff albums, the album contained two story-driven vocal cut-up tunes, 'Shanty Town', which sampled various children's programmes including *Thomas The Tank Engine,* and a jolly ode to eating fish, which is aptly titled 'Fish'. The album would see a very famous fan in Madonna.

Continued Hits Despite Big Beat's Ongoing "Death"

One act that did make an impact in big beat's twilight year of main-stream success was Manchester duo Mint Royale (Neil Claxton and Chris Baker). Their breakthrough track was their remix for rock band Terrorvison's single 'Tequila', which reached No.2 in the UK charts. Their earlier releases (such as 'Deadbeat' and 'Rock & Roll Bar') were championed heavily by Norman Cook, and because of the fact their pro-ductions sounded very similar to his, many people thought that Mint Royale may be another of the many pseudonyms for Cook. Their first album was also released that year, *On The Ropes* - while not a big sales hit, it was a cult classic and contained the track 'Don't Falter' with singer, comedian, and TV presenter Lauren Laverne from the band Kenickie (who they previously remixed), which reached No.15 in the UK singles chart.

1999 saw the release of the acclaimed DJ mix CD, *FSUK Vol.4 by Cut La Roc*. From start to finish, this symphony of modern electronic music is absolutely mind blowing - up there with other revered mix CDs such as Coldcut's *70 Minutes of Madness*. In an interview for this book in October 2017, Cut La Roc remembers making this masterpiece of a mix CD: "Martin 'Krafty Kuts' introduced me to the Ministry Of Sound dude behind those compilations; it was a really fun thing to do actually, and not many people know about this, but I insisted that I recorded it live (there was one small edit made after the mix was recorded as a record jumped) onto a DAT tape, so that mix comp was recorded in the living room in a flat I was renting in Brighton one afternoon. It's raw, it's as you'd witness at a gig, no computer trickery, just me, 2 turntables, a mixer and a DAT machine."

The year also saw The Prodigy do a mix CD of their own *The Dirtchamber Sessions Vol. 1* (named after the studio Liam uses to record his tunes) which was based on a DJ mix Liam Howlett did for BBC Radio 1's Breezeblock Show.

For licensing issues, the mix was re-recorded for its commercial release as its Radio 1 prototype contained many high-profile tracks, such as tunes by The Beatles, Jimi Hendrix and the Sex Pistols, which would have cost an arm and a leg to license. Sadly, a Volume 2 never came to be.

1999 also saw Skint Records becoming shirt sponsors to the football team Brighton & Hove Albion FC, something the label's manager (Damian Harris) was very proud of - the sponsorship lasted for nine years. Ironically at the time, the football team were on the edge of bankruptcy, so having the word 'Skint' etched onto the T-shirts seemed rather cruelly apt (also funny to think now the team are doing really well, and are in the Premiership!). Four years after the sponsorship, Fatboy Slim would later play two successful 'Big Beach Bootique' shows at the then-recently opened stadium for Brighton & Hove – The Amex Stadium.

1999 was also the year of the infamous Y2K scare. Several singles were made to cash in on it, including one from big beat producer Fuzz Townsend called 'Y2K – The Bug Is Coming' which featured Jim's Stereo Superworld and most notably, music legend Ian Dury. In an interview for this book in December 2017, Fuzz remembers working with Dury: "I only worked with Ian for a single day, I think Sept 4th or 6th 1999. I went to his Hampstead apartment, along with Bobby Bird from H.I.A. as my sound engineer. Ian worked so fucking hard; it was for a 'Millennium Bug' cartoon that was never released. He pulled out a bottle of brandy and took sips from it, offering the same to me and Bobby. Others present were Mick Gallagher and Rainbow George Weiss. After recording, Bobby and I went around to Rainbow George's mews house and were treated to a listen of his cassette tapes, featuring his neighbour, the then recently late Peter Cook. A unforgettable few hours."

Despite the big baggage behind the single, it failed to chart.

To end the year - and to ring in the start of the new millennium and the 21st Century - a lot of the big beat artists did high-profile New Year shows including the Chemical Brothers at Fabric in London, and Fatboy Slim for the club night Cream at the Ice Arena in Cardiff, Wales. This was broadcast on BBC Radio 1, and I remember listening to it as a 12-year old boy on New Year's Eve 1999 and being blown away.

Alex Gifford from the Propellerheads' most fond memory of being a Propellerhead was ringing in the new millennium to the sound of their Shirley Bassey collaboration 'History Repeating', as told to me in March 2018:

"On News Year's Eve 1999, Theo from The Wiseguys called me up at midnight from Sydney, Australia, and yelled down the phone that the local radio station was playing 'History Repeating' and that you could hear it booming out of sound systems all over the city. To know that a great city on the other side of the planet had chosen to see in the new millennium to our tune was incredibly moving. Well proud."

Despite being considered "dead" by the critics, 1999 was another strong year for planet big beat.

A Little Less . . . Big Beat's Curtain Call (2000-2)

New Decade – New Hits

By the year 2000 however, big beat was on its last legs, thanks to the critical backlash the genre received the year earlier, despite the continuing success of several of its artists. One big tune did come out at the very start of the year – 'Because Of You' by Scanty Sandwich (Richard Marshall), which was based on 'Shoo Be Do Dah Day' by a very young Michael Jackson, and was released on Fatboy Slim's Southern Fried Records – it got to No.3 in the UK charts. In an interview for this book in October 2017, Scanty Sandwich himself explains how he felt about the track's unexpected success, and how the tune came to be:

"It was pretty amazing really. I remember it was Christmas 1999, and we were in New York with the record label. One of the pluggers got a call from Radio 1 to say that 'Because of You' had just been put on the A-list. This pretty much meant a guaranteed Top 40 entry – maybe even Top 10 - but I don't think anybody was expecting a Top 3!

"What's funny is that it's a track that came into existence through a complete stroke of luck. I'd just popped into my local corner shop and there was a box of discount CDs on the counter. I'm a great believer in spontaneous purchases for sampling potential, and there was this 1971 Michael Jackson album called *Ben* – I think it was 99p – I had to buy it. I stuck it on when I got home, and although it's a nice enough album, there wasn't really much potential for sampling – and then right at the end of the album a track came on called 'Shoo-Be-Doo-Be-Doo-Da-Day'. I remember thinking 'hello...!'"

And did the King of Pop himself, Michael Jackson, approve of being remixed big beat style?

"I never got to meet him in person, but the story goes that he used to personally approve any samples of his work, so I have to believe that he listened to the track himself, and the fact that we got clearance means I guess he probably liked it."

So - MJ may have been a big beat fan?

Fatboy Slim released his third album that year called *Halfway Between The Gutter & The Stars*, a title which reflected how Norman felt at the time. "Halfway between the gutter and the stars was exactly how I felt at the moment," stated Norman in an interview for *DMC* magazine in 2012. "'Cause I was DJing at the Oscars party, but still getting drunk and thrown out [laughs] - so you can take the boy out of the gutter, but you only get halfway to the stars." [79]

More on that Oscars party later in the book!

Commercially, the album did well (but not as well as the previous one) reaching No.8 in the UK albums charts, No.11 in the US Billboard Top Dance/Electronic Albums, No.6 in Australia, and was even No.1 in the UK Independent Albums Chart, selling over 2 million copies worldwide. For Norman himself, the more moderate success was a relief for him, as the astronomical success of his previous album, *You've Come A Long Way, Baby* was all a little too much.

The album contained a very popular spiritual follow on to 'Fucking In Heaven' called 'Star 69' - a "smash house" track, which featured house singer Roland Clark on vocals going "They Know What Is What But They Don't Know What Is What They Just Strut - What The Fuck" ad infinitum, which was a big hit underground, but not mainstream (for obvious reasons). The album also contained the tracks 'Weapon Of Choice' (best known for its iconic Grammy award-winning video), which featured vocals from Bootsy Collins of Parliament-Funkadelic fame, as well as the laid-back 'Sunset (Bird of Prey)', which sampled the late, great Jim Morrison from The Doors. Other highlights included the rock-orientated 'Ya Mama', (originally made for *You've Come A Long Way, Baby* under the working title of 'Kettle') which featured a hilarious music video directed by the acclaimed team Tracktor, two collaborations with soul queen Macy Gray ('Demons' and 'Love Life') as well as a sort-of Freak Power reunion on the Daft Punk-esque track 'Retox' with the vocals of Ashley Slater (Ash also co-wrote the track 'Weapon Of Choice'). Like *You've Come A Long Way, Baby*, a rare "clean" version of the album was issued for more conservative US stores. This self-titled "Kiddie's Clean Version" sadly removed 'Star 69' entirely (despite a cleaned up version existing) and removed the track's reprise in the final track - the 10 minute house epic, 'Song For Shelter' - a tribute to the US house club night, Shelter, and a secret remix of the Roland Clark & Roger Sanchez house anthem 'I Get Deep'.

Skint's main man, Damian Harris aka Midfield General, also released his own album *Generalisation* that year. The reviews were good (despite the fact that big beat was considered by critics to be yesterday's news at the time), and it contained several noteworthy tracks including the funky disco house inspired 'General of the Midfield' and the 'Praise You'-esque 'Reach Out' with the vocals of Linda Lewis. The album is probably best known for the track 'Generalising', which features spoken word from the soon-to-be famous comic Noel Fielding. "As a solo producer I was always looking for vocal content to make tracks more interesting," recalls Damian Harris on his bio for the Skint Records website. "I'd always really liked the idea of telling stories over my music. One night I saw a very early TV performance from Noel Fielding on Channel 4. He was telling these very funny surreal rambling stories and I thought he'd be perfect. So I tracked him down and he liked the idea, recorded some pieces for me and I put them over my music. I remember a lot of the reviews at the time didn't quite get it, but it became something of a cult track, people were making T-shirts with quotes from the song on them. All very bizarre." [49] In charge of making the black and white animated music video for the track was Ste McGregor (future Kidda), who in a previous chapter mentioned how making it was one of his proudest moments. At this time Skint Records, because of diminishing returns, with the exception of the Fatboy (and Kidda later on), would change direction to a more house orientated sound.

Another Skint artist, Cut La Roc, also released his debut long-player that year with *La Roc Rocs*. The album was scheduled to be released earlier, but due to sample clearance issues it was frequently delayed. It contained several tracks that were originally on previously released EPs (such as the Sugarhill Gang sampling 'Hip-Hop Bibbedy Bop') and also featured collaborations with MC Det, TC Islam, Gary Lightbody and most notably a reworking of his 1997 single 'Post Punk Progression' featuring an up-and-coming UK indie rock band, Snow Patrol, who would later see huge success in the 2000s and 2010s.

Bentley Rhythm Ace also released their second (and final) album in 2000 *For Your Ears Only*. To promote the album, they made TV spots on shows such as *The Priority* on Channel 4, where they played the first single from this release 'Theme From Gutbuster', which did moderately well in the UK singles charts reaching a healthy No.29. "I remember reading somewhere that Bentley Rhythm Ace's second album *For Your*

Ears Only was the 'end' of big beat, it was 'too much, too crazy'," recalls Lee Mathias (aka Stepping Tones) in a 2018 essay. "I would argue that it was one of big beat's magnum opus moments, a glorious record, admittedly not quite for everyone and it's definitely out on a musical limb, but it sure is fun! Their debut album had a summer theme, whereas *For Your Ears Only* had a wintertime vibe about it, such a shame they never made spring and autumn albums too. I think the winding down of this style was more due to tempo. Big beat could be hectic and unpredictable; after the year 2000 onwards, it seemed the masses wanted slower, more constrained and concentrated beats, not 'clunky' music."

Justin Robertson also decided to close shop with his Lionrock project that year too. "We got dropped from Deconstruction which was going through a bad financial phase, and folded soon after," Justin told me in January 2018. "That was a good point to stop I thought, the project had been going a few years and been through quite a few stylistic changes from dub house to psych beat, and I wanted to try something new. It just felt like it had run its course."

The underground big beat scene saw (as he describes himself) 'Plymouth's 14th Best DJ', release his debut record on wax - Aldo Vanucci. He was one of the scene's biggest underground successes, which kept the flag flying for the genre during its wilderness years. "I put my first few EPs out in 2000, there is a track called 'Big Dogs Rok' which is blatantly the big beat sound," remembers Aldo in an interview with me in September 2017. "I've always been better at ideas and samples than actually producing. All my early output was with Scott Whyte; we first got together when 'Strike : U Sure Do' came out, as I had a nice piano loop and vocal that would work well in a similar vein."

2000 saw the release of the comedy movie *Kevin and Perry Go Large,* a spin-off for the Kevin The Teenager character created by comedian Harry Enfield for the BBC TV Series *Harry Enfield And Chums*. The film features Kevin and his friend, Perry (played by Kathy Burke), going on holiday to Ibiza to lose their virginities. The film gained a very mixed reception, but it does have a cult following. The soundtrack to the film is quite heavy on big beat tracks - most notably a special remix of 'Love Island' by Fatboy Slim (previously used in the Manumission movie) as well as his remix of Underworld's 'King Of Snake', and the classic 'Ooh La La' by The Wiseguys. The soundtrack also featured the big beat inspired track 'Big Girl' by the Precious Brats (Judge Jules and Matt Smith) with the fictional characters of Kevin and

Perry on vocals. This big beat novelty track went to No.16 in the UK singles charts, and one of the remixes was by Shaft, who are none other than a pseudonym for big beat producers Skeewiff.

Random Stories

The year 2000 also saw The Prodigy's Liam Howlett open for Madonna at her show at Brixon Academy in London in November, with a DJ set (coincidently, the US release of The Prodigy's *Fat Of The Land* was distributed by her label, Maverick Records). Because of this musical mishmash, and being Madonna's first UK show in a long time (with the more appropriate Richard Ashcroft and Charleen Spiteri from Texas also on the bill), ticket sales were phenomenal with some tickets going for £1000. Rather than tailoring his set to Madonna's fanbase, Liam played a mixture of classic hip-hop such as Public Enemy and The Beastie Boys and proto big beat-ers Bomb The Bass and Meat Beat Manifesto - naturally, Madonna's fanbase weren't digging it and Liam himself didn't enjoy the experience.

It was also the year when Leeroy Thornhill from The Prodigy de-cided to leave the band. In a May 2000 issue of 7 magazine, here is what he had to say on the matter: "At the end of the day, I didn't want to dance no more. It's got to the stage now where I don't find throwing myself around mentally challenging. I've been doing it for nearly ten years and now I want to concentrate on my music, and I couldn't do that with the band." [106]

Thornhill would later have a solo career, and still performs to this day as a DJ. He is still friends with the band.

On a more humorous note, dance music tribute acts started to emerge, and big beat artists got their fair share of tribute acts - most notably Fatboy Tim (Timothy Davies, who co-runs Tall House Digital label, and is a member of house music collectives Bronx Cheer and Stuttering Munx), who had a massive following on the Student Union circuit in the 2000s. In an interview for *Thump* magazine in 2015, Tim recalls the genesis of Fatboy Tim:

"I used to DJ in a club in Clapham and I'd wear really loud shirts. I had quite a few people who'd come up to me and say, 'Oh, you look like Fatboy Slim!' I went back to my house with a mate after a gig once, and we started talking about becoming the first tribute DJ. My initial reaction was 'no thanks' but he asked me to do a mixtape - which shows how long ago it was - and said he'd be able to get me a few gigs. So I did this mixtape in the style of Fatboy Slim and he managed to get me a gig at Dundee University. I got paid three or four times my usual fee to play so I thought 'why not?'" [50]

The first year of the new decade ended with The Boutique touring in conjunction with Rizla - the 'Bands & Booze Tour' - in November. This tour went round pretty much the entire UK with stops at Northampton, Cardiff, Warwick, Edinburgh, Aberdeen, Newcastle, Norwich, Leeds, Cambridge, Portsmouth, London and of course Brighton. Acts that were featured included the Lo Fidelity Allstars and The Dirty Beatniks for the live acts and the DJs included Midfield General, Scratch Perverts, Cut La Roc, Xpress2, Jon Carter and Scanty Sandwich.

Big Beach Boutique

The following year (2001) saw Fatboy Slim start a new spin-off of the Boutique entitled the Big Beach Boutique, which took place on Brighton beach. This event started off humbly as an afterparty for Channel 4's cricket coverage, but then evolved into its own thing. To put things into perspective, Channel 4 had set up a giant screen and a sound system to show the cricket on Brighton beach. England had unfortunately lost the match, but that didn't dampen the spirits of the organisers, who booked Fatboy Slim to perform for the post-game entertainment. The first event (which was nicknamed "Normstock" by the fans) was a free entry gig, and took place on the 7th July (with support coming from Groove Armada). It attracted 65,000 happy party people, and highlights were even broadcast on Channel 4. For Norman, this was the greatest gig of his career. When asked by the web magazine *Higher Frequency* in 2006 what his favourite gig was, Norman said: "I think the first Brighton beach party, when we had no idea whether it would work or not, how many people would come, and 65,000 people came. My own hometown, and the weather was good and just the love that I felt from the crowd, because I live in Brighton and not in London. A lot of people in Brighton are very proud of me, because I didn't move to London. And they all came out to show their appreciation. And they brought their kids, and everybody smiled and danced. Just the pride and triumph of returning home. Yeah, like 'you're one of us and we're proud of you'." [51].

One of the punters who remembers the first Big Beach Boutique show was fellow DJ, Tony "Slackshot" Gainsborough. In January 2018, he told me what it was like to be at this groundbreaking concert:

"When I heard the rumour that there was going to be a Big Beat Boutique on the beach (and remember, this was pre-internet days, so there was no way of substantiating such rumours) my brother, Adam, and I decided we'd just jump on the train, head over there and see what's what. We were best mates and loved an adventure if it meant music was involved! Yet we simply had absolutely no idea what lay ahead of us.

"The BBB was already our 'go to' club night of choice. It always offered a great night out, with friendly, welcoming patrons from a huge cross section of different walks of life, and of course the music was always on point. So we knew we should be expecting a decent night out at the very least.

"As soon as we got off the train, we could not only feel but also see the buzz. You could see from a mile off anyone that was heading down, and the level of camaraderie was off the scale. We headed towards the sea front, and like any event that we were excited for, we got there a couple of hours early. Once we got down to the beach we spotted the stage and laid claim to our 'spot' on a foot tall sea wall located side stage left, which we knew would give us a vantage point. But we'd overlooked bringing refreshments. There was no point going to any of the nearby bars, as the place was rammed. So we waited. It didn't take long for a busy prom to become a festival field full of punters waiting for the main act. But it just kept getting busier. And busier.

"Being the friendly herberts we were, we made friends with a couple of girls who just so happened to end up standing next to us. Then Groove Armada took to the stage and rocked it, but everyone was waiting and really saving their energy for Sir Norm. Then the time was upon us. The lights focused on the stage, The bass rumbled for which seemed like a lifetime. And then there he was. Fatboy Slim. Smiling from ear to ear with a look on his face that seemed to say 'How have I done this?' as he cast his view over the immense crowd of partygoers. It wasn't long before it dawned on me that this might possibly be one of the best events I'd ever been too. And we were completely straight. Notable memories being: crazies climbing the lamp-posts, people waving from every single visible balcony, boats pulling up on the water to watch the show on the mainland, hearing Basement Jaxx's 'Where's Your Head At' for the first time (which felt soooo fitting for the moment as it was just plain crazy) and of course the music getting stopped, on account of the amount of people 'avin' it' in the sea. I'd never been to an event like it and with a few more years of hindsight behind me, nor have I ever been to anything like it since!"

2001 – A Big Beat Odyssey

On the opposite end of the spectrum, Fatboy Slim also did the Oscars Vanity Fair after party. In an article for *Sabotage Times* in 2013, Damian Harris (Midfield General) reminisces about this infamous "event":

"I was at the 2001 Vanity Fair Oscars Party in Morton's Restaurant Hollywood. The party is in two sections. Firstly, the Oscars ceremony is shown on a big screen while guests eat dinner. Afterwards those attending the Awards arrive at the party and move to the spectacularly decorated back room for the disco and meat raffle. For the first hour, it was just like the early stages of a school disco, people milling around the edge of the dance floor, too shy to start the dancing, except, instead of nervous hormonal teenagers, it was the likes of Tom Cruise, Renee Zellweger and Sarah Jessica Parker. The dancing did eventually get going, thanks to Helen Hunt and (I think) Sally Field with some top Auntie dancing.

"Part of the deal for any entourage is to show support for your leader, so we established a little base camp near the DJ box, shuffled around a bit and made enthusiastic party noises when needed. We would take it in turns to go on little sorties round the venue and report back with fresh sightings, whilst trying to keep the giddy excitement in check. After a brief interlude from a live band Norman went back on. Now, as a DJ, there are times when you should push the dance floor to its limits, take them on a journey with cutting edge new music - and there are times you just stick on 'Superstition' and 'I'm Every Woman'. I love the fact that he went down the more challenging route but, in hindsight, Norm should've probably played the wedding set. It did lead to the funniest moment of the night. Luke Slater's 15 minute long acid techno classic 'Waiting To Exhale' was reaching a climax and John Cleese had had enough. In full *Fawlty Towers* mode, he walked angrily across the dance floor and shouted to Norman to turn that bloody awful racket off." [52]

The Freestylers also released their second album *Pressure Point* in 2001. Despite healthy review scores, the album was not as successful as their first (*We Rock Hard*). It did, however, spawn a hit in the US with 'Get Down Massive' featuring vocals from Navigator, which reached No.16 in the Billboard Dance Charts in 2002. Further albums from them included *Raw As Fuck* in 2004, *Adventures in Freestyle* in 2006 and *The Coming Storm* in 2013. Like many people, their sound had moved on from the big beats of old, but this was however a natural evolution, not bandwagon jumping. "There was no master plan," remembers Aston Harvey from the Freestylers. "We just started making tunes using other influences that we didn't delve into on the *We Rock Hard* album. We both have very eclectic taste, so the music we were making seemed to roll out freely. We've always tried to do our own thing, which makes it easier than trying to chase a trend or style. Obviously when you start getting positive feedback that helps you push your sound even further."

One artist who was flying the flag for big beat that year, after its mainstream popularity peaked on the more mellow tip, was Manchester producer/DJ/drummer Jon Kennedy. "I joined the scene in 2001 with my first release," Jon told me in an interview in September 2017, "so was watching this year you mention from afar. I was taking a lot of acid at that time." He was good friends with fellow Mancunian Mr. Scruff, who frequently played his early output on his radio show *Unfold*. "We were friends prior to him discovering me. I had been making music for years, since the age of 12 or so, 4 track recorders etc. I handed him a CD of ideas and he played a couple on a Brighton radio station where it all started." He was picked up by Brighton label, Tru-Thoughts, and during this time, he moved to Bristol. His first three 12 inch singles and his debut album *We're Just Waiting For You* were released between 2001-2 on Tru-Thoughts. In 2003, he moved to Manchester label, Grand Central Records (run by Mark Rae), where he released his second and third albums *Take My Drum To England* in 2003 and *Useless Wooden Toys* in 2005, as well as several singles. 2007 saw him establish his own independent label The Jon Kennedy Foundation, which continues to this day, as well as recording for Organik Recordings, where he released his fourth album *14* in 2009.

The Boutique (formally Big Beat Boutique) also celebrated its fifth birthday in April 2001. To celebrate, Midfield General recorded a well-received cover mix CD for *Musik* magazine.

Big Beat's Mainstream Swan-Song

Moving on to 2002, this year saw the release of the Chemical Brothers' fourth studio album *Come With Us* on the 28th January - a total departure from the classic big beat sound, but still a very good release featuring the fan favourites 'Star Guitar' and 'It Began in Afrika'; it sold well worldwide and was even No.1 in Australia and New Zealand.

By 2002 the scene was more or less completely dead... though one really big track did slip through the cracks. Dutch DJ Junkie XL (Tom Holeknborn) remixed the at-the-time-obscure track 'A Little Less Conversation' by the not-so-obscure Elvis Presley. "It was very important to me in remixing the track that I kept the original track intact as much as possible," recalls Junkie XL in an interview for elvisinfonoet. "I wanted to preserve the original vocal as far as I could - to add something to it without altering the original. It was already a funky and uplifting track and had elements I really liked, but I wanted to beef it up. I totally respect Elvis's music and wanted to maintain its integrity." [54]

The remix was initially made for Nike's 2002 FIFA World Cup advertising campaign, and it was so popular it got a release (though the Presley family objected to the name Junkie XL, so it went under the name of JXL). It was a gigantic hit at the time, reaching Number 1 in 13 countries, and was one of the biggest selling tracks of the 2000s (as well as being the biggest selling single in the whole big beat genre) - not a bad achievement for a music genre that was getting massive persecution at the time.

Paul Oakenfold would emulate the Junkie XL formula with this own Elvis big beat remix 'Rubberneckin' in 2003. While still pretty successful, reaching No.5 in the UK singles chart, it didn't have quite the same impact that the 'Little Less Conversation' remix had. After the success of the Elvis remix, Junkie XL would later team up with Hans Zimmer several times for many big name movie scores including *The Dark Knight Rises*, *Megamind*, *Man Of Steel*, *Batman VS Superman* and *Wonder Woman*. To top this off, he was nominated for a Grammy for his remix of the Madonna song '4 Minutes'.

The Prodigy saw the release of their poorly received single 'Baby's Got A Temper'. Despite reaching the Top 5, the single did have a negative impact because of its lyrics relating to the drug Rohypnol and Liam Howlett would later disown the single (though fans disagree) and it was even removed from their upcoming album.

US big beat DJ Freddy Fresh also released a new album for BML (Brooklyn Music Limited) called *Music For Swingers* - a compilation of previous singles including stuff on his Howlin' imprint. It most notably contains the ironically titled track 'Death Of Big Beat' - a diss track aimed at the journalists who bashed the genre in its twilight years. In this track a robotic female voice loops "Big beat has changed its name to rock & roll", while also doing a roll call of several artists in the big beat genre. The track ends with the same robotic voice saying "Kiss .. my .. ass!"

Mr. Scruff also released his third long player, *Trouser Jazz*. It contained the uptempo banger 'Sweet Smoke' as well as some rather humorously titled tracks such as 'Valley Of The Sausages', 'Come On Grandad' and 'Ahoy There!', which sampled the famous Monty Python comedy sketch 'Buying A Bed'. The album sold well, with an excess of 100,000 copies worldwide and went to No.29 in the UK albums chart, as well as gaining positive review scores from the critics.

Because big beat was considered yesterday's news by most people at this stage, getting big beat records out during this period wasn't easy, an example being the debut album from an up-and-coming act called Sir Vere (formed 1997 consisting of Craig White aka Craig Hammond, Gary Morland and Stevie Vega). Their debut album, *Paranoid and Crucified,* was scheduled for a 2002 release... but didn't come out 'til 2014! Craig from the band explains: "After releasing our first single 'Have A Nice Day' on promo 12", we recorded 30 or so tracks for *Paranoid & Crucified* album. We had started to create a real buzz, which led to high level meetings with Virgin, EMI & Wall of Sound records. In the end though, we went for a new record company called E park who had big financial backing. The album was finished and due for release early 2002. Then unfortunately E park went bust after the Swiss bankers pulled the plug. This put us in complete limbo for a while. I managed, with time, to get all the tracks and artwork back, and I managed to get Ravesta records in Florida to get it out in 2014. We are about to reissue this album, as well as its sister album *Paranoid Originals Remasters*. It's a very good insight to how the early scene was."

Big Beach Boutique Returns

July 13th 2002 saw Fatboy Slim probably play his most well-known gig - Big Beach Boutique II, which was part of Brighton's 2002 City of Culture Festival, which took place during their bid for the European 2008 Capital of Culture (they lost out to Liverpool).

"It was a major thrill, though equally a headache," remembers Fatboy Slim for the Rane website in 2013. "Both the police and myself knew that there were far too many people there to guarantee safety, but equally knew it would be more dangerous to cancel it and have that many people walking the streets unhappy. It truly felt like a Woodstock of my generation, seeing all the tribes descend on one place to celebrate their music and culture."[55]

As stated by the Fatboy, getting the gig to finally happen was a real struggle. The Sussex police were keen on shutting the gig down, fearing it potentially could cause a tragedy. The event did however come off, as they feared that a riot could take place if the gig didn't happen.

It was another free entry event - this time, 250,000 happy punters attended (four times the estimated crowd size) and it was even front page news in the UK. In the *Guardian* broadsheet in 2004, Norman reminisces: "The thing is, I can only see the first 10,000 anyway." [56] The night was a celebration of all that was great about British dance music, and it even got its own DVD release later that year. Support came from Midfield General and John Digweed - Midfield General also opened for Fatboy during his Kick 'N' Spin tour during the Japan/South Korea 2002 World Cup and coincidentally the biggest gigs of his career happened in this one year. "It was pretty terrifying... I tried not to look up," recalls Damian Harris, the Midfield General, when speaking to me in 2018. "I would never usually prepare a set beforehand, but this was the first time I felt I should, as I knew I only had an hour. Once I got going I was fine. I'm still very proud that I played the Dahlbak remix of 'The Real Jazz' to that many people."

Norman's now-legendary set began with a pre-recorded spoken introduction from former Freak Power singer Ashley Slater naming various Brighton landmarks over a droning sound (taken from 'Phunkee Wind' by Track 7 slowed down to 33 RPM) then announcing 'Welcome to Brighton Beach', while Fatboy baby scratched into the happy funky house anthem 'It Just Won't Do' by Tim Deluxe. The following 90 minutes contained some notable bangers from the likes of Mint Royale,

Basement Jaxx, Kid Creme, Layo & Bushwacka, a Nirvana bootleg (not included in the DVD version for clearance issues), Glen Masters, a mashup of 'Born Slippy NUXX' by Underworld with 'Right Here Right Now', the rather potty mouthed 'Star 69', a Space Cowboy (formally Loop Da Loop) cover of Prince's 'I Would Die 4 U', and rather amusingly, climaxing with a special big beat re-edit of... girl band the All Saints (I'm totally not kidding!). The set was supposed to be two hours but ended early due to safety concerns from the police, but that didn't dampen the spirits of the punters (or Norm for that matter).

Big Beach Boutique would later become a ticket-only event, and was moved to a smaller part of the beach in subsequent years (2007 and 2008), and was later revitalised under the slightly-revised name of 'Big Beach Bootique' at the Amex Football Stadium in June 2012.

Sometimes I Feel So Deserted - The Wilderness Years (2003-2010)

Wilderness Hits

In 2003, nothing of any major significance happened in the world of big beat... except for the Propellerheads announcing that they would take a hiatus, and The Chemical Brothers doing a re-working of Aussie pop star Kylie Minogue's hit 'Slow'.

The year did however see the launch of Skint artist Cut La Roc's brand new label, Rocstar Recordings. "From our debut release (on vinyl I might add!) from my 'Many Styles Vol 1 EP' to our current day digital releases, we have always strived to be as much of a cutting edge record label as possible. Not strangled by genre, we pride ourselves on having a musically open minded approach with the label, and our back catalogue is testament to this," stated Cut La Roc in an exclusive interview for this book. "Rocstar Recordings was launched back in 2003 by Marco Distefano and me. I had just come out of a deal with Sony/Skint and me and Marco shared a love for cutting edge music. We pooled together our resources and the label was born, initially releasing music from prolific artists like Chad Jackson, The Beat Traffikers (9 Lives The Cat) and of course myself; we also managed to hook up featuring vocal artists such as Kool Keith, Rasco & Donald D to name a few. Fast forward to today and the label is still signing and releasing new and exciting music. The label is something we're extremely proud of, and we're pleased to be able to offer up and coming acts (and of course established acts) a firm base on which to release their musical creations across the planet."

2004 was a much busier year for big beat, considering its status as a "dead" genre of music. Fatboy Slim released his fourth studio album, *Palookaville*. This album was more vocal-orientated and featured Damon Albarn from Britpop band Blur, the return of P-Funk legend Bootsy Collins covering the Steve Miller track 'The Joker', Justin Robertson from Lionrock (singing rather than producing), Sharon Woolf, US Rapper Lateef the Truth Speaker and local Brighton band Jonny

Quality. In an interview for Andrew Drever in 2004, Norman told him that "I personally think it's [*Palookaville*] the best thing I've ever done, and a lot of people are saying that, but it's kind of scary, because if it gets as big or bigger than *You've Come a Long Way, Baby*, I'd probably run a mile. It's not what I wanted. You don't want to be in the goldfish bowl. I never wanted to be the centre of attention all the time – only some of the time!" [56].

Justin Robertson (formerly of Lionrock) remembers how he got the singing gig on the *Palookaville* album in an interview for this book in January 2018. "I've known Norman for a few years and used to drunkenly sing to him when we were at various parties, much to my subsequent embarrassment - still it was fun at the time! So when he was putting his album together, he asked if I would like to contribute a song, which I was more than happy to do. It's a song about heartbreak, there is an acoustic version somewhere that is quite melancholic."

Also helping him with sample sourcing on the album was none other than Fatboy superfan, Aldo Vanucci:

"Imagine a boy who has never drunk alcohol, never smoked weed, never took drugs, all he did was go to parties and clubs and buy records. Everyone has influences in their life and musical heroes, Norman was all my heroes rolled into one, I bought everything he made, everything he sampled, every song he mentioned, I went to every gig I could, whether Beats International, Freak Power or DJ gigs as himself or Fatboy Slim; on nights off I would drive to Brighton and hear him DJ whenever I could. So to get to supply samples which made up four tracks for *Palookaville* then to co-write a song on his Greatest Hits literally meant the world to me."

Sadly, despite the album's high quality, it only made a fairly modest impact, and got a mixed reception from critics at the time, despite featuring some great tracks such as the Outkast-esque 'Wonderful Night' and the John Martyn sampling 'North West Three'.

The Prodigy also released their fourth album *Always Outnumbered Never Outgunned*. Despite strong sales, reviews at the time were mixed, but over time, the release has been vindicated with French house act Justice including it in the *NME* list of '100 Great Albums You've Never Heard'. This album was more guest vocal heavy with appearances from Princess Superstar, Juliette Lewis, Ping Ping Bitches, Kool Keith (again), Louis Boone, Paul Jackson, Matt Robertson and most impressively, both Noel and Liam Gallagher from Oasis on the final track,

'Shoot Down'. The album also contained the banger 'The Way It Is', which sampled the famous Michael Jackson song 'Thriller'.

The Freestylers had a big hit single in 2004 with the P-Funk inspired track 'Push Up' - from humble origins as a white label, to a big hit, which went to No.22 in the UK singles charts, and was No.1 in Belgium and No.2 in Australia and The Netherlands. Aston Harvey remembers how this really funky track came to be: "I had an idea to do an updated 'P-Funk' sounding track. I'd been sitting in the studio all day working on another track, which wasn't sounding very good, and just as I was about to leave for the day I had a brainstorm. I always loved the song 'It Doesn't Really Matter' by 'Zapp' and wanted to make a track influenced by this, so quickly got the initial idea done in about an hour, which I then sent to my publisher to see if we could get a song written over it.

"About two weeks later we got this song called 'Push Up' back, and we were absolutely blown away by it. I was convinced it was a hit, there was nothing like this out there. Just to test the water, we decided to press up some white labels under the name 'Ghetto Funk' and it worked a treat as nobody knew it was us at first. We were hearing that some people thought it was Justin Timberlake or even Prince himself. We started getting daytime Radio 1 play from Jo Whiley, who started championing the track even before it was sent to them officially, to get on the play list, so we knew we were onto something potentially big then. Subsequently the track got released in Europe and Australia which went on to be massive for us, with help of a great video that was shot on Oxford Street and featured a super hot girl that everyone used to ask us about, but I couldn't answer, as we weren't there at the video shoot. Haha. "

The super hot girl in question in the 'Push Up' video was dancer Kate Eloise Whitfield.

Another big beat tune to get recognition that year was one by Max Sedgley (formally of Organic Audio), who was signed to Rob Da Bank's label, Sunday Best. His tune 'Happy' (not to be confused with the Pharrell Williams track of the same name) was a minor hit in the UK charts, where it reached No.30 in July 2004, and was used by ITV for their coverage of the Euro 2004 football tournament, as well as a promotional advert for one of the most acclaimed video games of all time – 'Super Mario Galaxy' for the Nintendo Wii in 2007. The tune also got a remix from Fatboy Slim. "I have to say it felt great!" Max told me in February 2018. "I'd had a bit of success before with getting

216

my music on to TV shows in the US, but nothing like what happened with 'Happy'. To get Fatboy Slim to remix it... one word: awesome!"

One band which was big in 2004, drawing heavily from the big beat sound at the time, was popular Brighton indie band The Go! Team, formed in 2000. Their sound was heavily inspired by the eclecticism of big beat - mashing up garage rock with hip-hop, Bollywood, blaxploitation funk, plunderphonics etc. Their single 'Ladyflash' was a minor UK hit reaching No.26 in the charts, and their debut album *Thunder Lightning Strike* was certified gold by the BPI. The band have become a cult favourite and continue to this day, with three more successful albums and several singles.

2004 also saw DJ Touché becoming the main resident at the Boutique (January 23rd to be exact). The year also saw him do the BBC Radio 1 Essential Mix where he mixed everything from early electro house, obscure German krautrock, hip-hop acapellas, former Wiseguy DJ Regal's Bronx Dogs banger 'Closing in', indie rock such as Primal Scream... and even the Sugababes! This incredibly diverse mixture, while not 100% big beat, did feel like the movement's spirit was still alive in 2004, thanks to Touché's open minded eclecticism as a DJ as, by then, clubs (for the most part) returned to a more homogenised music policy. He would later return to do the Essential Mix in 2009 - this time under his (at the time) latest pseudonym, Fake Blood.

The mid-2000s was also the time the nu-skool breaks movement was at its peak. By then, the genre's name was shortened to simply "breaks", as it wasn't exactly "nu" at the time. One popular sub-genre from this movement was tech-funk, which was pioneered by former big beat producer Simon Shackleton (Elite Force), who in an interview for this book in September 2017 remembers the genesis of this new sub-genre:

"Yeah that's an interesting one really, and it dates back to a personal distaste I'd always had for straightjackets and the tedium of genres. I've always seen music as music - it's either good, bad, or indifferent to me - and I've always had an independence of spirit that never bowed down to playing within restrictive tramlines. The term 'tech funk' was designed to be a wilfully 'grey' term that was inclusive rather than exclusive; it was supposed to tell people that they could expect a range of non-genre-specific styles ranging from electro to techno, to breaks to house music, and all points in between."

The following year, 2005, saw the release of The Chemical Brothers' fifth album *Push The Button* on January 24th, and featured the massive hit 'Galvanize' (No.3 in the UK singles charts) - a Middle-Eastern inspired track in the unusual time signature of 6/4 and featuring guest vocals from Q-Tip from the seminal hip-hop outfit, A Tribe Called Quest. The album also featured guest spots from Tim Burgess from The Charlatans on the big beat throwback track 'The Boxer', Kele Okereke on 'Believe' - a live favourite, and also Anna-Lynne Williams, Anwar Superstar and The Magic Numbers.

Outside of *Push The Button*, 2005 was another quiet(ish) year for the big beat ship; rumours of a big beat revival were circulating but never came to fruition (probably because of the continuing Top 40 hits from the Big Three). Mint Royale released their third album *See You In The Morning* in August of that year, which is notable as two of the tracks ('Something New', and 'Little Words') featured guest vocals from someone who, three years later, would become a massive star in her own right - Welsh songstress Duffy (does anyone know what happened to her?). The album also featured the famous breaks re-working of the Gene Kelly song 'Singing In The Rain', which was famously used in a Volkswagen Golf advert, as well as the winning entry on *Britain's Got Talent* in 2008 by dancer, George Sampson - the track reached No.1 when it was re-issued that year.

At the end of the year, Japanese big beat artist Hideki Naganuma composed another big beat-inspired soundtrack to a video game, this time for the highly popular 'Sonic Rush' - one of the many entries in the massively successful Sonic The Hedgehog series by Sega, released for the Nintendo DS handheld console in November of that year. "It's an honour to be a help to Sonic games," remembers Hideki. "Since I became an official employee of Sega, I was thinking that I wanted to do music for Sonic games someday. But actually, it was so tough to use the Nintendo DS internal sound chip and sequencer. The data capacity was only 256k per song. It was challenging work. But I had so much fun to make catchy music for kids."

Its big beat inspired soundtrack was met with critical acclaim, with the popular gaming site Gamespot calling it "all very fitting and very catchy" [58] - the site 1up.com also called it "bright [and] buoyant" [59]. The game would later sell over 3 million copies worldwide. For much of Sonic's fanbase, which consists mainly of young children, it was their first exposure to big beat and sampling; hopefully it will bring in a new generation of younger crate diggers in the process!

The next year (2006) saw the release of Fatboy Slim's greatest hits album *Why Try Harder*. The compilation was a success, and featured two new cuts, the laid-back 'That Old Pair Of Jeans' and the proto-Moombahton track 'Champion Sound' both featuring US West Coast rapper/singer Lateef, who previously provided vocals on 'Wonderful Night'. The latter track sounded quite ahead of its time, and wouldn't feel out of place with the likes of Diplo and Major Lazer. To promote this release, Fatboy headlined the very first RockNess Festival, at Loch Ness in Scotland on the 24th June, to a sell-out crowd. RockNess carried on with Fatboy Slim returning in 2008, 2010 and 2013 to headline, but sadly, that was the last one, because the festival ended that year due to increasing competition.

On August 6th, The Boutique celebrated its tenth birthday at the Turnmills venue in London. Headlining was techno legend Dave Clarke (not to be confused with Dave Clark from the Dave Clark 5) and French house act Cassius. Also appearing on the night was old Wiseguy favourite, DJ Touché. Not long after that, Gareth Hansome pulled the plug on the Boutique after ten years of legendary parties.

New Big Beat Acts Start to Emerge and Old Acts Re-emerge

2006 also saw the formation of a new big beat (and also funky breaks and later nu-funk/ghetto funk) label called Breakbeat Paradise Recordings. Set up by BadBoe from the USA and Wiccatron from Denmark, Breakbeat Paradise Records (or BBP for short) started life as a website in 1996, but ten years later would become a fully-fledged record label. In an interview for this book in November 2017, Wiccatron told me how this label came to be:

"We started as music buddies over the web and made music in the same vein, so it was always easy to share ideas with each other's music. I started helping Boe out with graphics, as he maintained the website Breakbeat Paradise. It started as a huge community of breaks enthusiasts and breakbeat warriors. You were able to upload tracks and share with others, and get sample packs. You could also participate in contests held, and I remember we were judges at these breakbeat music contests. At the time, I read, and had, almost every issue of the *Future Music* magazine, and I read about the advantages of online music services like CD Baby and the micropayment system as a way to put out music - we see it today with streaming services like Spotify and iTunes.

"We started visiting each other and making music and tracks over a few days together. Later on, we also lived in the same city, which made things much easier. While I studied to become a teacher, we would hang out and spend time in BadBoe's basement, equipped to put beats and raps together, and to hang out with the local aspiring rappers and hip-hop lovers and friends. I presented the label idea to BadBoe, and gave him copies of all the material I was reading about the digital distribution business. BadBoe was sure this idea could materialise, and that his business degree now somehow would come in handy. A few months later in 2006, I was designing early versions of the BBP logo as we see it today. We also wanted to still have both a web shop and community, and made the shorter spellings of Breakbeat Paradise with BBP and BBP Recordings."

In the chapter 'Beats International – Big Beat Overseas', I mentioned an American funky big beat duo called the All Good Funk Alliance (Frank Cueto and Rusty Belicek). In 2006 they had the honour of one of the biggest support slots imaginable – opening for Mr. Dynamite himself, James Brown, at a show in Baltimore at the Ramshead Theatre. 2006 was a great year for the AGFA, as it was off the heels of their acclaimed debut album *On The One* and its follow-up *Social Comment* with Swamburger and Alexandrah, as well as running the popular indie funky breaks label Funk Weapons – the icing on the cake was opening for the hardest working man in showbusiness in his final year before he left this earth to the great Funk Train in the sky.

In March 2018, Rusty from the band told me what it was like opening for the Godfather of Soul:

"We were honoured to open for James Brown on May 29, 2006, shortly before his death on December 25, 2006. We had been DJing and producing as All Good Funk Alliance for a while by 2006, and we had just dropped 'Super Jam', which was one of our biggest selling records. Calls came in and we were playing a bunch of little gigs but nothing super big. We had played a few times for a promoter and DJ from Baltimore named Love Grove or LG as we called him and he knew our sound.

"Apparently, James Brown's people didn't want an opening band as it was a small stage and they wanted to keep the timeline tight. LG said he thought about all the DJs he knew and thought we would be perfect for this gig. This was a great opportunity so we took the gig and started putting together records. The first two songs of our set were Tom Tom Club's 'Genius of Love' which we mixed into Grandmaster Flash and The Furious Five's 'It's Nasty' which of course samples 'Genius of Love'. From there it was a blend of newer midtempo songs like our own 'Call it' with songs from Flow Dynamics, Fort Knox Five and Dr. Rubberfunk with classics like Roy Ayers etc. They set us up on the balcony overlooking the stage and allowed all our friends up in there with us, I think we had 15 or so people with us.

"Shortly before the show one of James Brown's people came up and told us, no James Brown songs and no rap. We were a little shocked, as we had planned on playing that Grandmaster Flash song as our second song. We looked at each other and said let's just play what we have and see what happens. So, we begin and people start filling the space, and we look down and people are actually dancing and getting into it. It was pretty magical, given most shows with no opening band or just DJs opening up you don't usually see a lot of dancing, but they were feeling our set. About 3/4 of the way through the set one of our crew accidentally dumped a beer all over our record crate. Like the good friends they are, they all jumped in and got the beer cleaned up and had it somewhat contained so we could finish off without a hitch.

"Near the end, we got a nod from the band and as we faded down, they started up with some really funky instrumentals. We had a great vantage point so we could see that they opened up the back door to the alleyway and a limo pulls up and out comes James Brown with a younger white woman and he strolls straight in and grabs the mic and takes control of the band. We watched the whole show from our awesome balcony and were in awe of his energy at his advanced age, it was a really stellar show. We really wanted to meet James Brown, so we made our way down to the stage after the show. But when JB finished and bowed, he walked right back down the hallway into his limo and he was out. His band leader came over and told us they really liked what we played and that we were a great opening act, which was a cool moment. It almost seemed shocking that he died later that year, because the energy he put off on that show, he was still on fire."

On New Year's Day 2007, Fatboy Slim hosted Big Beach Boutique 3. Like the first two, this was on Brighton beach (but moved lower down the beach) - unlike the sweaty sunshine of the first two, this time it was in the cold, damp rainy New Year weather, making it very difficult to mix (the records were constantly skipping). Supporting him on the night was a French pop house DJ who would end up super famous in his own right - David Guetta. Poor Dave's CDJ decks were damaged midway through his set, and he had to finish early. Unlike previous BBBs, this one was ticketed, and only for people with Brighton postcodes, to avoid the over attendance of 2002's event. Despite these minor hiccups, the event went well, without any newsworthy incidents.

In 2007, Stateside Records (a major label) signed Liverpool artist Sonny J, a big beat artist who received some moderate buzz at the time. His debut single 'Can't Stop Moving' unfortunately flopped in the charts, reaching only No.80, but the single did see a renaissance a year later, when a fan published a popular viral video on YouTube featuring clips from the old 1970s Jackson Five cartoon series - this time it reached No.40 in the UK singles charts, and was even No.8 in Japan. His debut album *Disastro* was released in June 2008, and spawned the singles 'Enfant Terrible' and 'Handsfree (If You Hold My Hand)' with the late soul queen Donna Hightower. Unfortunately it wasn't commercially successful, and critics at the time gave it a bashing - it is presumed he was dropped by Stateside not long after that.

2007 also saw The Chemical Brothers release their sixth album *We Are The Night* on the 27th June. Despite moderately mixed reviews, the album was successful commercially, going straight in at No.1 in the UK albums charts, and featured hit singles - the insanely catchy 'Do It Again' and the humorous 'The Salmon Dance' with rapper Fatlip from The Pharacyde. The album also won a Grammy for 'Best Electronic/Dance Album' at the 50th Grammy Awards and was certified gold by the British Phonographic Industry.

It was also the year my own musical career would take off. Before Soundcloud, Spotify etc. the de-facto place to share your music online in the mid-late 2000s was MySpace (don't look for my account - it's not there anymore, I shut my MySpace down in 2013). I've never been comfortable with social media (still feel this way) and I wasn't sure how my own compositions would be received on the World Wide Web circa 2007 when I was 19. On the 12th of July of that year, with much persuasion, I set up a MySpace account, and immediately starting mass friend-requesting big beat legends such as Fatboy Slim, Chemicals, Prodigy, Touché from the Wiseguys etc. While Touché sent some positive words back, the response that really stood out was when I sent the link to my page to Freddy Fresh, and much to my surprise, he responded

222

back - and he loved what I'd done, although it was very different to what he'd been putting out: it was more chillout, hip-hop instrumentals with a 'trippy' vibe. This was incredibly heartening, and by the end of the month he signed me to his Howlin' Records label... my debut album *Cosmic Child* was born and I made four subsequent albums on his label that were mostly big beat orientated, with other genres thrown in to keep it interesting.

2007 also saw Theo Keating (formally DJ Touché from The Wiseguys) try out a new pseudonym, Fake Blood, to produce music. At the time, nobody knew who he was, with a lot of people trying to guess who this mysterious Fake Blood was. "One person thought it was Tiësto," said Theo Keating in an interview for *DJ Mag* in 2012. "You couldn't tell which ones were serious guesses and which ones weren't, it was like names out of a hat really. Random stabs in the dark. I thought it was pretty obvious myself, but apparently not."[60] After the massive underground success of his single 'Mars' in 2008 there was even a blog at the time with conspiracy theories to who this "Fake Blood" was. It was officially revealed in a January 2009 issue of *Mixmag* that the former Wiseguy was the man behind the name (though people had already found out when he started performing live).

Moving on to the year 2008, Ste McGregor's DJ alias Kidda graduated from music video director/cartoonist to being a fully fledged Skint artist. Unlike most Skint artists at the time, who were aiming for a more house and techno direction, Kidda recognised Skint's roots and his tunes were a beautiful hark-back to the big beats of old. His debut album for Skint *Going Up* was released in July of that year to critical acclaim. One of the singles of the LP, 'Under The Sun', was snapped up for a popular advert for Bacardi, but unfortunately, the royalty money wasn't there. "All good til EMI snapped up all the money," stated Kidda in an interview with me in September 2017. "Capitalism is a pigsty. Aside from that, there was a simple magic to making a tune in the front room and travelling around the world, only to arrive back in your front room and see and hear it on the telly." The track also received a popular remix from "Fidget" house producer, Herve, that was championed by many DJs at the time. Another single from the album, 'Strong Together' was a hit in Europe and charted in Italy, Belgium and Holland, but despite the success Kidda never reaped the rewards. "I didn't really feel or see any of that success here, they made their own video and occasionally

I'd hear about chart positions or do a live phone call thing, but ultimately I was still broke and riddled with doubt and anxiety about the future at that point." Kidda would eventually release another album for Skint called *Hotel Radio* in 2011.

In Europe it seemed that a serious attempt at reviving big beat was on the cards...

2008 was the year the record label BigM Productions formed in Germany - wait a minute - a big beat label in 2008? Yes, that's true. The label was set up by Michael Grub (Mick from Production duo Mick & Marc) and was a spin-off of the underground house label Twin Town Productions. The first releases were a series of big beat remixes of popular songs called the 'BigM Bootie' series, which were well-received among people in the 'nu-funk' scene of the time. The label developed a strong cult following with signings from RamSkank, Chris Awesome, Telephunken from Spain, Ewan Hoozami, DJ Prosper, Funkanomics, Stickybuds, Rams Le Prince, myself and even big beat veteran Freddy Fresh did a couple of releases on the label.

Ramon Ott, who produces under the name of Rams Le Prince, was a signee to BigM Productions back in the day, and remembers his time working with the label when I spoke to him in November 2017:

"I used my own radio as a platform to test my music for the perfect target audience. I think almost all the people I know from the big beat scene was through an initial contact through the bigbeat.ch site. One of those contacts was Mick from Mick & Marc. He contacted me to publish some music on the Big M label after he heard some tracks of mine on the radio. I never met him in person... he was always a very friendly and nice guy (as all the people I got to know in the big beat scene). I mean, he even pressed some vinyls with my crappy music on it. For that alone I will be forever grateful."

Unfortunately, the label folded in 2013, but in its five years of existence it brought some of the best bangers from the big beat scene post-mainstream popularity.

Another new big beat artist emerged that year with PulpFusion (aka Terance Thoeny from Switzerland), who would start to develop a big underground following by 2009. "I always played guitars, I was maybe 13 years old (1987) when I started playing guitars..." remembers Terry. "I always wanted to produce my own stuff, but it was too complicated and too expensive to do it on your own... the only thing I did at that time was on tape! I think I started in 2006 with the first releases coming out

224

in 2008. The Prodigy and The Chemical Brothers changed the way I saw and played music, I have a lot of influences, big beat is just one of them, and, to be honest, big beat is a collection of influences which stand alone."

He also set up his own label that year called Pig Balls Records.

"I didn't find a label at that time, so I decided to do my own," he recalls. "Maybe my music was way too hard, crazy, noisy and/or dirty for the masses... That's why we did Pig Balls Records. The first release was a single I did 'Turn On Tune In and Drop Out' and it is still such a monster track. For me it's definitely big beat, and the Miles Philips remix is still one of my favourite tracks... I mean, whoah, what a killer track!"

The label would see releases from the second wave of big beat artists, which included Johnny Pluse, Ewan Hoozami, DJ Prosper, RamSkank, Ictus and myself.

Other big beat revival labels that would emerge in 2008 would include Timewarp Records in Greece and XLNT Records and Tru-Funk, both based in Poland.

It was also the year when big beat's successor genre, breaks (formerly nu-skool breaks) finally started to wane, almost exactly 10 years since big beat itself fell from grace. The genre evolved to sound almost identical to electro house, except without a 4/4 beat (this style was initially nicknamed plod, as the beats sounded like a horse trotting). To quote Lee Mathias aka Stepping Tones: "As a budding DJ, I felt this was good enough for me and carried my record bag through the beginning of the noughties. It would seem that the nu skool breaks scene was eventually consumed by the deep house mafia, but luckily the evolution of funky breaks rolled through a muddy hole in the fence."

Midfield General also released his second (and so far latest) album *General Disarray* in April of 2008. The album contained the disco and early hip-hop inspired single 'Disco Sirens' as well as collaborations with Miami Bass pioneer M.C. Ade, Ralph Brown, Pat Stallworth, Lucky Jim, Robots in Disguise and the return of comedian Noel Fielding on the track 'Seed Distribution'. Unlike his big beat-centric debut album, this release was more inspired by the sounds of the time, but keeping the distinct Midfield General feel. "When I was making my last album," recalls Damian on his bio on the Skint Website, "it was very tempting to try and make tracks influenced by the new music and current sounds that I find so inspiring. Every time I'd get blown away by a new Justice, Sebastian or Switch track, I'd have a go at making something like that. But usually to no great success! And it made me realise that I shouldn't neglect the characteristics that are, well, me. Their influences are in there, but I would like to think I kept my own identity." [49]

The year also saw Mr. Scruff release his fourth album *Ninja Tuna* - this album was notable for containing the track 'Kalimba', which had a second life because it came with every single computer which ran the Microsoft Windows 7 Operating system - making it, in many ways, Mr. Scruff's best known and best selling track, and technically outselling every artist mentioned in this book - thanks to 'Kalimba' alone! The album also contained the uplifting ode to music 'Music Takes Me Up' with the very talented Alice Russell on vocals, as well as another collaboration with Roots Manuva ('Nice Up The Function') and collaborations with Quantic, Danny Breaks, Andreya Triana and Pete Simpson. The album also received strong reviews as well as decent sales selling 30,000 in Europe alone (though a lot more if you count all the "sales" of 'Kalimba').

Also in 2008, Fatboy Slim hosted another Big Beach Boutique event in September on Brighton beach, which was another ticketed event. It was also the year when the extraordinary popular film came out, the Batman movie, *The Dark Knight*. The reason for mentioning this is because Japanese big beat duo The Boom Boom Satellites' track 'Scatterin' Monkey', was used in the scene where Batman apprehends the gangster Sal Maroni in a nightclub. Good to see that big beat was still living on in Gotham City circa 2008! Also from the same movie, The Crystal Method got the opportunity to remix the score with their reinterpretation of 'Why So Serious?' (The Joker's Theme), which was issued by Warner Sunset Records in December. Other remixers included Paul van Dyk, Mel Wesson and Ryeland Allison.

For those who loved Junkie XL's remix of Elvis Presley's 'A Little Less Conversation' (or Paul Oakenfold's 'Rubberneckin' for that matter), Italian producer (and obvious Elvis super fan) Spankox (Agostino Carollo) did an official remix of the Elvis song 'Baby, Let's Play House', which, ironically wasn't a house track but - shock horror - a mainstream big beat release in 2008; to quote Bill Murray in *Ghostbusters:* "cats and dogs living together, mass hysteria!" Surprisingly for a big beat remix in 2008, this tune was a hit in Europe, reaching No.1 in Italy, No.2 in Spain, and charted high in Scandinavia too, though it was sadly ignored by the UK, where it reached only a measly No. 84 in the

UK singles charts. The success of this remix in Europe lead to another Elvis/Spankox remix, this time 'Blue Moon Of Kentucky' and then, wait for it - a full album of Elvis/Spankox remixes called *Re:Versions* in September of that year. A second volume called *Re:Versions 2* was released the following year, and a whole slew of Elvis/Spankox remix albums, which include *Re:Loaded*, *Re:Live*, *Re:Generation* and the more generically titled *Re:Mixes* - there was even an Elvis/Spankox Christmas remix album (I don't even think I've listed all of them!) Surprisingly, Spankox's discography does contain tracks that aren't remixes of Elvis.

Norman Cook started a new project in 2008, under the name The BPA (Brighton Port Authority). It consisted of collaborations with punk legend Iggy Pop, the very talented David Byrne from the Talking Heads, UK rapper Dizzee Rascal, Emmy The Great and even fellow producers Ashley Beedle, Justin Robertson, Cagedbaby (Thomas Gandey) and Norman's sound engineer Simon Thornton providing vocals. The album (2009's *We're Going To Need A Bigger Boat*) was sadly greeted with commercial apathy, and has unfortunately since been forgotten in the sands of time (though it did bring a good mashup of the Iggy Pop track 'He's Frank', a Monochrome set cover and 'Washing Up' by Thomas Anderson, which Norman uses in his live sets). The only real attention the album got was for the controversial music video for the track 'Toe Jam' (the David Byrne and Dizzee Rascal track), which was a recreation of a 1970s softcore orgy, which played around with censor bars, and featured a cameo of a naked Fatboy Slim (!).

The following year saw Fatboy do another project with David Byrne called *Here Lies Love* - a musical about Imelda Marcos, wife of Filipino dictator Ferdinand Marcos. "David Byrne is one of my childhood heroes and to work with him was fantastic," stated Norman for the *Daily Record* in 2008. "Woody (Norman's son) really likes David Byrne and does puppet shows for him and charges him a dollar." [71]

The album for the musical was more successful than the BPA, and received favourable reviews. It featured guest vocals from Florence Welch (from Florence & The Machine), Cyndi Lauper, the late soul queen Sharon Jones, and even country star Steve Earle. The musical would later tour during the decade to decent receptions in both the UK and USA.

As the 2000s closed, The Prodigy released their 5th album in 2009, *Invaders Must Die*, which was both a critical and commercial hit and had the singles 'Omen' and the title track. One would imagine with the success of this album, the big beat ship could rise again... but it didn't. The same year also saw The Prodigy curate a one-day music festival called Warriors Dance Festival in Tokyo Japan. The lineup included, as well as themselves, Pendulum, Hadouken!, MSTRKRFT, AutoKratz and South Central. The success of this led to the festival returning in 2010 at Milton Keynes Bowl in the UK, with their headline set making it to DVD and Blu-Ray the following year, under the title *World's on Fire*. The festival returned again in 2011 at Kalemegden in Serbia and the latest one in 2013, again in Serbia, but this time at Novi Sad.

While big beat may have "died" in the 2000s, several of its artists were keeping the spirit of the genre alive in the first decade of the 21st century.

Back Once Again . . . The Possible Return of Big Beat (2010-Present)

The Spirit Lives On

Many other short-lived genres have had lives that have paralleled that of big beat, most notably the dubstep sub-genre brostep, which saw tremendous success from around 2011-2014 (aka the sub-genre that most people think of when they think of dubstep). Pioneered by DJ and producer Rusko, the most popular act in brostep was US artist Skrillex (Sonny Moore), who was also part of the new wave of 'Stadium Jocks' (people like David Guetta, Calvin Harris, the late, great Avicii etc.) lumped into the "EDM" craze. If anybody were to listen to brostep and big beat back to back, you could probably see where brostep got some of its inspiration from - the loud, intense and sometimes obnoxious synths, the hip-hop vocal cut ups - you can thank big beat for that. "I had a moment watching Skrillex the other week," muses Norman Cook in 2012 for the liner notes for the Ministry of Sound Compilation *Big Beat Anthems*. "Dubstep's [brostep] got the hooligan elements with the energy of dance music. It's definitely the niece and nephew of big beat." [72].

"Yeah, I think [Skrillex] he's a pioneer," stated Liam Howlett from The Prodigy in a Q&A Session for *Spin* magazine in 2015. "The whole EDM thing in the U.K., it's so boring. But in America you have people like Diplo, Skrillex, they're the guys who started the new wave of it all." [19]

Brostep had a very similar history to big beat, becoming extremely big for a few years before being laughed at, and discarded like an old sock. Brostep was in some ways the spiritual successor to big beat. Coincidentally, Skrillex is signed to a label called Big Beat, a New York label that was set up in 1987 by Craig Kallman and is part of Atlantic Records.

Another scene that had a lot of big beat's spirit was the electro house sub-genre, fidget house (aka blog house, as the tunes would often get bootlegged and posted for free on blogs at the time). It was big in the underground club scene around 2006-2009 and, like brostep, had some of big beat's tropes. One of the scene's biggest DJs (or somebody who got lumped into the genre) was Fake Blood, formerly DJ Touché from The Wiseguys, but probably the most well-known DJ from the fidget movement was a guy called Hervé (Joshua Harvey), who is a Fatboy Slim super fan and, like Fatboy, goes under different names for different projects, such as Voodoo Chilli (for disco house) and Action Man (for techno). In fact, Fatboy Slim and Herve did an acid house track back in 2010 called 'Machines Do The Work' - a Fatboy (and Herve) track that sampled a Jim Henson (of Muppets fame) documentary on technology.

The author (Rory Hoy) with big beat legends, Cut La Roc and Jon Carter circa June 2011 when we DJed together at the Big Beat Reunion night in Preston. Photograph by Tom Hoy

By the mid-2000s, the big beat scene was merely just a relic of the mid-late 1990s... until the year 2010. At the turn of the new decade, Cut La Roc started a brand-new club event that would revitalise the spirit of big beat called Big Beat Reunion at the Concorde 2 in Brighton. The first night was on the 23rd April 2010 in aid of the Rocking Horse charity, and the bill was a big beat fan's dream come true including

Bentley Rhythm Ace, Cut La Roc, Jon Carter, Midfield General, Hard-knox, Wildstyle Bob Nimble... and even Fatboy Slim doing a special classic big beat vinyl set.

"The Big Beat Reunion shows literally came about on a whim to see my old gang, Lindy (Hardknox), Norman, Jon Carter etc. so what better idea than to have one last blast at Concorde 2 (which then actually led on to a string of shows)," remembers Cut La Roc in an interview for this book in October 2017. "So I made a few calls and it just happened! Have to say, the Brighton show was one of the best nights I'd had for a long, long time; the weather was perfect, sunny all day, warm at night and it just felt like it was 1997 again, lots of happy smiling people in a sold out venue, just like it was back in the day. It was lovely to meet you, Rory, when we both did the BBR gig in Preston."

For me it was a great honour DJing alongside such big beat legends as Cut La Roc and Jon Carter at the Big Beat Reunion in Preston.

Posters for Big Beat Reunion nights

Simon Shackleton aka Elite Force, who was in the big beat group Lunatic Calm, reminisces about when he played at a Big Beat Reunion night in Brixton, London in 2011:

231

"I remember it being a struggle to source the music in a digital fashion… in retrospect I should just have played off vinyl, but I wanted to put together a bespoke set that involved lots of re-edits as well as moving through the gears from mid tempo up to peak time mosh pit. It was a fun night for sure and the response was great."

Also in 2010, breaks DJ Timmy Schumacher recorded the big beat tribute track 'Bring Back Big Beat' for Rocstar Recordings, which gives out a roll call of all the classic big beat artists set to a retro big beat backing. "I'd always wanted to pay homage to a really special period in my musical development," remembers Schumacher in an interview with me in September 2017, "and I kind of knew Cut La Roc would have the balls to release it, so I just followed my instinct. I wanted to speak to the people who were as deep in it as I was. The smashy drums and acid line are definitely inspired by Fatboy Slim's early material (e.g. 'Big Beat Soufflé'). I did the breakdown roll call using the voice generator on the Monkey Mail website because I thought it sounded cool - kinda 'refined'."

The start of the new decade saw The Chemical Brothers release their seventh album *Further* on the 14th June. Despite positive reviews and healthy sales figures, the album was banned from being featured in the UK albums charts because it contained a competition to win an iPad and UK Chart Regulations forbid prizes being used as enticements to buy albums. It was nominated for a Grammy, but lost out to the self-titled debut album from La Roux.

The new decade also saw a new big beat artist getting a buzz from the major labels - Brighton DJ/producer Benji Boko (Benjamin Gordon). "I remember getting a NOW CD compilation when I was a kid with all this pop music on it and 'Gangster Trippin' by Fatboy Slim was on there," Benji told me in January 2018. "I was totally obsessed with it. I think I just liked the explosive, raw energy of big beat. Its energy applies to a lot of the music I'm still writing now, even though it's not big beat."

He got his big break at the end of 2010, when he shared the bill with Calvin Harris, Deadmau5 and Justice at a New Year's Eve party at the famous O2 Arena in London. "It was amazing. That night holds a special place in my heart," Benji remembers. His eclectic and electric DJing style grabbed the attention of BBC Radio 1 DJs such as Zane Lowe and Rob Da Bank, who considered what he did to be unique. As well as recording solo stuff for Tru-Thoughts, including his debut album *Beats, Treats & All Things Unique*, he was commissioned to remix a slew of major label artists - these included Rizzle Kicks, Chiddy Bang, Pixie Lott, Nelly Furtardo, Maroon 5 and Little Dragon - a remix that went to No.4 on the worldwide Hype Machine Charts in 2013, as well as doing remixes for big beat veterans Fatboy Slim and Kidda.

Despite being a popular act on the festival circuit in the early-2010s, including acclaimed sets at Glastonbury and Bestival on multiple years, his production and DJing output slowed down in the middle of the decade, and he decided to rename himself IamBenji and became more hip-hop orientated, as well as pursuing a side career as a photographer. His second album is on schedule for 2018.

2011 was a quiet year on the big beat ship, but Norman Cook did produce a hit tune for UK hip-hop duo Rizzle Kicks with the infectious 'Mama Do The Hump', which reached No.2 in the UK singles charts, making it the band's biggest hit, and one of the best party tunes of the decade... and there was much rejoicing from Fatboy Slim (and Rizzle Kicks) fans (Yay!).

Also in 2011, after 22 years in the business, DJ Regal (Wiseguys & Bronx Dogs) decided that enough was enough and it was time to hang up the headphones and switch off the decks. "Upon returning [to Australia] and after a brief first year of some nice gigs at the Big Chill, plus joining my homeboys on Icecold FM every Friday night, laying down funky breaks and hip-hop classics, my mental state pretty much collapsed, and it took me a few years to deal with it," remembers DJ Regal. "But nowadays, thanks to my little lady, who has saved my soul, I am at peace with being retired from it all. I still hunt down new discoveries of old music online virtually every day and the size of my Spotify playlists will make your eyes water! These days it's Blue Note, euro 70s, soul 45s, Cuban & Afro rhythms that soothe the soul and get me going. I'll never stop searching for an unheard breakbeat or dope sample, but they're for me and my homies only now."

The next year, 2012, saw the release of the Ministry of Sound compilation *Big Beat Anthems* on the 26th March. Despite featuring some classic big beat tracks including some of the great "B-Cuts" from the genre, such as 'That Green Jesus' by Mr. Natural, the compilation did feature several non-big beat tracks, but this was sort-of excusable, as the non-big beat tunes they did select fitted in well with the compilation (such as hip-hop classics 'Jump Around' by House Of Pain and the 45

King's 'The 900 Number'). A similar CD was issued in 2016 on Sony Music called *Big Beats (38 Essential 90s Anthems)* which contained several tracks in the genre, but this release was even more loosely connected with the big beat movement, and was mainly a release to capitalise on the 1990s nostalgia craze of the 2010s.

2012 was also the year Fatboy Slim held two more Big Beach Boutique shows under the slightly revised name of 'Big Beach Bootique' - this time at the Amex Football Stadium in Brighton on the 1st and 2nd of June with support coming from Carl Cox, DJ Fresh, Annie Mac, Nero and more. Both nights were big successes - attracting over 40,000 people - considering the heavy rain in Britain during the summer of 2012, and the fact they clashed with the Queen's Diamond Jubilee; it even saw a DVD release later that year, and remains one of the shows Fatboy is most proud of. He also did a set at the London 2012 Olympics closing ceremony. The Chemical Brothers also composed a special track for the Olympic events called 'Velodrome'.

Late 2013 saw Fatboy Slim have another hit single in collaboration with house producer Riva Starr and voice actor Beardyman, with the acid house throwback, 'Eat Sleep Rave Repeat', which reached No.3 in the UK singles charts. Part of the success of this lies with a remix from Scottish commercial EDM Producer, Calvin Harris, who, at the time, was at the height of his fame (as well as the whole "EDM" thing being at its peak).

Big beat producer (and drummer for Bentley Rhythm Ace) Fuzz Townsend made a comeback that year - though not in music! This time, he was the presenter of the popular TV show, *Car SOS*, which airs on Channel 4 and the National Geographic Channel and has been running since 2013 - a show focusing on vintage cars. "I sort of went via a circuitous route from writing and recording, to owning a bar, to college lecturing and freelance bus museum merchandising, to magazine writing, commissioning and editing to workshop owning to TV presenting," he told me. "I just roll with it."

April 2014 saw Skint Records being bought out by major label Sony BMG. In the same month, a brand-new big beat label was formed in Russia by Alex Hornet called Criminal Tribe Records. This label would end up being one of the most successful big beat labels in recent times with several of its releases topping the Beatport Breaks charts and with tracks on this label getting support from several of the genre's veterans such as Fatboy Slim, The Prodigy and The Crystal Method. "I founded

Criminal Tribe Ltd in April 2014," stated Alex in an interview for this book in November 2017. "I was the initiator of this project. Together with me, helping to build the project, was a number of our first artists, who I met on big beat internet forums and in other communities. The person who created this label together with me was Dmitry FB Force Shinkarchuk. Thanks to him, we rightfully became a fully fledged recording studio. I was responsible for creating the private company and all the promo and info, and he was responsible for the sound. A number of friends were an invaluable help in the initial stages of the project, such as designer Eugene Wertos Georgiev, with whom we developed our replacement logo, and drum and bass producers, Dmitry Dizzy Muzzy and Anna Anngree."

Mr. Scruff also released his fifth album that year, *Friendly Bacteria*, a moderate departure from his trademark sounds, with a more sparse and electronic sounding palette, with many of the tracks featuring vocalist Denis Jones (as well as Vanessa Freeman and Robert Owens).

Late 2014 saw internet radio broadcaster Digitally Imported securing a channel dedicated solely to big beat, run by US big beat mega fan, Frank Smith.

"I began throwing events and spinning records in 2005, and noticed over the course of time that the big beat sound was all but nonexistent in the whole rave universe and eventually something just kind of clicked," remembers Frank. "I started delving deep into the genre around 2007-2008, and decided I needed to do whatever I could to save and preserve this amazing movement. I started buying up all the CDs, vinyl and mp3s I could, and scoured the internet for all of the independent artists I could dig up, eventually discovering the Russian big beat scene on promodj.com, and a bad ass producer by the name of Countertop Hero who really inspired me to dedicate my skills to big beat music. At some point I was basically creating an archive for the whole big beat genre, because who else was going to do it?

"The idea to pitch a station to Digitally Imported Radio came in 2014. At that point, I had amassed about a half terabyte of indie big beat music, several crates of big beat vinyl and several boxes of big beat CDs. They were all about the idea, and had been unsuccessfully looking for a big beat guy for years. It was a perfect fit. Finally all of this incredible music could be dusted off for the masses to hear.

"The highlights so far from running the station are too many to count. The recurring mixes from Rory Hoy and Wiccatron have been nothing short of spectacular. Russian mega-producer Mercenary (SPB) doing a promo mix for the station is definitely up there on the list. A 4.5 hour recording of a Criminal Tribe Records party in St. Petersburg, Russia is definitely up there as well. My favourite part is the tradition of throwing Eazy-E – 'Merry Muthafuckin' X-Mas' into the rotation every December."

Moving forward, 2015 saw the release of two big albums from big beat legends The Chemical Brothers and The Prodigy. The Prodigy's sixth album *The Day Is My Enemy* came out on the 30th March and was recorded over a timespan of six years. Reviews were mostly positive and the album went straight to No.1 in the UK albums charts, outselling its competitors such as Ed Sheeran and Sam Smith. It was hinted that this may well be their final full-length release, as Liam Howlett stated in some interviews that they would switch their focus to EPs instead - though in September 2017, it appears they changed their minds, as their Facebook page announced that they will be releasing a new album in 2018 via BMG Records.

The Chemical Brothers' new album, *Born In The Echoes* (their eighth) was released on the 17th July 2015 and debuted at No.1 in the UK albums chart, making them the dance act with the most number one albums ever in the UK. The album was successful with both critics and audiences and included the hit single 'Go' featuring Q-Tip, who had previously done vocals on 'Galvanise' ten years before. The tune was used on the E3 trailer for the Playstation 4 video game 'Need For Speed' as well as 2016 adverts for Cedar Point.

2015 also saw Freddy Fresh release a new album - the very ambitious and diverse *Play The Music*. The album featured guest vocals from dancehall legends Tanto Metro & Devonte on three of the tunes (including the opera-meets-electro hip-house inspired title track), Ashley Slater and Scarlett Quinn's 'Kitten & The Hip' project with the very catchy and commercial sounding 'Epic Fail', Matisse (whose real name is Jon Carter, but not THAT Jon Carter!), rapper Mikey Dredd, and even Freddy's own children as well as production collaborations with Andy Ictus, Countertop Hero and myself.

"Working with Freddy was an honour, and a lot of fun," remembers Countertop Hero, who worked with Freddy on the track 'I Don't Like You' on the album. "Knowing that my music has been heard by someone whose albums I've bought and someone whom I consider myself to be a fan of, is exciting, but then to have them reach out to you to

236

collaborate is just an encouragingly surreal experience. The ideas shared between us really inspired me, influencing and promoting some very creative directions that seemed to come from the ether. Being able to include myself among the illustrious list of Freddy Fresh collaborators is something that I hold in high esteem, as is being part of Freddy's prolific catalogue of music."

Despite a decent promotional campaign and healthy support for the accompanying music videos from MTV in the US, the album didn't receive the recognition it deserved.

The next year, 2016, was a quiet year big beat-wise. Fatboy Slim celebrated the 20th anniversary of his debut album *Better Living Through Chemistry* in September, appropriately at the Social bar in London with support from Damian Harris (Midfield General). He played the album in its entirety.

Sadly, Michiuki Kawashima of Japanese big beat act Boom Boom Satellites tragically died of a brain tumour on the 9th October 2016, and the band disbanded with their final release being the EP 'Lay Your Hands On Me'. Mint Royale also disband that year with their final single coming out, entitled 'Time'.

The following year (2017) was another quiet one for team big beat, and mainly consisted of Hannah Grace covering Fatboy Slim's 'Praise You' for a Lloyd's Bank advert, and pop star Katy Perry sampling the Fatboy Slim classic 'Star 69' in her song 'Swish Swish' . The year did however (other than a couple of low-key Fatboy Slim singles) see the announcement, as mentioned before, that The Prodigy are going to release a new album on major label BMG records in 2018... so maybe a big beat revival might come after all, seeing as it's 20 years since big beat peaked.

Moving on to 2018, Wiccatron (who runs Breakbeat Paradise Records with BadboE) and PulpFusion (Pig Balls Records) set up a new big beat label called Big Fat Mama Beats Records. The first release on this new label in February 2018 was an EP by myself, Rory Hoy, 'The Other Side Of Forever' featuring collaborations with Quincy Jointz from Germany, Under Influence from Russia, Pecoe from Australia and Jack & Jointz from Germany. The label also saw releases from PulpFusion, Wiccatron, Under Influence and One Dead Jedi (aka DJ Spatts from Environmental Science).

The Chemical Brothers also announced that a ninth studio album is in the works, not to mention that Fatboy Slim's magnum-opus *You've*

Come A Long Way Baby got a reissue in March of that year. Fatboy also played a sell-out gig at London's famous Alexandra Place venue, and The Chemical Brothers sold out two shows there scheduled for October in record time!

Big Beat Memories

Despite the fact he doesn't really play Big Beat anymore, Fatboy Slim still, to this day, sells out arenas and headlines major music festivals all around the world (and you still hear the odd classic of his used in an advert). Both The Chemical Brothers and The Prodigy are still major draws, with both releases and live shows. Also, classic big beat duo Bentley Rhythm Ace have some big plans for 2018: "We are trying to sort out a 21st anniversary re-issue of the first album with some bonus tracks from the early singles," Richard March from BRA told me in December 2017. "Hopefully it will be released spring 2018. We are also looking at some festival shows for next year."

Both Skint Records and Wall of Sound are still going strong today. In an interview for this book in January 2018, Damian Harris recalls some of the highlights of his time as label manager of Skint: "I have quite a few proud moments. I was lucky enough to work with some phenomenal artists, so I'm very proud of pretty much all their records and videos. However, getting number one single and album was pretty special, seeing the 'Praise You' video for the first time. The Lo Fidelity Allstars selling out the Astoria was a pretty triumphant night. X-Press 2 and David Byrne on *TOTP* was fun, and being able to give my dad a gold disc was also nice."

"Time is immaterial with many things that have happened," remembers Jon Carter from the liner notes of the 20th Anniversary edition of Fatboy Slim's *You've Come A Long Way, Baby* album. "It makes you think, how much happened in 88-90, how much has happened since – we have new scenes, style revivals and now 20 years on, we're in a period of looking back at classic albums, and reliving them. We've all been on different journeys and orbits since dance music exploded – 30 years since acid house, 25 years since *Screamadelica* by Primal Scream, 20 years since big beat. Those days were the very heart of everything that's good and pure in music. When we played on the beach in Rio, these waves on the beach turned into waves of people. The technology was turning from hardware to software. The music itself rode a wave, like the surfing scene in *Apocalypse Now*, with rockets and helicopters – DANCE MUSIC IS COMING! You could say It seemed like a victory, but we weren't fighting anyone – it was a victory for the people. It was the dance music Beatles... The Big Beatles!" [105]

Freddy Fresh, when I spoke to him in September 2017, states how the big beat genre is timeless and can still be relevant today.

"Frankly, as I am also a DJ and I always look for killer tunes, it didn't surprise me in the least that this music still relates and resonates with the public. When the UK music magazines said that big beat has 'moved on' and is no longer relevant, I likened these comments to sounding like saying 'Water is no longer in fashion'. Just absurd. When most everyone jumped ship, I continued making big beat. In fact my Howlin' big beat record label was formed the same year as big beat's proclaimed 'death' as you well know, seeing that you are one of my star artists Rory, as was Andy 'Ictus', Dynamo Productions etc."

"I rarely played at any 'big beat' events, although I had some good gigs with Jon Carter and The Chemical Brothers," remembers Mr. Scruff. "For me, the mid-late 1990s were about playing as many different gigs as possible all over the world, meeting people, and learning from the travel and DJing about all this amazing music, and where I fitted into that crazy mess. Much of my travel was done with Grand Central Records and Ninja Tune. One of my favourite memories was from a Ninja Tune night in Zurich. We saw Lee Perry around town in the day, and invited him to the gig. He turned up at the venue, and as I was the only DJ who had any reggae records with me, he came and sang/chatted over my DJ set for half an hour, mostly about the internet and how it could be used to communicate with Jah. Properly surreal, and a real night to remember."

"That whole period was massive wasn't it?" remembers Barry Ashworth from the Dub Pistols. "I think it spawned more hits than any other genre of dance music in that period. The amount of success was massive, though not many acts from that period have survived. After the initial big beat backlash, the album (*Point Blank*) came out - and we got called 'The sound of Norman Cook's sweaty jock strap' but we were lucky enough to strike a deal to go off to America - we kind of avoided the pitfalls of everyone else, who dropped off. Went over to America for four years - came back and it was still alright to be us, and I think we're still having our best moments now. We're doing some of the biggest shows we've ever done, and the whole thing's just going off for us, and we've had our biggest-selling album to date."

When I spoke to Pete Houser (Bassbin Twins) in April 2018, he told me what his favourite big beat memory was:

"Always the music itself: music you'd hear and instantly feel changed. It was a collision of so many things that I loved rolled into one."

"I got to play most corners of the globe and see sunrises in more countries than I ever thought I'd visit, all thanks to playing big, silly, fun party music that was all about good times," remembers Canadian big beat DJ, Myagi. "There was no better way to spend my twenties. I think the highlights for me were always getting a chance to work or tour with people I'd idolised as a teen. Phil Hartnell from Orbital, The Crystal Method guys, Freddy Fresh, etc... these dudes provided me with so much happiness. Having been retired for a few years now from music, and living the glamorous life of a small restaurant owner, I can honestly say it was a lifetime ago that these things happened for me... and I'm even more amazed now than I was at the time."

"I've made some amazing friends over the last ten years DJing, but my proudest moment was when my friend Emil from Romania (who has booked me to play there a number of times in Bucharest) asked me to be his best man at his wedding. Such an honour," reminisces James Glenton aka Lebrosk, who now writes for *Mixmag*.

"Pride is a strange thing for Countertop Hero. I feel an overwhelming sense of pride with each track I create, but there's always a feeling of wanting more," Countertop Hero told me in February 2018. "Specifically, to create more, to create something new, something better than I've ever done before. The moment I realized that Freddy Fresh had contacted me, was quantifiably the proudest I've ever been of my music; however it absolutely ignited the desire to do even more. The songs that promoted this moment were important, and were arguably the best I had created so far, but I knew—even in that moment—that I could do better. I could hear the sounds, melodies, and beats of that next level. I believe that my proudest moment as Countertop Hero has yet to happen, and it feels like it's right around the corner."

"Fatboy Slim blowing me a kiss in the middle of one of his sets was pretty cool although I turned several different shades of red," remembers Max Sedgley on his favourite big beat moments. "My DJ set in the

Dance Tent at Glasto 2007 was very special for me… I always preferred live gigs with the band, but this was the one time when I had a total blast behind the decks. It helped that there were about 10,000 people in the tent absolutely losing it of course."

The power of big beat is still out there. In fact (with the help of Grace Jones, famous soul diva), Wall Of Sound founder Mark Jones proposed to his future wife, DJ Lottie, at the Secret Garden Festival, as he told to me in December 2017: "With Grace Jones - they say 'Never work with your heroes', but I thought - fuck that! She was amazing, but interesting to deal with - I got her to headline the Secret Garden Festival, there's a track on the album she did for Wall of Sound (*Hurricane Dub*) called 'Williams Blood' - I got Grace to dedicate the song to Charlotte (Lottie) - I got the visuals on each side of the stage to read 'Are you going to be here, Jones?' because that's the chorus, and Lottie looked at it and was like 'What?', and I went down on one knee and proposed - how could she say no!"

Norman Cook aka Fatboy Slim is still an inspiration to millions everywhere. In fact he helped a fellow fan find his dreams of becoming a DJ himself. Dave Winship, who runs a special charity for vulnerable people called Inspired Support, based in Newcastle, has a roster of DJ tribute acts, special volunteers taking on the roles of famous DJs. One of them is Fatboy Slima (real name Joe), who's a tribute to Fatboy Slim, and when the man himself heard about what Inspired Support do, Norman endorsed what this amazing charity does as explained by Dave himself:

"When we set up Inspired Support we had a man called Joe who came to us and asked us for support to change his life. Joe had been going to traditional institutionalised day services, and therefore had been isolated from the joys of real life. Joe had a love of music, but had not been exposed to the joys of dance music. We introduced Joe to DJing and we did a project about Fatboy Slim. Through the research, Joe absolutely loved the music and imagery of Fatboy Slim and decided that, as part of the project, we should recreate the sights and sounds of a Fatboy show.

"After a long enjoyable process, we had Joe DJing in the style of Fatboy and we were recreating visuals and stage sets to match the fun and ethos of the original man himself. The concept of Fatboy Slima was born and a chance booking enabled Joe and the Inspired team to take the show to a live audience. Mighty Dub Fest was the first time out for

Fatboy Slima, and we did not know how it would go down. We built the stage set on a budget, using a lighting setup that we had cobbled together, but that created amazing visuals utilising lasers and smoke, and projectors that we had borrowed to stream the visuals. The stage was adorned with smileys, we had dancers with smiley masks and an MC to raise the crowd. Was the concept going to work??

"At 10pm Fatboy Slima took to the stage in front of a small gathering of festival goers. By 10.30pm the crowd had swelled to close to a thousand. The crowd watching the main stage headline act had heard rumours of what was happening on our outdoor stage. The main marquee emptied and Fatboy Slima had stolen the show. What can only be described as a landmark moment had been created – the likes of which are reserved for, well, yes, the likes of Norman Cook. The crowd bounced, sang and came together as one to the sounds of Fatboy Slim courtesy of Fatboy Slima.

"In 2014 Stuart Mair, who was a commissioning manager in West Sussex Council, contacted us to find out more information about Fatboy Slima and Inspired Support. When he realised what amazing work we were doing, enabling people with autism and learning disabilities to develop their lives and experiences, he asked if we minded him telling Norman about our work. It turned out that Stuart was one of Norman's very good friends, and he thought that Norman would love our work and the Fatboy Slima concept. Stuart contacted Norman and relayed a message to us that Norman had seen our videos and that he would be in touch on his return to the UK.

"Months went by and a parcel arrived at Inspired Support. On opening the parcel, I was blown away to see a load of signed merchandise and a personally written letter from Norman to Joe. Norman had put a lot of his own personal time and effort in to sending us the parcel of goodies, but it showed what a top man he is, and it created the beginnings of a bond between our small social care organisation and one of the best DJs in the world. Norman gave his best wishes to Inspired Support and Joe and the work we do and basically gave his backing and love to the Fatboy Slima concept, finishing the letter saying "hopefully one day we can DJ together" - now there is a true legend.

"The following year Norman was DJing at Majorca Rocks when I was due to be on a family holiday in Majorca. Joe and the rest of the guys at Inspired insisted that I met up with Norman and gave him some of Inspired's merchandise as a thank you for his gift to us. It just so happened we had hoodies that were emblazoned with smileys and the strap line 'Eat, Sleep, Inspire, Repeat'. Norman invited me and my girl-friend to the show for a meet and greet. Norm made us VIP and it was an absolute pleasure to meet the man himself - they say never meet your heroes, but this man is an absolute gent and a top man. Norm put the hoodie straight on and took great interest in the work we do at Inspired. Norm went on to blow Majorca Rocks away in true Fatboy style.

"In 2016 Fatboy Slim announced a big outdoor show in Newcastle and this proved to be the ideal opportunity for the guys, and more spe-cifically Joe, to meet Norman. Norm organised for the guys to be VIP at the show and a meet and greet was all lined up, Fatboy Slim was going to meet Fatboy Slima for the first time. The meet and greet was amazing, with Norm making the guys very welcome and chilling with them back stage. Once again the friendship and bond was further sealed between us all. Fatboy Slim went on to play an amazing set with the Inspired team raving in the VIP lounge.

"What can we say about Norm, he is a top man, a DJ icon, a UK superstar and an Inspired Legend."

Is It Time For a Revival?

Do I think big beat will ever get a serious mainstream revival? It would be really cool, but there are a few hurdles. As big beat is usually very sample-heavy and sample clearance is ridiculously expensive (in fact, even some major pop stars sometimes use replayed or soundalike sam-ples if they want to "sample" anything) it makes it almost impossible to reproduce the authentic classic sound. However, now would be the best time to try it, as the genre is pretty much forgotten about by the general public at large (except for Fatboy, Chemicals and The Prodigy) - for many people, if big beat came back tomorrow, for them, it would be a brand new type of music.

As stated previously, there are still a number of people producing big beat music to this day - one of these is Jason Ard from the USA, who goes by the DJ name of Old Flame. In an interview for this book in September 2017, Jason explains how his love for big beat got him to produce music of his own: "I was a bedroom DJ for years, as you should be. I started playing out as Old Flame around 2007 and have been nearly every weekend since. Big beat was a huge influence on both my DJ and production career. I released my first EP in 2013. I have followed up with several more, collaborating with artists like Rory Hoy and RamSkank."

Another artist who keeps the big beat torch going is Bristol producer Ewan Hoozami. When I spoke to him in November 2017, he told me how the spirit of big beat lives on in his music and how big beat influenced his own musical output:

"Hugely, even if I didn't really know it at the time. I was young, inexperienced and short of technical skill - just fooling around with my MPC, looking for my sound and my place. I started looking to make music that was more propulsive than the head-nod beats of the hip-hop guys I was mixing with, which I attribute to the big beat music I was DJing with, as well as stuff like DJ Format and RJD2. Big beat had this sense of fun that was lacking from a lot of music at that time, too. I always wanted to facilitate dancing and good times, but I couldn't understand house music, and didn't want to play D&B.

"Coming from Bristol at that time, there was really only two other options - reggae or hip-hop/funk (later dubstep, too - which I hated). When big beat came along, it showed me it was possible to make proper dance music using hip-hop tools and techniques. If it influenced my production, it was even more an influence on my DJing. I'd never play a 100% big beat set but would almost always finish on it as it was so fun and such a natural progression from hip-hop. I loved the way people in that scene were so open to eclectic and unusual sounds, too. It was a fun period in music and certain big beat records didn't come out of my DJ bag for years."

"Whether the name 'big beat' sticks around or not doesn't matter, because there will always be artists looking to do what big beat set out to do: try new things and have fun while doing it," American DJ Josh Gaudioso told me back in 2017.

"It's funny that you don't realise how dramatically your present is influenced by your past until you actually go back and revisit your history," remembers Australian DJ, Kid Kenobi. "I've been doing a lot of that recently with some of my 'classic' mixtapes. It's insane how much I took from that era and how much of it is still locked away deep in my subconscious. Fatboy Slim's remix of 'Renegade Master' still has one of the most epic breakdowns and build ups of all time and deep down, I'm probably still trying to recreate that in everything I do today! Plus beyond actual production, I think there is a certain tough, yet fun, party sensibility created by big beat that still gets me going today and that you can certainly hear in a lot of my productions. That ethic hasn't left me after all these years, despite the many shifts in music culture."

Will the Propellerheads reform and maybe release their super-long-awaited second album? I asked Alex Gifford from the band on the matter, and this is what he had to say:

"Funny you should say that... well, we never actually broke up, so it wouldn't really be a reunion, more of a reactivation. I think the secret to what we did back in the day was that we really enjoyed doing it — we had the motivation, means and opportunity, and the motivation was really strong. We were on a mission to put some fun and individuality back into the dance music scene, which at the time felt like it was taking itself way too seriously. Together with others, we achieved that, and it nearly killed us. That particular motivation became weaker when it stopped being fun. Other people took up that baton and ran with it in their own ways, which is how it should be. But times change, people change, and new challenges emerge. So, yes, watch this space."

Despite big beat's contemporary maligning, if you're lucky, you may sometimes hear the odd big beat tune in a modern DJ set. "I've occasionally heard back-room and warm-up DJs admit that they just play as many big beat records as they can get away with!" Lee Mathias stated in a 2018 essay.

But will there ever be a proper big beat revival? I asked a few people to have their say on the matter:

Fatboy Slim - Not really, the whole point of big beat was to break away from the norm and mix genres and sound different, but it ended up just all sounding the same. The evolution continued with breaks and dubstep etc. but you gotta keep moving forward...

Freddy Fresh - If all the songs and music from the artists I just mentioned [in this book] were suddenly heard drowning out the Kanye Wests and Justin Biebers here in the USA, I promise you the infectious melodies and crashing beats would quickly find favour. In my personal multi dimensional reality, I still dance each night to big beat... but of course the crowds are pretty small in my dreams... Big beat still kicks ass. The best way for a revival is to have many of the original artists get together and just have a good time and dust off the old records and play the ones that they had produced but were afraid to release due to the

245

power of the UK press declaring it dead. I'll bet there are many unreleased JAMS waiting to still be played. I often come across insane samples today, as I sell rare records and 45s for a living, in fact I am working on another book on breakbeats and killer riffs for producers.

Aldo Vanucci - All music comes around again in waves, I read that it's usually 20 years, so big beat is due, I would say though, that it doesn't come back like before, if you look at the current crop of acts like Disclosure who were influenced by 90s house and garage, they put their own spin on those influences, so it would be producers who grew up fondly remembering big beat, and then doing something new with it. Big beat was also very wide influences-wise. Yes, there were a lot of hip-hop samples and styles, but if you take a look at the sound the Chemicals came out with, what Norman put out, labels like Blowpop, it is a very wide ranging sound. Big beat had everything from funky little jazz samples through to raging massive Stretch and Vern tracks. It also had a cheeky sense of humour a lot of the time, it was a very fun clubbing era, but also a reaction to what was around at the time, so maybe the new era of big beat needs something to go against.

Frank (All Good Funk Alliance) - Music is so cyclical and I wouldn't be surprised if it reappeared, but with a different skew on it.

Rusty (All Good Funk Alliance) - I'd like to see it come back, but I feel like it's still alive in certain aspects of EDM culture. Look at Jersey Club music, it uses breaks and cut up vocal samples, you could probably say it wouldn't really be a thing if big beat wouldn't have happened.

Ben Willmott (*NME/Guardian* journalist) - Let sleeping dogs lie I say. The best things about big beat culture - the freestyle nature of the DJ sets, that crossover with rock, funk and hip-hop - were things that I don't think have ever left dance music culture ever since. They'll probably be around forever. So, yes to the spirit of big beat, but no to a revival. You'll see elements of it in new dance music movements for generations to come.

Simon Shackleton (Elite Force/Lunatic Calm) - Well everything in music is cyclical so I wouldn't rule it out. That being said, I can't see myself being involved in it really. Times have changed and I'm not one for dwelling in the past.

Deadly Avenger - I'm too old to bring it back… :) !!!

Kidda - I'm not sure about revivals, it's always an attempt to re-frame the past and I'd rather that stayed where it was. I always think about the Mods in Brighton, the old fat lads driving about on scooters that were too small for them a long time ago, and how true modernists were concerned with culture being pushed and moved forward - like when The Style Council started making house records and pissed off a load of people who only watched *Quadrophenia* .

I love some of those records, they still sound as fresh and immediate as the day they came tumbling out of the Akai, and I'd rather maintain my relationship with those tunes as and where they were in my life, rather than try to make those times happen again. In terms of new music, it's the same old adage - there's only two types of music, good and bad. For me, it's more important to just keep creating without worrying about whether it's from one genre or another.

Danielsan - Well, Prodigy, Chemical Bros and Fatboy Slim still headline big shows, so why not? The people who were into it are at a good age to reminisce. Nostalgia sells! I watched Oxide and Nutrino, DJ Luck and MC Neat and Heartless Crew do daytime sets at the Port at Bestival and they went down a storm. You could do the same with 3 or 4 big beat DJs, though they have to be party jocks. Big Tunes all the way.

Scanty Sandwich - I think you're the man to do it Rory – big beat's future is safe in your hands!

To put my two cents on the matter - reviving an old music genre successfully is not an easy task, as you have to observe what worked and what didn't work with the genre and see where it went wrong the first time round. If big beat was to have a proper mainstream revival, I would say yes to the music itself, as well as the 'anything-goes' DJing ethos, but no to the boozy subculture that went with it. Like Mark Ronson & Bruno Mars with 'Uptown Funk!' in 2014, I would love to see a big beat throwback tune become a gigantic hit in the charts, maybe get a pop star of the moment to do the vocals with heavy airplay and promotion to go with it, and viola! - Big beat's back, Baby!

Big Beat Top-5's and Top 10's

In this chapter, I have contacted several people who were involved in the Big Beat Scene, and asked them to give me their Top-5 Records (and some Top-10's and even a few Top-20s) in the genre, in alphabetical order - here is what some of them had to say . . .

Aldo Vanucci Top 10 (Good Living Records)

1. Dylan Rhymes - Naked & Ashamed
2. Lionrock - Rude Boy Rock
3. Capoeira Twins - Stump Juice Theme
4. Deadly Avenger - Live at the Capri
5. Midfield General - Coatnose
6. Scanty Sandwich - Because Of You
7. Cirrus - Break In
8. ETA - Casual Sub (at 33RPM)
9. Monkey Mafia - Retreat Wicked Man
10.   Krafty Kuts - Gimme The Funk

Aldo Vanucci's Top 5 Norman Cook Tracks

1. Pierre Henry - Psyche Rock (Fatboy Slim Malpaso Mix)
2. Cheeky Boy - Once In a Plastic Time
3. Fatboy Slim - Michael Jackson
4. Deeds Plus Thoughts - The World's Made Up Of This And That (Fatboy Slim Remix)
5. Stretch & Vern - I'm Alive (Fatboy Slim Remix)

Alex Gifford (Propellerheads) (Wall of Sound)

Mmmm that's a tricky one too, cuz I'm not sure how you would define Big Beat. Well, here's a list of five tracks which, in one way or another, loom large in my memory of the mid to late 90s, when it might be said I was busy being a full-time Big Beater (Big Beatist? Big Beatle?)

House of Pain: Jump Around — for the original possession with intent.
Masters At Work: The Nervous Track — for the sublime, rolling deepness.
David Holmes: My Mate Paul — for the relentless slinkiness.
The Wiseguys: Ooh La La — for the shameless largeness.
Soul Coughing: Super Bon Bon (Propellerheads remix) — for the bobsled-run insanity.
I know that the last one is one of our own remixes — it's just that, for me, it perfectly captures that moment in time.

Alex Hardee (CODA Agency) Top-3

1 The Freestylers - Ruffneck
2 Monkey Mafia - Lion In The Hall
3 The Wiseguys - Ooh La La

Alex Hornet (Criminal Tribe Records, Russia)

1. Ils - Cherish
2. The Prodigy - Breathe
3. Fatboy Slim - Right Here, Right Now
4. Ils - No Money on Trees
5. The Chemical Brothers - Hey Boy Hey Girl

The All Good Funk Alliance (Funk Weapons, Super Hi-Fi, USA)

1. The Prodigy - Outer Space
2. Fatboy Slim - Give the Po' Man a Break
3. The Dust Brothers (aka Chemical Brothers) - Chemical Beats
4. Propellerheads - Take California
5. M.S.P. - Done and Dusted

Andrew Divine (Hi-Karate) (Scotland)

"I'm struggling a bit here and it's possibly due to the 'Big Beat' tag. I keep pulling things out and thinking "nah, that's a Techno track" or "nah, that's a Drum 'n Bass track" and at Hi Karate, we'd just mash everything up - Hip-Hop, Breaks, Funk, Indie, Big Beat, Techno, Reggae etc. I suspect if we continued the night now, we'd probably just cast the net even further. It was always more of an "eclectic" night, than a "Big Beat" night - but here's five tunes which (in my opinion) could be classed in that genre..."

1 DJ Shadow 'The Number Song' (Cut Chemist Party Mix) (FFRR 1997) 'Entroducing' is obviously a hugely important record in Big Beat's evolution, and whilst the album track is a quality cut'n'paste mash-up, Cut Chemist just takes it to a whole new level.

2 Jedi Knights 'Catch The Break' (Evolution 1997) Looping a sample from Dennis Coffey's 'Theme From Black Belt Jones' and, inevitably, adding an infectious break - this is the sort of track I loved mixing the original sample sources in and out of...

3 Plaid 'Scoobs In Columbia' (Black Dog Productions 1991) Possibly an "accidental" Big Beat record, from dons of "intelligent" Techno Black Dog, when they were still making Breakbeat/Rave tracks like 'Virtual'- except here they used Latin samples, making a Breakbeat club anthem.

4 Hiroshi & Kudo feat. DJ Milo 'Return Of The Original Art-Form' (Major Force 1988) Way ahead of its time, and obviously influenced by Steinski's 'Lessons' but possibly even more club-friendly. A DJ secret weapon when Mo Wax finally re-issued it in 1997.

5 Depth Charge 'Shaolin Buddha Finger' (Vinyl Solution 1994) J Saul Kane is undoubtedly one of the true pioneers of gritty underground sample based instrumental Hip-Hop (or what we now more commonly refer to as "Big Beat") and the 'Nine Deadly Venoms' album was a defining moment.

Andy Ictus (Howlin' Records)

1. The Chemical Brothers - Chico's Groove
2. Freddy Fresh - La Lyrica
3. The Prodigy - Poison
4. The Wiseguys - Start The Commotion

5. 2 Inda Bush - Nutty Drumstick

Bassbin Twins (Pete Houser) (Bassbin Records, Skint Records, Southern Fried Records)

1. Quite
2. Honestly
3. Everything
4. Norman
5. Cook

Bee&See (Thomas Binzegger) (X-Tra Records) (Switzerland)

1 Ceasefire – Trickshot
2 Mekon – Fatty's Lunchbox
3 DJ Tools – Rusty Goes Gaga
4 Fatboy Slim – The Weekend Starts Here
5 The Chemical Brothers – Leave Home

Ben Willmott (Music Journalist/Author – NME/Guardian etc.)

1. Fatboy Slim - The Rockefeller Skank
2. The Wiseguys - Ooh La La
3. D.O.S.E. featuring Mark E Smith - Plug Myself In
4. GTO - Dub Killer
5. TC1992 - Funky Guitar

Captain Funk (Sublime Records, Model Electronic) (Japan)

1. **Stretch 'N' Vern presents Maddog - Get Up! Go Insane! (Rock 'N' Roll Mix)** - I played this so many times that the crowd almost misunderstood that it was my own remix. Of course, it was not.
2. **Bassbin Twins - Two Turntables and a Crate of Skint** - It gets me back to the old school.
3. **Freddy Fresh - Chupacabbra (Bassbin Twins Remix) (USA)** - I loved the building middle part.
4. **Fatboy Slim - Punk To Funk** - I think the title represents the spirit of Big Beat.
5. **Captain Funk - Home Sweet Home** - the biggest floor-killer at the

251

party (as well as 'Twist & Shout').

Countertop Hero (Howlin' Records USA)

"This one is tough, as I have so many favorites that I want to give shout outs for ('Fire Like This', 'A Cellar Full of Noise', 'Blowin Ya Brainz', 'Morning Lemon', etc.; the list keeps going). I'm also excluding some music that is incredibly important to me, but only because it doesn't quite fit in the Big Beat genre (like the Avalanches). These are in no particular order" -

Fatboy Slim – Mad Flava
'Halfway Between the Gutter and the Stars' was an album which I eagerly counted down the days and minutes until its release. I begged my parents to drive me the forty-five minutes into the city so I could buy Fatboy's newest. I bought it at K-Mart. Immediately popping it into a portable CD player, the album was great but different from what I had expected. Intently absorbing the new songs, the album came to 'Mad Flava'. As soon as the piano dropped in the intro, I felt immediately at home in the dripping Funk. This song is the "I-don't-care-I'm-just-here-to-have-fun" anthem of what Big Beat really means to me.

Mint Royale – Space Farm
Songs that make me feel more than a single emotion really mean a lot to me, especially songs which transport me to another place or time. The feeling and melodies of Mint Royale's 'Space Farm'—off their album 'On the Ropes'—give a glimpse into a world of open, endless possibilities. It's energetic, deep, eccentric, introspective and an absolute favorite of mine.

The Go! Team – Get It Together
At the risk of including a song loosely categorized as Big Beat, I submit The Go! Team's 'Get It Together' off their album 'Thunder, Lightning, Strike'. The album fits perfectly into my shifting musical preferences at that time, having been introduced to the Strokes by a friend. This Garage Rock version of Big Beat was a staple in my Summer soundtracks. Fast-forward to years later. I'm playing the first level of 'Little-BigPlanet', and 'Get It Together' starts playing halfway through the

stage. That moment solidified both that game and that song as two of my favorites in their respective categories.

Air – Kelly Watch the Stars (Moog Cookbook remix)
When I was younger, I used to have my alarm clock set to the local college radio station when I woke up. There were times where it barely came through, being far away from the station itself. One morning, I came to consciousness as the Moog Cookbook's take on Air's 'Kelly Watch the Stars' was already in the midst of its sonic journey. I remember anxiously waiting for the radio DJ to announce the name of the song, which never came. I learned of the Moog Cookbook and this song much later after becoming well-versed in all things Big Beat and it's one of my favorites to this day.

Lo Fidelity All-Stars – Kasparov's Revenge
I didn't initially understand 'How to Operate with a Blown Mind'. It was slow and meandering when it wasn't Disco-heavy, and I just wasn't ready for it at the time. This album has since become one of my all-time favorites, rewarding each listen with new layers and emotional perspective. Along with 'Battleflag', one of the standout Big Beat tracks is 'Kasparov's Revenge', a hostile, Funky, Kubrick-esque stomper. This song still has an attitude that can be appreciated today.

Indian Ropeman – Your Own Enemy
"Dis is da way, I am da way, dis is da way, da way I am." The dusty keys, the indecisive synth, the cleansing sitars; all make this one of my favorite tracks. The composition of this song contains so much movement and it feels so right when it's brought right back home to the rhythm of the vocal delay. 'Elephant Sound' has some of my favorite Skint songs ever released by the label, making 'Your Own Enemy' a telling choice.

Craig White (from Sir Vere) (Wall Of Sound, Big Fat Mama Beats)

1. Dub Pistols - There's Gonna Be A Riot
2. The Chemical Brothers - Block Rockin' Beats
3. Fatboy Slim - The Rockefeller Skank
4. Daft Punk - Da Funk

5. The Wiseguys - Ooh La La

Crawford Tate (Resident at Hi Karate) (Scotland)

1 Bassbin Twins - Vol 1 Side B Track 2 - It still astounds me that this came out in 1992, so it's cheating in a way, but you can't really call this anything except Big Beat. I think probably more than anyone they presaged the style.

2 Chemical Brothers - Life is Sweet - When I first heard 'Chemical Beats', it was just a bit too mental for me, but of course within days I'd come round and bought it, and that was a bit of a turning point. However, this remains my favourite Chems track - it's so joyous and epitomises the coming together of Indie and Dance that was so important.

3 Bronx Dogs - Tribute to Jazzy Jay - I remember the weekend when this just seemed to be in the window or on the wall of every record shop in London I went to - and with good reason! Not a great deal to it, but I love sample-based stuff and cut-ups.

4 Dylan Rhymes - Naked and Ashamed - I loved this the first time I heard it, we were doing student radio at the time and I felt that qualified me to ring up the label and demand a promo. So I did :)

5 Ceasefire - Trickshot - I remember hearing Pete Tong play this on his Friday night show on Radio 1, including the sweary bit! Probably one of the earlier Big Beat things I heard.

Cut La Roc (Skint Records, Rocstar)

1. The Chemical Brothers - Chemical Beats
2. Cut La Roc - Post Punk Progression
3. Definition Of Sound - Outsider (Lunatic Calm Remix)
4. Fatboy Slim - Everybody Loves A Carnival
5. Les Rythmes Digitales - Jaques Your Body

Daniel Curtis AKA Danielsan (Skint Under 5's)

1. The Prodigy - Poison
2. The Chemical Brothers - Chemical Beats
3. Fatboy Slim - Everybody Needs A 303
4. Kurtis Mantronik - King Of The Beats
5. Lo Fidelity Allstars - Vision Incision

Dave RMX (Hardly Subtle)

1. Fatboy Slim - Going Out Of My Head
2. Sound 5 - Spray + Tag
3. Wax Assassins - Waxadelica
4. Suburban State - It's Yours
5. Propellerheads VS The Jungle Brothers - Take California And Party

Deadly Avenger (Illicit Recordings)

1. Deadly Avenger VS Ceasefire - Evil Knievel
2. Deadly Avenger - Live At The Capri
3. Deadly Avenger - Brooklyn Scraps
4. Deadly Avenger - Charlie Don't Surf
5. Anything by the Chemical Brothers

Decky Hedrock (Japanese Popstars, Gung Ho! Recordings) (Ireland)

1. Fatboy Slim - Rockafeller Skank
2. Hedrock Valley Beats - Radio Beatbox
3. The Prodigy - Poison
4. The Prodigy - We Are The Ruffest
5. Mr Spring - BlaxxTraxx 3

DJ Buba (BubaKing)

1. Fatboy Slim - Everybody Loves a 303
2. Midfield General - Go Off
3. Dub Pistols - Cyclone
4. ETA - Casual Sub

5. Propellerheads - Velvet Pants

DJ Hadj (Ba'Da Boom, North Wales)

1. The Chemical Brothers - The Private Psychedelic Reel
2. Freestylers - Ruffneck
3. Fatboy Slim - Everybody Needs A 303
4. Beastie Boys - Body Movin' (Fatboy Slim Remix)
5. Josh Wink - Higher State of Consciousness

DJ Prosper (Howlin' Records, Boxon Records) (France)

1. Bassbin Twins - Vol.2 Track 2. (Funkiest track ever)
2. The Chemical Brothers - Chemical Beats (I played it so much)
3. Propellerheads - Dive EP (such a great EP from a great label)
4. Lionrock - Packet Of Peace (Chemical Brothers Remix) (Just perfect)
5. Saint Etienne - FIlthy (Monkey Mafia Remix) (Jon Carter was my hero at the time)

DJ Regal (The Wiseguys, Bronx Dogs) (Wall of Sound, Marble Bar, Funk Weapons)

1. SHADES OF RHYTHM – 'EXORCIST' 1990
So simple, so damn HUGE! ... made the mistake of playing this from the start of our set in Barca – it took the roof off, but the next 1hr 55 mins was hard work!! ... This is the awesome sound of quality Rave and Techno producers getting dirty on JB's 'Funky Drummer'. Magic!

2. PRODIGY VS METHOD MAN – 'RELEASE YO' SELF' 1995
Another mid-tempo barnstormer ... Hip-Hop 12" remixes had always been a step up from the album cut, but this was the next level. Tearing up the GCS break 'The Jam', with sirens from hell... only the Meth could sit on top of this and still stomp imperially. HYPE.

3. BLUEBOY – 'REMEMBER ME' 1997
Remember Richard Sen dropping this on white label for the first time, at one of our Fun Gallery parties... Another non-hip outfit rocking a

classic B-Boy break, with that ridiculous Marlena Shaw sample on top … genius.

4. RESIN DOGS – 'DAILY TROUBLE' 2000

My time in Oz was supremely kicked off by touring with the mighty Resin's in late 2000 and then staying on after. These boys threw the kitchen sink and more into their debut album, but this, their chart-topping single, slayed all before them. The Corner Hotel gig in Melbourne was just a riot, and this track had them touching the ceiling! Massive tune and forever the sound of good times.

5. DEADBEATS – 'FUNKY FOR YOU' (MARK RAE REMIX) 2003

They don't all have to be mid or uptempo to roc' of course … as proved here by one of the greatest remixes of all time – period.
Rae outdid himself on this short but sharp dope-ass groove. Mix this in the right spot, with P.E.'s 'Don't Believe The Hype' and it's fucking heaven. A benchmark for all wannabe instrumental beat heads.

DJ Rehab (USA)

1. Fatboy Slim - Give the Po' Man A Break
2. Slab - Rampant Prankster (Monkey Mafia Remix)
3. Bassbin Twins - Mash Up
4. The Chemical Brothers - Not Another Drugstore
5. Propellerheads - Velvet Pants

DJ Trev Broadbank

1. The Wiseguys - Ooh la la
2. The Chemical Brothers - Setting Sun
3. Fatboy Slim - Everybody Needs A 303
4. Lionrock - Rude Boy Rock
5. Freestylers - Push Up

Doc Moody (BlowPop Resident DJ) (Particle Zoo Recordings)

1. Son Of A Cheeky Boy VS Blackstreet - Comma/No Diggity
2. The Wiseguys - Ooh la la

3. The Chemical Brothers - Block Rockin' Beats
4. Groove Armada - I See You Baby
5. The Dope On Plastic Series (It ran right through the Big Beat era - you can hear the history unfolding in the time line if you play them from one to eight. You can see where Big Beat came from in the early Albums and later how it gave way to Nu Skool Breaks)

Ewan Hoozami (Particle Zoo Recordings, Pig Balls Records)

1. **The Wiseguys - Ooh La La.** Absolutely never fails to make the dancefloor go nuts
2. **Freestylers - Dogs and Sledges.** Has that tempo switch where you can segway from Reggae/Hip-Hop to something meatier, which you need to, to keep up with the absolutely banging tune. Hard as nails.
3. **Evil Nine - Crooked feat Aesop Rock.** Another gritty one, but I think it's wicked. Often a little much for my audiences but I still played it to death.
4. **Fatboy Slim - Praise You.** Stone-cold classic and deserves to be in my list.
5. **Red Snapper- Wesley Don't Surf.** Were Red Snapper Big Beat? Amazing live act at that time, who I saw quite a few times in Bristol at intimate venues like Fiddlers. 'Wesley Don't Surf' has all the characteristics I loved most about Big Beat; raw and Funky drums; looping, prominent bassline and a bit of grit.

Fab Samperi AKA The Captain (Beatnik City) (Italy)

1 Fatboy Slim – The Rockafeller Skank
2 The Chemical Brothers – Block Rockin' Beats
3 Lionrock – Rude Boy Rock
4 The Prodigy – Smack My Bitch Up
5 Fatboy Slim – Soul Surfing

Fatboy Slim (AKA Norman Cook) (Skint Records, Southern Fried Records)

1 The Chemical Brothers - Leave Home
2 Cut & Paste - Forget It
3 Bassbin Twins - Out of Hand

258

4 Incredible Bongo Band - Apache
5 The Crystal Method - Busy Child

Fatboy Tim (Fatboy Slim Tribute Act, Tim Davies) (Tall House Digital)

1. Fatboy Slim - The Rockafeller Skank
2. The Wiseguys - Ooh La La
3. The Chemical Brothers - Block Rockin Beats
4. Cut La Roc - Freeze
5. Scanty Sandwich - Because Of You

Featurecast (Bombstrikes, Ghetto Funk)

1. The Wiseguys - Ooh La La
2. Captain Funk - Twist and Shout
3. Fatboy Slim - Gangster Tripping
4. Krafty Kuts - Latin Bounce
5. Propellerheads – Bang On

François Deman - Creator of fatboyslim.org/Normancook.info - The most well known Fatboy Slim Fan Site (France).

1. Fatboy Slim - Song For Lindy
2. The Chemical Brothers - In Dust We Trust
3. The Wiseguys - Ooh La La
4. Elvis VS JXL - A Little Less Conversation
5. Propellerheads - Take California

Frank Smith (Manager of the Big Beat Channel for Digitally Imported Radio, USA)

1. The Chemical Brothers – Life Is Sweet
2. The Grassy Knoll – Culture Of Complaint
3. Deeds Plus Thoughts - The World's Made Up Of This And That (Fatboy Slim Remix)
4. Lo Fidelity Allstars - Deep Ellum... Hold On (Featuring Jamie Lidell)
5. Countertop Hero – Same Ol' Song

Bonus: The Lovin' Spoonful - Summer In The City (Maxim Portnenko Remix)

Freddy Fresh (Howlin' Records, Eye-Q) Top-20 (USA)

1.Atomic Soul Experience - Get Right 45 - 7" Single PEP Japan
2.H2SO4 - Imitation Leather Jacket - (PVC Mix) - Recon Records UK
3.Freddy Fresh feat. Fatboy Slim - Badder Badder Schwing - Eye Q Records UK
4.Big M - 7th Son – Big M Germany
5.Pucker Up! - Pucker Up - Round Records UK
6.B-Boy - Front to Back - Caged UK
7.Captain Funk - Twist & Shout - Reel Musiq - Japan
8.Andy "Ictus" Halstead - Do the Crazy Mouse (Part 2) - Howlin'
9.Scanty Sandwich – Slam Dunk - Acetate UK
10. DJ Polo - Taxman - Test Pressing UK
11. Cut La Roc - Post Punk Progression – Skint UK
12. Rory Hoy - Y'Know What I'm Sayin' - Howlin'
13. Akakage - She is a Pretty Girl - Low Blow - Japan
14. Fantastic Plastic Machine - Bachelor Pad - Nippon Columbia Japan
15. Freddy Fresh - Creeper - Howlin'
16. Shmelja - Bad Girls - Pomishane
17. JJ Flash Vs. The Beach Boys - Acetate
18. Countertop Hero - Like Jello (unreleased)
19. Freddy Fresh & Jerry Kosak - Red Pierce - Howlin'
20. Maxim Portnenko - La La La - Russia

The Freestylers (Freskanova)

1. The Wiseguys - Ooh La La
2. Fatboy Slim - The Rockafeller Skank
3. The Freestylers - Ruffneck
4. Ceasefire VS Deadly Avenger - Evil Knievel
5. Les Rythmes Digitales - (Hey You) What's That Sound?

The Funky Boogie Brothers (Tru-Funk) (Belarus)

1. The Wiseguys - Ooh La La

2. Wildchid - Renegade Master
3. Skeewiff - Highspeed Heist
4. Deeds Plus Thoughts - The World's Made Up of This and That
(Fatboy Slim Mix)
5. Elvis VS JXL - A Little Less Conversation

Fuzz Townsend (Bentley Rhythm Ace) (Parlophone Records) (His favourite Big Beat track)

Bentley Rhythm Ace - 'Carbootechnodisco'"....or whatever it's called (I still don't know the song titles)...... actually, I'm not good with re-membering individual tracks. If you've lived life as a human cartoon, it's hard to turn back the pages. It was all nuts and all great and I worked with some beautiful, talented lovely people along the way, some of whom we've lost and others who are still going bananas, even if only part-time."

Hideki Naganuma (SEGA, Sonic Team) (Japan)

It's very hard to choose. Also Big Beat is a genre which is very hard to define. Well... this time I choose very happy and fun "Big Beat-ish" tracks. Digital Rock/Breakbeat (Like The Chemical Brothers, The Prodigy, The Crystal Method or Propellerheads) tracks, and Fatboy Slim, his own tracks were excluded. Because there are too many fa-vourites!

1. Deeds Plus Thoughts - The World's Made Up of This and That
(Fatboy Slim Remix)
2. Wildchild - Renegade Master (Fatboy Slim Old Skool Mix)
3. The Wiseguys - Ooh La La or Start The Commotion (Can't choose!)
4. Bassbin Twins - Vol 1 Side 2 Track 2
5. Hardknox - Come In Hard

I don't know whether I can call these tracks Big Beat or not. But I like these very much, too.

1. Junkie XL, Elvis Presley - A Little Less Conversation (Elvis vs JXL)

2. Beastie Boys - Body Movin' (Fatboy Slim Remix)
3. Timo Maas - To Get Down (Fatboy Slim Remix)
4. Elite Force - Call It Brisco (And Why Not?)
5. Apollo 440 - Stop The Rock
6. Tim Deluxe - It Just Won't Do
7. Basement Jaxx - Do Your Thing"

IamBenji (formally Benji Boko) (Tru-Thoughts)

1 Fatboy Slim – Gangster Trippin'
2 The Prodigy – Diesel Power
3 The Wiseguys – Ooh La La
4 Backyard Dogs – Baddest Roughest
5 Groove Armada – If Everybody Looked The Same

Jadell (Ultimate Dilemma)

1. The Wiseguys - 'Oh La La'
2. The Beastie Boys - 'Body Movin' (Fatboy Slim Remix)
3. Jadell - 'Brand New Sound'
4. The Hightower Set - 'Escucha Mi Funk'
5. Major Force - 'The Return of the Original Artform'

James Glenton AKA Lebrosk (Mixmag)

1. The Wiseguys - Ooh La La
2. Propellerheads - Take California
3. Fatboy Slim - Everybody Needs a 303
4. Freestylers - B-Boy Stance
5. David Holmes - My Mate, Paul

Jane Winterbottom AKA Funk Boutique (Resident at Molotov Pop, Manchester)

1. Mantronix - King Of The Beats
2. Silver Bullet - 20 Seconds To Comply
3. Afrika Bambaataa - Planet Rock (808 State Remix)
4. Genaside II - Narra Mine
5. Bug Kahn and the Plastic Jam - Made in Two Minutes

Jari AKA James Spectrum (Pepé Deluxe) Top-6 (Catskills Records) (Finland)

Fatboy Slim - Rockafeller Skank. The quintessential feel good, catchy-as-hell party track. 60's soul groove reborn & supercharged.

Chemical Brothers - Block Rockin' Beats. Killer drums and bass from the era when Dance music was more Rock'n'Roll than Rock.

Beastie Boys – Intergalactic. Big beats, a classical music sample and a most genius-ly stupid vocoder hook. These guys were the three Mozarts of our times.

Led Zeppelin - When the Levee Breaks. The original Big Beat tune, with a beat that will be resurrected forever.

The Millenium – Prelude. A quite unknown, yet timeless, gem, that could almost be a Pepe Deluxé tune: big drums with lovely triplet fills, a harpsichord riff and a funny but Funky tuba bass.

KLF – The Unwritten Tune. Had KLF ever produced a Big Beat anthem, I believe we would have world peace AND colonies on Mars. It could still happen you know?

Jason Laidback (Boshi Records)

1.Laidback - Rock Your World (Bolshi)
2.The Dust Brothers - Chemical Beats (Dust Up Beats)
3.Ceasefire - Trickshot (Wall Of Sound)
4.Rasmus - Johnny K (Bolshi)
5.London Funk Allstars - Sure Shot (Ninja Tune)

Jason King (BubaKing)

1.Scanty Sandwich - Because of You
2.Bentley Rhythm Ace - Bentleys Gonna Sort You Out
3. Sound 5 - Spray & Tag
4. Captain Funk - Twist & Shout

5. Dirty Beatniks - Latin Head

Jemma Kennedy (Wall of Sound Label Manager)

1. The Propellerheads – Take California
2. The Chemical Brothers – Block Rockin' Beats
3. Lionrock – Rude Boy Rock
4. Mekon feat. Skooly D – School's Out (Deckwrecka Remix)
5. The Ganja Kru – Super Sharp Shooter

Jem Stone (Soul of Man, Finger Lickin' Records)

1 – Fatboy Slim – Gangster Trippin'
2 – Freestylers – Freestyle Noise
3 – Fuselage – Seize the Time
4 – Cut & paste – Watch Me Rollin'
5- Ceasefire vs Deadly Avenger – Caipirahna

John Gosling (Mekon, Agent Provocateur) (Wall of Sound)

1. Kenny Dope Presents The Mad Racket - Supa (Deep In Brooklyn Mix)
2. Renegade Soundwave - The Phantom
3. Original Concept - Can You Feel It
4. Blade - Mind of an Ordinary Citizen (Instrumental)
5. Bad Boy Orchestra - Its Just an 808

Johnny Pluse (Bulabeats Records) (Ireland)

1. Cut La Roc - Freeze
2. Monkey Mafia - Work Mi Body
3. The Prodigy - Voodoo People (Dust Brothers Remix)
4. DJ Zinc - Ready Or Not
5. Natural Born Chillers - Rock The Funky Beat

Jon Carter (Monkey Mafia, Heavenly Records, Wall of Sound)

1. Chemical Brothers - The Private Psychedelic Reel
2. Violet - Burn the Elastic
3. Monkey Mafia - The Whore of Babylon

4. Micronauts - The Jag
5. Ceasefire - Trickshot

Kidda (Skint Records)

1. The Dust Brothers - Chemical Beats
2. Fatboy Slim - Santa Cruz
3. Lo Fidelity Allstars – Kasparov's Revenge
4. Fatboy Slim - Everybody Loves a Filter
5. The Chemical Brothers - Life is Sweet

Kid Kenobi (Ministry of Sound) (Australia)

1 Sabres Of Paradise – Tow Truck (Chemical Brothers Remix)
2 Wildchild – Renegade Master (Fatboy Slim Old Skool Mix)
3 Ceasefire – Trickshot
4 Propellerheads – Dive
5 Freestylers – B-Boy Stance

Kounchilhouse (Simon Tagg)

1. Prodigy - Diesel Power
2. Leftfield - Phat Planet
3. Meat Beat Manifesto - Radio Babylon
4. Chemical Brothers - Let forever be
5. My Bloody Valentine - Soon (Andy Weatherall Mix)

Lee Mathias (Stepping Tones) Top 20

1. Captain Funk- Twist & Shout
2. Fuzz Townshend – Big Tasty Ed
3. Deeds Plus Thoughts - The World's Made Up Of This And That (Fatboy Slim Remix)
4. Bentley Rhythm Ace - Kenny Beats (Part One)
5. Fruitloop Feat. Cantankerous – Jumpin'
6. Mint Royale – Loca
7. Freak Power – No Way
8. Hardwire – Dope Jam
9. Psycho Cowboys – Come On Baby

10. The Scammers – Sally Walk
11. Freddy Fresh – Swing Time
12. Lionrock - Rude Boy Rock
13. Surreal Madrid – Rockin' On The Radio
14. Fatboy Slim – Es Paradis
15. Cut & Paste – Watch This Sound
16. Indian Ropeman – Dog In The Piano
17. Psychedelicasmith - Who's Gonna?
18. El Magnifico - Tha Nu Style (Athletico Borough)
19. Resident Filters – Big Train
20. Loop Da Loop – Hazel

Liam Howlett (The Prodigy, XL Recordings) Top-5 Prodigy Tracks

("It changes each month, in no order")

Take Me To The Hospital
Smack My Bitch Up
I Need Some 1 (New Album Track)
Poison
Out of Space

Mako of Mako & The Hawk and Mako & Mr Bristow (editor of the website, monkeyboxing)

1. Beastie Boys - Body Movin' (Fatboy Slim Remix)
2. Resident Filters - Big Train
3. Depth Charge - Poison Clan '95
4. Chemical Brothers - Leave Home
5. Scuba Z - California Paranoia

Mark Jones (Founder of Wall of Sound Records) Top-10

In no particular order

Daft Punk - Da Funk
Propellerheads - Take California
The Wiseguys - Ooh La La

Basement Jaxx - Where's Your Head At
Fatboy Slim - Right Here Right Now
Chemical Brothers - Dig Your Own Hole
The Prodigy - Smack My Bitch up
Ceasefire - Trickshot
Propellerheads - Bang On
Faithless - Insomnia

Matty Blades (Bulabeats, Tru-Funk) (Australia)

1. Propellerheads Feat. Miss Shirley Bassey - History Repeating
2. The Wiseguys - Start the Commotion
3. Fatboy Slim - Rockafeller Skank
4. The Chemical Brothers - Alive Alone
5. Freestylers Feat. Tenor Fly - B-Boy Stance

Max Sedgley (Sunday Best) Top-6

1 The Chemical Brothers – Chemical Beats
2 Propellerheads – Velvet Pants
3 Überzone – Botz (Synthetik Mix)
4 The Wiseguys – Ooh La La
5 Euphoria - The House Crew (Nino's dream mix)
6 Red Snapper – Hot Flush

Michal Borczon (BMD, XLNT) (Poland) Top-10

1 Frank Popp Ensemble – Catwalk
2 Mighty Dub Katz – Magic Carpet Ride (Fatboy Slim Ska Acid 3 3
Breakbeat Mix)
3 Mint Royale – Take It Easy
4 Fatboy Slim – Love Island
5 Propellerheads – Crash!
6 The Wiseguys – Oh La La
7 The Three Amigos – Louie Louie
8 Telephunken – Don't Wanna Hear About It
9 Fatboy Slim – Kalifornia
10 Dub Pistols - Cyclone

Midfield General (Damian Harris – Skint Records founder)

1 Daft Punk – Da Funk
2 Dexter Wansel – Life On Mars
3 Madonna – Into The Groove
4 The Rolling Stones – Gimmie Shelter
5 Public Enemy – Public Enemy No. 1

Mike Atkinson (1990's-2000's Music Journalist for the Guardian)

1. Cornershop - Brimful Of Asha (Norman Cook Remix)
2. Chemical Brothers - Hey Boy Hey Girl
3. Surreal Madrid - Girls Of The Nite
4. David Holmes - My Mate Paul
5. Pierre Henry - Psyche Rock (Fatboy Slim Malpaso Mix)

Mr. Scruff (Ninja Tune)

1. Renegade Soundwave - The Phantom
2. Outlaw Posse - Original Dope (Instrumental)
3. Fish - Can You Feel It
4. The Wiseguys - A Better World
5. The Dust Brothers - You Kling To Me, I'll Klong To You

Myagi (Howlin' Records) (Canada)

My top Big Beat track of all time would have to be **Fatboy Slim's 'Everybody Loves a Filter.'**   A sort of remix of 'Everybody Needs a 303' this tune was a huge influence on me... It was big and manic and had some low slung House sounds in It, vocal chops galore.... it became my template and standard for a remix for years. Still brings a huge smile to my face. Catching it up or slowing it during the mix in was a bitch though... rapid pitch change on those vocal elements made you feel like you were at sea.

Next up - **Wax Assassins 'Rocking 2 the Rhythm'**. This was just a 'no holds barred' sample orgy. Funk, Rap, classic B-Boy elements, all on top of a rushy break with loads of quirky ear candy

Chemical Brothers 'Loops of Fury'. The main reason is the best edits at the end. Besides being an awesome track, this also includes about 45 seconds of some the coolest, most screwed up, sounding beat juggle elements as the outro. So much of Chems' early stuff should be on this list, the b-sides in particular.

Freska Allstars - 'Get Fresh'. If you don't know it, go look it up. Matt Cantor of Freestylers and Andy Gardner of the Plump DJ's with a total party bumper. Worked so well on the dancefloor.

Wubble U - 'Petal (Freestylers Remix)'. Still a great total 'feel good' track with B-Boy elements, a rolling break, the Stanley Unwin gibberish loud and clear, along with an emotive breakdown that felt so perfect when it dropped. Classic.

Neil McMillan (Hi-Karate) (Scotland)

1 Dust Brothers - Chemical Beats - They were really the masters of this for me at the beginning, especially as DJs, but this was the tune of theirs we probably rinsed the most.

2 Stik-E & The Hoods - Shake Watcha Mamma Gave Ya - Picked up on a trip to NYC in 97 that provided me with HK fodder for many years to come. The best of all those AV8-style party records.

3 Coldcut - Beats & Pieces - Could've put Steinski's Lesson 3 here, but let's tip the hat to the UK remake. We were all big fans of the cut'n'paste style. Equally, Cut Chemist's remix of Shadow's 'Number Song' was on heavy rotation.

4 Cutty Ranks - Limb by Limb - Hard to pick a representative dancehall track from HK, but this is probably it. Brutally infectious.

5 Beck - Loser - There were a few favourite end-of-nighters, but this is the first I thought of!

Nick Faber (Parlorphone Records, Marble Bar)

1. **Appleseed - 'Mile High Express'** I know this is my own tune but it was massive for me, great fun to make, smashed dance floors and got onto an Adidas TV commercial.
2. **Hightower Set - 'Escucha Mi Funk'** - another one of my own tunes but the reactions to this have been mega, and it still gets played out in clubs today.
3. **Common Ground - 'Get Yourself Together'** - a Big Beat tune without drums… how does that work?
4. **The Wiseguys - 'The Real Vibes'** - the tune that started me on my journey to making sample-based Breakbeat music. Perfect.
5. **Jadell - 'Brand New Sound'** - one of the few tunes I wish I'd made, from my best pal and musical mentor.

Noko (Norman Fisher-Jones from Apollo 440) (Epic Records) Top-9

Cor, that's a question.
It's impossible to talk about Big Beat without referencing Norman Cook - there's got to be some Fatboy in there..
Wildchild "Renegade Master (Fatboy Slim Old Skool Mix) is genre-defining flash genius, but I think his best is his remix of '**Brimful of Asha'** by **Cornershop**. It's one of those 'transparent' remixes that cuts to the chase and simply excavates the inner party tune already in there and makes it more, without any unnecessary distraction : immaculate work - we salute you, Sir.
I think what defines a 'Big Beat' track, as distinct from any regular Breakbeat one is the single-minded, visceral party agenda with a big 'kick-off' moment - this is proper DANCE music that also rocks.

The staccato assault of '**Block Rockin' Beats'** by the **Chemicals** (Chemical Brothers) certainly fulfils that criteria.

The explosive 'one' downbeat of '**Firestarter'** by **Prodigy** satisfies this remit and was a major milestone and I'd even go as far as to suggest **Knife Party's** "Bonfire" with it's explosive jump-around moments and general exhilaration.

In fact, **Pendulum's remix** of 'Voodoo People' is almost Big Beat too!

'**Disco To Disco**' by **Les Rhythms Digitales** is another great one that takes the 4-to-the-floor 'Da Funk' route.

I always felt that **Aphrodite** had an unspoken influence of a lot of the great Big Beat records with his builds and drops even though the beats were different. - summat like '**I Need a Woman That Rolls**' or '**King Of The Beats**'

Old Flame (Jason Ard) (Division Bass Digital) (USA)

1. Fatboy Slim - Sho Nuff
2. Mint Royale - Shake me
3. Scanty Sandwich - This One
4. Junkie XL - Billy Club
5. Freddy Fresh - What it is

PulpFusion (Pig Balls Records) (Switzerland)

1. Prodigy - Poison
2. Chemical Brothers - Block Rockin' Beats
3. Propellerheads - Take California
4. Professor Kliq - Elephantitis
5. Colombo - Gods

Quincy Jointz (Top-4) (Big Fat Mama Beats) (Germany)

1.Chemical Brothers - Leave Home
2.Fatboy Slim - Praise You
3.Prodigy - Poison
4.The Wiseguys - Ooh La La

Rams Le Prince (Founder of Internet Radio Station bigbeat.ch AKA bigbeatradio.com) (BigM Productions) (Switzerland)

- Apollo 440 - Stop The Rock
- The Prodigy - Breathe

- The Chemical Brothers - Leave Home
- Stereo MC's - Warhead
- Terrorvision - Tequilla (Mint Royale Shot)

Can't rank them really

Rasmus (Bolshi Records) (Sweden)

1. Fatboy Slim - Acid 8000
2. Monkey Mafia - Lion In The Hall
3. Laidback - Cold Rock Noise
4. LHB - Sometimes
5. Mr Natural - Go Crazy

Richard March (Bentley Rhythm Ace) (Skint Records, Parlophone)

1. Fatboy Slim - Everybody Needs a 303
2. Lionrock - Rude Boy Rock
3. Cut La Roc - Post Punk Progression
4. Propellerheads - Take California
5. Pigmeat Markham - The Trial

Robert Luis (Tru Thoughts, Deeds Plus Thoughts)

1. David Holmes - My Mate Paul (Go Beat)
2. Masters At Work - Blood Vibes (Cutting)
3. Fatboy Slim - Praise You (Skint)
4. The Wiseguys - Ooh La La (Wall Of Sound)
5. Deeds Plus Thoughts - The World Is Made Up Of This & That (Fatboy Slim Remix) (Sophisticuts)

Robin Turner (Heavenly Social)

1. Jay Dee - Strange Funky Games And Things
2. The Dust Brothers - Chemical Beats
3. Justin Warfield - Pick It Up (Dust Brothers Remix)
4. Supersuckers - Dead Homiez
5. The Beatles - Tomorrow Never Knows

Rory Carlile (Dirty Beatniks) (Wall of Sound)

1. Coldcut: Beats & Pieces (original version)
2. KRS One: Sound Of Da Police
3. Hardfloor: Acperience
4. Leftfield: Open Up (Dust Brothers Remix)
5. Beastie Boys: Hey Ladies (Instrumental)

Scanty Sandwich (Southern Fried Records)

1. Think Tank - Hack One
2. The Dust Brothers - Chemical Beats
3. Wildchild - Renegade Master
4. Fatboy Slim - Everybody Needs a 303
5. Basement Jaxx - Fly Life

Scott Hendy (Dynamo Productions, Boca 45) (Illicit Recordings)

1. Double Dee and Steinski - Lesson 3
2. DJ Shadow - The Number Song (Cut Chemist Remix)
3. A-Skillz and Krafty Kuts - Tricka Technology
4. DJ Format - English Lesson
5. DJ Bombjack - Lesson 7 (The Next Lesson)

Simon Shackleton (Elite Force/Lunatic Calm) (Universal Music)

1. Dave Clarke - No One's Driving (Chemical Brothers Mix)
2. Sol Brothers - That Elvis Track
3. Wax Assassins - Rockin' to the Rhythm
4. Midfield General - Devil in Sports Casual
5. Cut & Paste - Cut it Nice

Steven Hall (A&R Man - Junior Boys Own Records)

1. Lo Fidelity Allstars - Battleflag
2. The Chemical Brothers - Chemical Beats
3. Dylan Rhymes - Naked & Ashamed
4. The Propellerheads - Take California
5. Fatboy Slim - Right Here Right Now

Timothy Adam AKA Timmy Schumacher (Rocstar Recordings) (New Zealand)

1. Deadly Avenger VS Ceasefire - Evil Knievel
2. Fatboy Slim - Big Beat Soufflé
3. Propellerheads - Drive!
4. Ceasefire - Trickshot
5. Aleem - Why Hawaii

Tony "Slackshot" Gainsborough (Splank! Records)

1. Bowser - Code Name Hard Hat
2. Deadly Avenger - Caipirinha
3. Freak Power - No Way (Norman's Club Mix)
4. Space Raiders - I Need the Disco Doctor
5. Scanty Sandwich - Because of You

Tony Green (Promoter of D:Funked – Leeds Big Beat Night)

1. The Propellerheads - Take California
2. The Freestylers - Freestyle Noize
3. Dub Pistols - Westway
4. Deadly Avenger - King Tito's Gloves
5. Bentley Rhythm Ace - Bentleys Gonna Sort You Out

Under Influence (Criminal Tribe Records) Top-5 Big Beat Artists (Russia)

1. The Prodigy
2. The Chemical Brothers
3. Fatboy Slim
4. Junkie XL
5. The Crystal Method

Wiccatron (Breakbeat Paradise Recordings, Big Fat Mama Beats) (Denmark)

1. Lo Fidelity Allstars - Vision Incision
2. Lionrock - Rude Boy Rock

3. The Prodigy - Smack My Bitch Up
4. The Freestylers - Ruffneck
5. Fatboy Slim - The Rockefeller Skank

Zenit Incompatible (Hungarian Playboy Magazine) Top-10 (Hungary)

1) Wildchild - Renegade Master (Fatboy Slim Old Skool mix) - Basically, the moment when I fell in love with the genre, and to this day, that's my all-time favourite.

2). NEO - Rambo 13 - Neo were a great Hungarian Big Beat duo, with a lot of hits including 'Aiiaiio', and a remix of 'The Pink Panther Theme', but this one always makes me smile because of the samples (also, the video is funny as hell)

3) Groove Armada - Superstylin' - can we call this post-Big Beat - or just call this a masterpiece?

4) Freestylers feat. Valerie M - Calling - every single Friday night was about this song for years. It's perfect.

5) Mint Royale - Shake me - you can't imagine a better soundtrack for your life when springtime arrives.

6) Three Amigos - 25 Miles - I love it when someone samples the good old Motown records, especially with these good synths.

7) Propellerheads with Miss Shirley Bassey - History Repeating - Okay, this one was in every movie in the late 90's, but here's a thing: it's incredible. (also: 'Where Do I Begin' by AwayTEAM?)

8) The Wiseguys - The Bounce - I thought I would mention "Start The Commotion", but the sampling, the heavy, fast post-rock drums just grows on me.

9) Utah Saints - Funky Music (Krafty Kuts Remix) - I still play this beauty whenever I can, it has everything anyone needs at 0:30am.

10) Blue Boy - Sandman (Phunk Phlava) - I searched for this song for years, and it was on my shelf the whole time with a smiley sticker on the cover!

. . . and if you're wondering . . . **Rory Hoy's** Big Beat Top-5 is

1 Wildchild - Renegade Master (Fatboy Slim Old Skool Mix)

I think this remix pretty much sums up the entire genre. I just love it to bits. This is one I play out on a frequent basis and people go . . . WILD!

2 The Wiseguys - Ooh La La

The first records I got in the Dance Music field when I was 11 were 'Right Here Right Now', 'Hey Boy Hey Girl' and this. Such a Funky track, and still sounds good today, plus it works on so many different styles of DJ-ing, whether it be a club, a festival, or even a wedding.

3 Fatboy Slim VS The Rolling Stones - Satisfaction Skank

Bootleg mashup of Fatboy Slim and The Rolling Stone's 1965 classic 'Satisfaction'. First heard this on Norman's 1998 Essential Mix, and eventually found it on a White Label. If I had to pick a version of 'Rockefeller Skank' - this is the one.

4 The Chemical Brothers - The Private Psychedelic Reel

Epic . . . just simply epic.

5 Freddy Fresh - Go Kat Go

It's unthinkable to have a top-5 Big Beat tracklist without including a track by Freddy Fresh (could have picked so many!). This isn't one of his most well known tracks, but a very infectious Rock and Roll workout with some catchy guitar licks and cheeky vocal snatches.

. . . and my honourable mention

The Beatles - Tomorrow Never Knows

Obviously a great influence to the Chemical Brothers - I think this is unofficially the first 'Big Beat' track.

276

To end this book and bring everything full circle, I feel I should share this picture of me with Norman Cook aka Fatboy Slim. I felt I'd come a long way (baby) from the little autistic boy dancing to 'Right Here, Right Now' at the school disco.

The author Rory Hoy with Norman Cook AKA Fatboy Slim backstage at the Warehouse Project in Manchester. Photo by Faye Woodhead

Referencecs

In addition to my own interviews, I have used the following sources, which I would like to credit.

[1] https://thump.vice.com/en_uk/article/gvn83y/big-beat-producers-retrospective-freestylers-rhythm-bentley-ace-cut-la-roc

[2] http://www.npr.org/2011/08/19/139754112/the-big-beat-revolution-11-essential-songs

[3] https://www.amazon.co.uk/Chemical-Brothers-Life-Sweet/dp/1873884869

[4] https://www.amazon.co.uk/Nineties-What-F-k-That-About/dp/0091871352/ref=sr_1_1?s=books&ie=UTF8&qid=1507634671&sr=1-1&keywords=The+Nineties%3A+What+the+Was+That+About

[5]Jon Carter interview
https://www.youtube.com/watch?v=0ZsNKlcb0g0

[6] Spin Magazine April 1998 Issue

[7] Melody Maker January 1996

[8] http://www.nme.com/blogs/nme-blogs/how-the-chemical-brothers-revitalised-uk-dance-with-their-lairy-house-and-hip-hop-hybrid-exit-planet-767788

[9] https://www.theguardian.com/music/2015/jun/17/chemical-brothers-classic-interview-1995-muzik-rocks-backpages

[10] http://www.bbc.co.uk/news/entertainment-arts-33778363

[11] https://www.mixcloud.com/Francisnotdead/28-10-2007-xfm-the-making-of-fatboy-slims-youve-come-a-long-way-baby-album/

[12] https://thump.vice.com/en_uk/article/gvn83y/big-beat-producers-retrospective-freestylers-rhythm-bentley-ace-cut-la-roc

[13] http://theprodigy.info/articles/Rolling_Stone_august_97.shtml

[14] http://theprodigy.info/articles/dailystarnov96.shtml

[15] https://www.m-magazine.co.uk/features/interviews/interview-the-freestylers/

[16] http://www.atomicduster.com/interviews/lofidelity_allstars/

[17] https://www.youtube.com/watch?v=yyzHuHsGxVk

[18] http://theprodigy.info/articles/melodymakeraug97.shtml

[19] https://www.spin.com/2015/04/the-prodigy-interview-new-album/

[20] http://theprodigy.info/articles/select98.shtml

[21] http://www.musicradar.com/news/tech/classic-album-richard-march-on-bentley-rhythm-aces-eponymous-debut-641613

[22] http://www.tranzfusion.com/music/features/2005/DJ_Touche_interview_Palpable_Hits/

[23] https://www.residentadvisor.net/features/434

[24] https://pitchfork.com/features/interview/9680-running-on-instinct-how-the-chemical-brothers-stay-vital/

[25] http://theprodigy.info/articles/electronic2.shtml

[26] https://www.vice.com/en_au/article/qbxdm7/jet-set-radio-shows-us-15-years-later-that-video-games-have-an-influence-problem-553

[27] https://www.amazon.co.uk/Funk-Soul-Brother-Fat-Slim/dp/1860744303

[28] https://archive.org/details/muzikmagazine

[29] http://www.breakspoll.com/blog/southern-sounds-freestylers-interview/

[30] http://www.slowmagazine.com/slow/interviews/02_MonkeyMafia.asp

[31] http://inthemix.junkee.com/dj-touché-gets-his-shot-of-money/775

[32} http://www.atomicduster.com/interviews/lofidelity_allstars/

[33] https://www.residentadvisor.net/dj/fckahuna/biography

[34] https://www.youtube.com/watch?v=h_wmxOgFgbQ

[35] http://web.ar-chive.org/web/19981205174204/http://www.skint.net:80/

[36] http://www.completemusicupdate.com/article/eddy-says-big-beat-theres-nothing-to-be-ashamed-of/

[37] https://www.allmusic.com/album/release/youve-come-a-long-way-baby-mr0000657715

[38] http://www.mtv.com/news/502419/fatboy-slim-feeds-new-album-with-vocals/

[39] https://www.theguardian.com/music/musicblog/2008/apr/09/bigbeat

[40] https://arstechnica.com/civis/viewtopic.php?f=23&t=467353

[41] https://soundcloud.com/ra-exchange/ra-exchange-349

[42] https://planet-dust.laserjay.net/pulse.htm

[43] http://www.nme.com/news/music/fatboy-slim-155-1391842

[44] https://www.youtube.com/watch?v=B1id_IABIYU

[45] http://www.users.globalnet.co.uk/~madeira/norman_cook_aka_fatboy_slim_aka_.htm

[46] https://soundcloud.com/freestylers/freestylers-live-glastonbury

[47] https://groovefm.wordpress.com/2011/01/03/my-imaginary-interview-with-djproducer-mr-scruff/

[48] http://theprodigy.info/articles/melodymakerjan99.shtml

[49] http://www.skintentertainment.com/artists/midfield-general

[50] https://thump.vice.com/en_uk/article/wna5bw/the-rockafeller-prank-meet-fatboy-tim

[51] http://higher-frequency.com/e_interview/fatboy_slim/index.htm

[52] https://sabotagetimes.com/tv-film/high-times-at-the-vanity-fair-oscars-party

[53] http://www.trackitdown.net/news/show/102502.html

[54] https://www.elvisinfonet.com/junkiexl.html

[55] http://dj.rane.com/blog/artist-spotlight-the-one-and-only-fatboy-slim

[56] https://www.fatboyslim.org/theguardian-where-did-it-all-go-wrong/

[57] https://www.fatboyslim.org/norman-cooks-brighton-port-authority-supergroup-experiment/

[58] https://web.ar-chive.org/web/20090309051248/http://www.gamespot.com:80/ds/action/sonicds/review.html

[59] http://www.webcitation.org/6U2UXAs5B

[60] https://djmag.com/content/blood-tracks

[61] https://planet-dust.laserjay.net/addict_1997.htm

[62] http://theprodigy.info/articles/select98.shtml

[63] https://en.wikipedia.org/wiki/The_Chemical_Brothers

[64] https://planet-dust.laserjay.net/history.htm

[65] https://en.wikipedia.org/wiki/Tatsuya_Oe

[66] https://www.amazon.co.uk/Adventures-Wheels-Steel-Rise-Superstar/dp/1841154334

[67] https://www.allmusic.com/album/decksandrumsandrockandroll-mw0000034516

[68] http://selectmagazinescans.monkeon.co.uk/show-page.php?file=wp-content/uploads/2011/05/singles1.jpg

[69] http://www.slowmagazine.com/slow/interviews/02_MonkeyMafia.asp

[70] http://theprodigy.info/solo/liam/liam-dj-gigs.shtml

[71] https://www.fatboyslim.org/dailyrecord-interview-6-june-2008/

[72] https://www.amazon.co.uk/Big-Beat-Anthems-Various-Artists/dp/B007ATBS8C

[73] http://simonreynoldsfavesunfaves.blog-spot.co.uk/2008/12/nineties-best-and-worst-by-simon.html

[74] https://archive.list.co.uk/the-list/1998-12-03/88/

[75] http://web.ar-chive.org/web/20080919043822/http://www.djhistory.com/inter-views/norman-cook

[76] http://web.ar-chive.org/web/19990224031600/http://www.popstars.de-mon.co.uk:80/wick.htm

[77] http://eartothetrack.net/my-afternoon-as-a-star-ugly-duckling-on-top-of-the-pops/

[78] http://www.hiphoprnbsoul.com/web/index.php?option=con-tent&task=view&id=84

[79] https://www.youtube.com/watch?v=GKBPDv0Q-pM

[80] http://www.popmatters.com/review/fatboy-slim-the-greatest-hits-why-try-harder/

[81] http://pitchfork.com/reviews/albums/3008-halfway-between-the-gutter-and-the-stars/

[82] http://www.encyclopedia.com/people/literature-and-arts/mu-sic-popular-and-jazz-biographies/fatboy-slim

[83] http://theprodigy.info/discography/offi-cial/Smack_My_Bitch_Up/

[84] http://www.songfacts.com/detail.php?id=7405

[85] http://www.nme.com/photos/the-50-best-remixes-ever-1410098#/photo/49

[86] https://www.youtube.com/watch?v=dlax9DkZV8o

[87] https://www.discogs.com/Co-Fusion-Freddy-Fresh-Pals-Torn-Open-A-Howlin-Christmas-Tune/release/112616

[88] http://thedjlist.com/djs/derek-dahlarge/info/

[89] http://www.bbc.co.uk/radio1/ibiza99/derekdahlarge.shtml

[90] https://djmag.com/content/game-changers-history-repeating

[91] http://www.theransomnote.com/music/interviews/richard-fear-less-talks/

[92] https://www.mixcloud.com/londonreal/fatboy-slim-youve-come-a-long-way-baby/

[93] https://www.residentadvisor.net/dj/fckahuna/biography

[94] http://www.nme.com/blogs/nme-blogs/oasis-at-knebworth-20-years-on-history-in-the-making-4430

[95] http://acidhouse.tripod.com/articles.html

[97] Jockey Slut December 1997 issue

[98] https://www.discogs.com/Various-Brit-Hop-And-Amyl-House/release/59048

[99] https://www.discogs.com/artist/7211-Midfield-General

[100] https://soundcloud.com/jimagreen/1998-02-01-essential-mix-freddy-fresh

[101] Simon Reynolds, New York Times, March 7th 1999

[102] Electronica Goes Straight To Ubiquity by Simon Reynolds, New York Times, June 6th 1999.

[103] https://www.youtube.com/watch?v=3CoguPNyhPI

[104] Jockey Slut April 1998 Issue

[105]   https://www.amazon.co.uk/Youve-Come-Long-Deluxe-VI-NYL/dp/B0788WSVTX/ref=pd_lpo_sbs_15_img_1?_encoding=UTF8&psc=1&refRID=7DHE12K3TRCD2FNT9VR2

[106] 7 Magazine May 24th 2000

Acknowledgements

I would like to thank the following people for making this book happen:

Abel Reynolds (Finger Lickin' Management)
Adam Gillison (Jumbo Records, Leeds)
Aldo Vanucci
Alex Hardee (CODA Agency)
Andy Ictus
Barry Ashworth (Dub Pistols)
Bee&See (Thomas Binzegger)
Ben Willmott (NME, The Guardian)
Carl Logan (Melody Maker, DJ Mag)
Captain Funk
Countertop Hero
Craig Hammond (Sir-Vere)
Christopher Lang
Claire Townend (Prodigy Management)
Claudia Nicholson
Crawford Tait (Hi-Karate)
Cut La Roc
Damian Harris (Midfield General – Founder of Skint Records)
Damon Baxter (Deadly Avenger)
Dan Lurinsky (Rubadub Records, Glasgow)
Daniel Curtis (Danielsan)
Dave Bushnell (Dave RMX)
Dave Winship (Inspired Support)
Decky Hedrock
Den (Funky Boogie Brothers)
Derek Dahlarge
Doc Moody (Resident BlowPop Bristol)
DJ Buba
DJ Prosper
DJ Regal (Wiseguys, Bronx Dogs)
DJ Rehab (Todd Miller)
DJ Spatts (Environmental Science)
DJ Trev Broadbank

Exploynk
Ewan Hoozami
Fab Samperi (The Captain)
Fake Blood (Formally DJ Touché from the Wiseguys)
Fatboy Tim (Fatboy Slim Tribute Act, Tim Davies)
Featurecast
François Deman (owner of fatboyslim.org)
Frank C. and Rusty B. (All Good Funk Alliance)
Frank Smith (Digitally Imported Radio, USA)
The Freestylers (Matt Cantor and Aston Harvey)
Fuzz Townsend
Gareth Hansome
Gary Maclarnan (Mr Scruff's Manager)
Graham Chalmers (Johnston Press)
Graham Scullin
Gramma Funk (MC on Groove Armada – 'I See You Baby')
Hadj
Henry Cobbold (Knebworth Park)
Hideki Naganuma
Howie B (Founder of Pussyfoot Records)
Iain Williams
IamBenji (formally Benji Boko)
Jadell
James Glenton (Mixmag)
Jane Winterbottom (Funk Boutique)
Jari (Pepé Deluxe)
Jason Ard (Old Flame)
Jason Laidback
Jason King
Jem Stone (Finger Lickin' Records)
Jemma Kennedy (Wall of Sound Label Manager)
John Gosling (Mekon)
Johnny Pluse
Jon Carter
Jon Kennedy
Josh Gaudioso
Justin Robertson (Lionrock)
Keith Flint (The Prodigy)
Kid Kenobi

Laurence Malice
Lee Mathias (Stepping Tones)
Leon Fijalkowski
Liam Howlett (The Prodigy)
Lindy Layton (Beats International, Hardknox)
Mako of Mako & The Hawk and Mako & Mr Bristow (editor of monkeyboxing)
Mark Jones (Founder of Wall Of Sound)
Matty Blades
Max Sedgley
Mike Atkinson (Music Journalist)
Mr. Scruff
Myagi (Andrew Mavor)
Neil McMillan (Hi-Karate)
Nick Faber
Noko (Norman Fisher Jones - Apollo 440)
Norman Cook (Fatboy Slim)
Paul Kelly (Heavenly Social)
Pete Houser (Bassbin Twins)
Quincy Jointz
Rams Le Prince
Rasmus
Richard Marshall (A&M Records)
Richard Marshall (Scanty Sandwich)
Robert Linney (Chemical Brothers' Management)
Robert Luis (Tru Thoughts Records)
Robin Turner (Heavenly Social)
Rory Carlile (Dirty Beatniks)
Scott Hendy (Dynamo Productions/Boca 45)
Simon Shackleton (Elite Force)
Simon Tagg (Kounchilhouse)
Ste McGregor (Kidda)
Steven Hall (Junior Boy's Own Records)
Tim Adam (Timmy Schumacher)
Tim Ellis (Molotov Pop Promoter)
Tony "SlackShot" Gainsborough
Tony Green (Promoter, Leeds)
Trent Lane
Under Influence (Criminal Tribe Records)

The Unknown DJ
Wiccatron (Breakbeat Paradise Recordings)
Zenit Incompatible

Extra special thank you to Freddy Fresh (Howlin' Records USA, big beat DJ Legend), without whom I wouldn't be where I am today. Thank you for all your inspiration and encouragement over the last 10 years.

I would like to thank all my friends and family.

. . . and of course to Mum and Dad for keeping me sane!

This book is dedicated to big beat lovers everywhere.

Remember, at the end of the day . . . music should just be fun!

About the author

Rory Hoy is a multi-award winning music producer/DJ and occasional film maker. He was discovered by big beat veteran Freddy Fresh, who signed him to his Howlin' Records label in 2007. March 2008 saw his very first album, *Cosmic Child*, released to critical acclaim. This was followed by five further albums.

He has also released hundreds of singles, EPs, remixes and collaborations on various worldwide labels including Skint, Wall Of Sound, Howlin' Records, Funk Weapons, Criminal Tribe Records, Tall House Digital, Tru-Funk, Super Hi-Fi Recordings, Bulabeats, Breakbeat Paradise Recordings, Division Bass Digital and Big Fat Mama Beats Records. He has DJed at many major festivals in the UK and his tracks have been used as syncs for the likes of Disney, Sony BET TV, ITV, Costco, Buzzfeed Yellow, FOX TV and Audi South Korea.

He is also a film-maker, with the multi-award winning film, *Autism & Me*, about his own personal experiences living on the autistic spectrum, released on DVD by Jessica Kingsley Publishers. He goes into schools and organisations where they show his film and he talks about autism.

He was the winner of the Yorkshire Young Achiever of the Year Award hosted by ITV, in the Arts category, which he won alongside actor Mikey North from *Coronation Street*. He won a Film 4 Youth Award, presented by film director Guy Ritchie at the showing of his film at the Waterfront Hall in Belfast. He was nominated for a Royal Television Society Award, has a UNICEF Award, 4Front Award and Wavemakers Award among others. He's Youth Patron of the London based charity Resources for Autism, and in this capacity was invited to a special reception at the House of Lords. He was a Centenary Ambassador for the national charity UK Youth, and featured in their promotional film. He continues to be an Ambassador for them. He was invited to be a Royal Commonwealth Associate Fellow. He is also an Ambassador for the charity Henshaws, which supports people with sight loss and other disabilities to go beyond expectations – something we should all strive to achieve.

Lightning Source UK Ltd.
Milton Keynes UK
UKHW01f0803110918
328693UK00010B/471/P

9 781912 587094